Democratic Crossroads

The Carnegie Endowment for International Peace offers decision-makers global, independent, and strategic insight and innovative ideas that advance international peace. Founded in 1910 as the first international affairs think tank in the United States, it is a global institution with centers in Beijing, Beirut, Brussels, Moscow, New Delhi, and Washington. Carnegie's network works together to provide analysis, shape policy debates, and propose solutions to the most consequential global threats.

The Carnegie Endowment for International Peace does not take institutional positions. Its scholars embody a variety of national and regional outlooks as well as the issues that transcend them. All views expressed in its publications are solely those of the author or authors.

Democratic Crossroads

*Transformations in
Twenty-First-Century Politics*

RICHARD YOUNGS

OXFORD
UNIVERSITY PRESS

Oxford University Press is a department of the University of Oxford. It furthers the University's objective of excellence in research, scholarship, and education by publishing worldwide. Oxford is a registered trade mark of Oxford University Press in the UK and certain other countries.

Published in the United States of America by Oxford University Press
198 Madison Avenue, New York, NY 10016, United States of America.

© Oxford University Press 2024

All rights reserved. No part of this publication may be reproduced, stored in a retrieval system, or transmitted, in any form or by any means, without the prior permission in writing of Oxford University Press, or as expressly permitted by law, by license, or under terms agreed with the appropriate reproduction rights organization. Inquiries concerning reproduction outside the scope of the above should be sent to the Rights Department, Oxford University Press, at the address above.

You must not circulate this work in any other form
and you must impose this same condition on any acquirer.

Library of Congress Cataloging-in-Publication Data
Names: Youngs, Richard, 1968- author.
Title: Democratic crossroads : transformations in twenty first-century politics / Richard Youngs.
Description: New York, NY : Oxford University Press, [2024] |
Includes bibliographical references and index.
Identifiers: LCCN 2024007792 (print) | LCCN 2024007793 (ebook) |
ISBN 9780197762424 (paperback) | ISBN 9780197762417 (hardback) |
ISBN 9780197762448 (epub)
Subjects: LCSH: Democracy—History—21st century. |
Political culture—History—21st century. | World politics—History—21st century. |
Globalization—History—21st century.
Classification: LCC JC421 .Y677 2024 (print) | LCC JC421 (ebook) |
DDC 320.473—dc23/eng/20240402
LC record available at https://lccn.loc.gov/2024007792
LC ebook record available at https://lccn.loc.gov/2024007793

DOI: 10.1093/oso/9780197762417.001.0001

Paperback printed by Marquis Book Printing, Canada
Hardback printed by Bridgeport National Bindery, Inc., United States of America

Contents

Foreword   vii

1. Introduction   1
   Threats and Catalysts   3
   Beyond the Crossroads   6

2. Democracy's Altered Context   10
   2010s Democratic Regression   10
   New Era, Altered Dynamics   16
   A Framework   25

3. Democracy and Climate Crisis   29
   Ecological Authoritarianism   29
   Green Trustee-Democracy   36
   The Micropolitics of Climate Action   41
   Climate Protests   46
   The Era of Climate Assemblies   55
   Assessment: Top-Down versus Bottom-Up Climate Action   59

4. Snapshot: A Global Climate Assembly   65
   Shortfalls in Climate Global Governance   65
   Global Democratic Deliberation?   67
   Assessment: Democracy Without Borders   71

5. COVID-19, Democracy, and Post-Neoliberalism   74
   Pandemic versus Democracy   75
   Mixed Trends   79
   Democratic Outreach   83
   COVID-19 and Community Mutualism   86
   Pandemic Protests   92
   Economic Shift: What Impact on Democracy?   96
   Assessment: Empowered States and Micromobilization   105

6. Snapshot: Europe's New Political Economy   109
   Benign Rethinking   109
   The Specter of Technocratic Statism   112
   Assessment: Unresolved Trade-offs   115

vi CONTENTS

7. The New Geopolitics and War on Ukraine 117
   Democratic Lethargy 118
   Partial Birth of Democratic Geopolitics 123
   Democratic Resolve 127
   Mixed Global Dynamics 139
   Assessment: A Democratic War, for Some 147

8. Snapshot: Ukraine's Democratic Resilience 152
   Accountability in War 152
   Civic Engagement 156
   Assessment: War Citizenry 160

9. Conclusion 162
   Crises as Political Driver 164
   Statism and Localism 168
   Democratic Transformations? 174

Bibliography 179
Index 193

Foreword

In rich and poor countries alike, democracy's fragile and fluctuating fortunes have become a defining story of our age. Democracies around the world have been grappling with myriad internal challenges, from internal friction and often-sclerotic responses to public priorities to governing institutions and political parties that no longer command the respect of their citizens to illiberal political entrepreneurs scheming to wrest power from them. Yet democracy is being reshaped not only by its own internal difficulties, but also by the impact of three defining crises that cut across the practice and process of governments purporting to respond to the needs and aspirations of their citizens: climate change, the COVID-19 pandemic and its socioeconomic fallout, and rising geopolitical tensions. These era-defining crises have dramatically compounded the strains on democratic governance. They are also causing severe difficulties for autocratic regimes and thereby impacting the balance between democracy and autocracy in ways that are far from straightforward or obvious.

Against such a backdrop, there is a pressing need to re-examine assumptions about what drives or hinders democratization, what strengthens or strains democratic institutions, and what underlying dynamics govern the authoritarianism that thrives as democracy recedes. That need is thoughtfully addressed in this compact, magisterial book. In this book readers will find a subtle dissection of how the crises of climate change, the COVID-19 pandemic, and the Russian invasion of Ukraine have each begun to reshape democratic and authoritarian dynamics. It goes beyond examining democracy's deepening troubles to look at how citizens are reacting to safeguard and improve democratic freedoms, taking us on an eye-opening journey through the remarkable range of efforts in democratic renewal that have multiplied globally.

What this book ultimately serves up is a commendably balanced view often lacking in the pessimistic political zeitgeist of today, artfully noting that the very severity of democratic erosion is what has spurred such intensity in attempts at democratic renewal. Yet is does not idealize recent political reforms and innovations and delivers a substantial account of their

viii FOREWORD

limitations. It discerns cross-cutting themes while retaining a laudable focus on local and regional contexts that inevitably shape the practice of democracy.

When I became president of the Carnegie Endowment for International Peace, I was determined that we should place democracy's struggling fortunes at the heart of our endeavors. The fortunes of democracy affect virtually every facet of our endeavors at the Carnegie Endowment: from our research on Europe and Asia to our efforts bridging theory and practice on sustainability and climate, technology policy, and global order. Today, analytical work on democracy is one of our core pillars, cutting across our different areas of research. This work is anchored by Carnegie's Democracy, Conflict, and Governance Program, which is recognized internationally for its high-quality and innovative analysis of global political trends. This searching book is another seminal contribution from that program and from an extraordinary thinker who in more than a dozen books over recent years, has illuminated countless aspects of the global state of democracy and the quest for effective international policies and programs to support democracy.

To succeed, such efforts must recognize that democracy is continually demanding of the people and communities that support and renew it. Amidst disruptions ranging from the COVID-19 pandemic to the climate emergency, democracy calls for both practicality and idealism. Only through a careful and intellectually honest appraisal of both these aspects of democratic process can we hope to protect the democratic enterprise effectively and improve it for future generations.

The book's powerful sweep delivers such an appraisal. It speaks to Carnegie's ambitions to provide original global maps, while its telling detail and policy relevance speak to Carnegie's drive to provide not just acute analysis, but insights that bridge the world as it is and the world as it may come to be. I'm certain you will enjoy and benefit from this book and am proud to add it to Carnegie's list of major big-picture offerings. By taking account of democracy's fortunes in light of major disruptions of our age, it develops subtle new strands of inquiry and sheds major new light on political debates and emerging policy challenges affecting virtually every corner of the planet.

—Tino Cuéllar, president,
Carnegie Endowment for International Peace

1
Introduction

Global democracy stands at multiple crossroads. A number of far-reaching changes and challenges are shaking and remaking the ground upon which open, liberal politics stand. Democracy has rarely been static and has always had to adjust to an evolving world and its own internal crises. Today, however, it faces wide-ranging sources of change with especially profound implications for the shape and viability of democratic politics. Not for many decades has such an intense array of crises probed different systems of political governance across the world. A clustering of transformations makes this a particularly crucial moment of redefinition for democracy's future.

Three strands of dramatic change are especially significant for democracy's watershed. First, climate change and ecological crisis. Climate and ecological stresses are becoming so acute in their effects that they are beginning to reshape political systems, international relations, and societies in fundamental ways. If responses to ecological disruption have been belated and still inadequate, they have in the last several years become more far-reaching. After many years in slow gestation, ecological crisis is now becoming epoch-defining in its immediate, tangible consequences. These consequences are increasingly not just physical and environmental but also political. Climate change and ecological emergency represent a profound test for democracy.

Second, the COVID-19 pandemic and its aftermath. COVID-19 not only had a direct and all-enveloping effect on people's everyday lives around the world, but also hastened moves toward new forms of economic policy and social organization, impacting in far-reaching ways on political systems. New forms of civic organization have emerged to deal with health and post-COVID recovery challenges, as the crisis has prompted societies to mobilize and counteract government failings. Governments have inched toward

---

Democratic Crossroads. Richard Youngs, Oxford University Press. © Oxford University Press 2024.
DOI: 10.1093/oso/9780197762417.003.0001

a new paradigm of economic policy based around higher levels of state intervention and guidance. If many were already moving tentatively away from neoliberalism after the ravages associated with years of austerity, the pandemic pushed them further in this direction. COVID-19, an emerging economic framework, and social reorganization have fused together in potentially tectonic change.

Third, geopolitics. Geopolitical reordering is deepening and accelerating, especially in the aftermath of Russia's war on Ukraine. In the years prior to Russia's full-scale invasion of Ukraine in February 2022, international relations were already subject to profound shifts in global power balances, a sharpening of interstate rivalries, the splintering of multilateral cooperations, and the growing assertiveness of authoritarian powers. Russia's invasion adds a dramatic inflexion point in this process of geopolitical change. It pulls the global competition between different powers, and between democratic and authoritarian systems of governance, into a more directly confrontational and frighteningly violent new phase.

These three crises can be understood as transformative moments that fundamentally change the context for democracy and democratization. While they are of course not the only issues influencing democratic adaptation, they are those that have in recent years added especially notable challenges to the reconditioning of global democracy. They are momentous not only in their own policy domains but also in the way they effect democracy and the prospects for democratization in diverse countries around the world. The three crises are very different from each other but each of them has far-reaching political ramifications.

The common thread linking together these transformative crises is that they all have profound spillover effects on the balance between democratic and anti-democratic political dynamics. Although in recent years most focus has been on the mounting threats to democracy, each of these three crises has also generated a new momentum of democratic renewal. The three crises have strengthened the demand for democratic transformation, yet governments and societies have thus far only partially met these demands. If democracy is to survive and deal successfully with the three sets of challenges, then it must raise its game. This book's central message is that, taken together, these three crises will require far-reaching transformation in the way democracy works. Some aspects of democratic renewal are beginning to take shape, but they remain short of the necessary far-reaching transformation.

Threats and Catalysts

For over a decade, a narrative of democracy floundering in deep crisis has become the norm. Much-cited democracy indices have registered year on year declines in the overall level of global democracy. Reflecting the general direction of political travel, a clutch of related terms has assumed a notable prominence: democratic regression, de-democratization, democratic erosion, authoritarian resurgence, and de-consolidation, among many others. A wealth of conceptual analysis has focused on explaining these trends, pointing to the multiple factors of economic, cultural, international, and technological change.

The range of these factors working to democracy's detriment is extensive—from systemic shifts down to local dynamics, from directly political strategies to identity and economic drivers. The litany of democratic woes has become familiar mood music of the era. However, the 2020s have also brought new dynamics and different dimensions of political adjustment. The dynamics of the 2010s and earlier years are still powerful, but now other factors have appeared over the horizon. They will have different kinds of impacts on democracy around the world. In this emerging context, it is crucial to ask whether autocratic and illiberal dynamics will remain the dominant story of global politics or whether other kinds of effect will make themselves felt.

In the 2020s, democracy is confronted with the emergence of three crises, associated respectively with climate change, the COVID-19 pandemic and its aftermath, and geopolitical conflict. These crises present challenges that invite far-reaching democratic transformation. This book argues that such a transformation is not yet being made, although many aspects of promising political change are gaining ground. The three crises can be conceptualized as critical moments that open the prospect of democratic renovation—to which democracies are so far underresponding.

The three crises have both positive and negative implications for democracy. Each has intensified the risks and difficulties that democracy faces in different parts of the world and in some ways given oxygen to authoritarianism. Yet trends have also gathered pace that nourish democratic commitment and potential. The current moment is so defining and complex precisely because it pushes and pulls democracy in contrasting directions. It animates and threatens democracy at one and the same time. The established discourse of democratic decline has become too narrow and unidimensional to capture this Janus-faced duality. While both negative and

4 DEMOCRATIC CROSSROADS

positive dynamics are gaining force, it is the latter strand of positive democratic renewal that is especially striking against the backdrop of a dominant concern with democratic erosion in the last one or two decades. Democracy is best seen as standing at the multiple crossroads of these different crises: the question is whether full democratic rebirth can emerge from the embers of climate, pandemic, and geopolitical crises.

Climate change and ecological crisis are not self-contained policy challenges but are having far-reaching impacts on political trends across the world. Climate change's political impacts have become more evident and increasingly approach a crunch point. The increasingly pressing imperative of dealing with ecological stresses has in many countries empowered authoritarian structures of governance. In others it has driven politics toward a more elitist model of "trustee" democracy in which governments have sought to take an increasing number of decisions out of the cut and thrust of open politics. Yet climate change is also galvanizing an extensive wave of citizen mobilization and participation that could eventually morph into democratic transformation as it feeds into high-level politics.

As the effects of climate change have become more tangible and damaging, the world has had to digest another equally dramatic and far-reaching watershed phenomenon in the shape of COVID-19. The pandemic and its attendant social and economic changes have fundamentally remolded the context for political development. As the health emergency receded, it left in its wake altered social and political dynamics. Authoritarian regimes benefitted in significant ways from COVID-19 and even democratic governments tightened their control over countervailing political and social actors. At the same time, new forms of social organization have flourished in the pandemic's wake, and these have set the foundations for an era of remodeled democratic engagement. As governments around the world have adapted their economic models for post-pandemic imperatives, their tentative and still partial moves beyond neoliberalism open new possibilities of democratic renewal. Still, multiple factors are holding these opportunities back from being fully realized.

The era's sharpened geopolitics are also having an impact on democracy. In the 2010s, authoritarian powers increasingly menaced democratic norms in multiple ways. In the 2020s, the Russian invasion of Ukraine has dramatically crystalized an already-accumulating authoritarian surge against democracy and jolted such latent reordering into a new era and to a heightened level of threat. As the shift has become so much more evidently hostile to democratic and liberal norms, some democratic states and other actors have adopted stronger commitments to defend liberal political values. As Chinese, Russian, and other authoritarian actions have taken on more obviously order-related dimensions, so the defense of democracy has crept back to the forefront of geopolitical struggles. This democratic agenda is muddied by geopolitical complexities, however, and still lacks full clarity.

If these three issues have all shaken and prodded and stretched global politics into an age of disquiet, they represent very different kinds of crisis. The ecological crisis is a slow-burn challenge that has been incrementally deepening in gravity over many years and that more recently appears to have crossed decisive tipping-points in its encroachment on patterns of political governance. The COVID-19 pandemic appeared suddenly, almost completely stopped the world in its tracks for much of 2020 and 2021, subsided in most places, and then led into a series of longer-term and underlying economic, social, and political changes. The geopolitical challenge is one that has taken shape out of deep and unfolding change to the structure of international order, before the outbreak of war in February 2022 superimposed on this an inflection point of violent tragedy.

The world has then faced three crises of very different genesis as these have either emerged or reached qualitatively different levels of intensity all within the same short period of time. Notwithstanding their different features, the three crises all impinge in powerful ways on the nature of political systems, both democratic and nondemocratic. It is this political impact that the following chapters unpack. The analytical aim is to decipher the contrasting ways in which the different crises are acting on global democracy. Analytically the book's overarching concern is to examine how strongly and in what ways these three crises have become explanatory factors in the evolution of democracy and autocracy. More politically and normatively, its aim is to assess how far the three crises are propelling a momentum of democratic renewal.

A key analytical frame that structures and runs through the book relates to two changing levels of political action. The different crises are pushing the center of gravity in political power upward and downward at the same time—that is, they push politics in more centered and decentered directions simultaneously. Across the different crises and wide range of change underway, one trend is toward the *empowered state*: public authorities have assumed new powers, responsibilities, and resources to address climate change, the pandemic, and geopolitical conflict. The other trend is toward

6   DEMOCRATIC CROSSROADS

what can be designated as *micropolitics*: a thickening of political and social action organized at a local level, often outside traditional or formal organizational structures. Chapter 2 defines these concepts and outlines how they have become the current era's two powerful, cross-cutting trends in political organization.

In some ways these dynamics of empowered states and micropolitics encapsulate a spirit of democratic renewal and are set to enable this to extend further. In some countries, these are the contemporary face of positive democratic renovation and the form that a reconditioned democracy increasingly assumes. The three crises have resulted in state powers being deployed more purposively to attenuate some of the key risks to democratic politics, while they have also fostered forms of local-level mobilization around a search for more effective democratic monitoring. Yet the two dynamics entail more problematic implications for democracy too: state power that evades democratic accountability and forms of local-level political engagement that sit uncomfortably with liberal-democratic norms. In sum, the empowered state and micropolitics are helping democracy deal with the shocks it faces, although they also introduce new risks for democratic renewal. These contrasting dynamics of political dual movement are a recurring theme through the book.

Beyond the Crossroads

Crossroads and watershed analogies are perhaps overused and often employed for moments that in practice fall short of warranting the label. This is not the first moment of juxtaposed crises that has powerfully reshaped political trends toward and away from democracy. However, it would be difficult to overstate the significance and combined force of the three crises examined here. The crises' impacts are amplified because they are happening in parallel with each other, and such a coincidence of transformative drivers has not shaken global politics for many decades. As the three once-in-a-generation critical shifts unfold simultaneously, their political impacts have clustered together in time, reinforcing their impact on global democracy.

For the best part of two years, political leaders repeated a mantra that the pandemic represented the most serious and existential challenge for a century. In 2022, Western (although not many other) governments moved into a rhetorical frame that Russia's invasion of Ukraine was now the most serious challenge in the modern era. And all the while, as extreme weather events made the effects of climate crisis ever more apparent, governments also presented ecological stresses as the defining crisis for the long term. The three challenges have competed in the same period of time for status as "most serious crisis ever."

Even on its own, each is dramatic; with the three occurring together, the implications are seismic. A return to war in Europe and the splintering of an international order that has underpinned global politics for seven decades. A global pandemic that killed millions and left a deep economic imprint. And the end of a whole way of life as ecological stresses become ever more apparent and overwhelming. The impacts of these crises will take time to play themselves out fully and this book offers what is simply a preliminary sketch of the issues likely to shape future trends in democracy and autocracy, yet it is already clear that this magnitude of change is sufficient to impact in major ways on political systems.

While these are very different crises, there are some similarities in the political changes they are driving. Important political dynamics have emerged that are common to the three of them. To some extent they can be interpreted as three dimensions of a single process of political crisis and democratic reordering. They each exhibit an emerging popular frustration with democracy's failings and lethargy that is giving birth to more immediate forms of democratic renovation. They are each driving a dual movement toward both empowered states and micropolitics. They each dramatically raise the stakes for democracy: they mean that democracy needs to perform better both to protect itself from authoritarian and illiberal alternatives and to show itself germane to the defining crises of the era.

The chapters that follow paint a mixed analytical assessment. The three crises have acted as strong shocks to global politics, in some similar and in some contrasting ways. In this sense, the climate, pandemic, and geopolitical crises need to be factored in more systematically to explanatory accounts of both democratic and authoritarian trends. They call for reworked analytical frameworks of political change. The book suggests that the three crises have opened pathways toward potentially profound political change. However, while the three crises need to be understood more fully as drivers of political change, they have not yet steered patterns of political governance through a

8 DEMOCRATIC CROSSROADS

clearly decisive breakpoint. The combined impact of the three crises is significant but without resulting in one clear, singular trend.

This analytical balance feeds the book's core political argument: the degree of positive democratic change evident to date falls shorts of what is needed to deal with the three crises and hold at bay undemocratic dynamics. A more far-reaching democratic transformation is required if democracy is to adapt to these three major exogenous challenges. In the absence of this transformation, the risk is that trends militate further against democratic politics. The three crises touch on such profound, existential issues—environmental catastrophe, mortal disease, and war—that they require a radically reworked and deepened democratic ethos. Further change will be needed to give citizens effective influence over such epoch-defining matters and help ensure that democratic values are more vigorously defended. The three issues require new narratives that resonate with citizens more concretely: democracy as the route to a green economy, democracy as fairer social and economic rebuilding, democracy as peace against authoritarian violence.

The book offers a comprehensive chapter on each crisis in turn, starting with the climate and ecological crisis, then turning to the COVID-19 pandemic and its socioeconomic aftershocks, and finally covering geopolitical tensions and the Russian invasion of Ukraine. After each main chapter, a mini–case study offers a more detailed example of democratic change associated with each respective crisis: these snapshots examine the holding of a global citizen assembly on climate change, the democratic impact of a post-pandemic European model of political economy, and the democratic resilience of Ukrainian society at war. The chapters examine the crises' impact on democracy understood broadly as liberal democracy, although part of their concern lies with uncovering new forms of democratic practice that have emerged. While this is not a theoretical book about different abstract models of democracy, its empirical accounts reveal how the three crises are giving rise to very practical debates about different kinds of political engagement and accountability that in some cases go beyond mainstream templates of liberal democracy.

The last decade has been blighted by a sense of almost permanent crisis, as financial collapse has been followed by a global pandemic, deepening ecological instability, and Russia's war against Ukraine. The unrelenting doom has been accompanied by a constant drumbeat of democratic recession and authoritarian resurgence. In many senses, the political pressures of the 2020s look even more unsettling and dispiriting for democracy than those of the century's earlier years. Yet another side to these trends has gradually and still hesitantly taken shape. Ecological crisis, the pandemic, and the invasion of Ukraine have all in their own way begun to raise the prospects of new democratic initiatives gaining impact and political relevance. Democratic actors will need to seize these openings and opportunities more completely if democracy is to fully mold itself to the emerging era.

2

Democracy's Altered Context

As a precursor to delving into each of the three crises, this chapter stakes out conceptual terrain. It outlines the state of play in analytical debates about political change and lays out preliminary thoughts on how ongoing events require an update to existing conceptual frameworks. During the 2010s the overall level of global democracy declined, and theoretical debates came to focus on explaining the dynamics of democratic regression. Analysts highlighted a wide range of political and structural factors that contributed to this trend. They differed in which of these factors they stressed most heavily, while generally agreeing that multiple drivers of democratic erosion were gaining strength.

These frameworks need to be updated fully to reflect newly emerging dynamics. Democracy not only stands at multiple crossroads; of equal analytical importance, the dynamics that will push it toward one path or others are changing. The chapter lays out the ways in which explanatory frameworks of democratization and autocratic trends need to adapt. It suggests that climate change, the COVID-19 emergency and its economic impacts, and current geopolitical conflict can be understood as transformative crises that open the possibility of political adaptation. The chapter defines two incipient adaptations that seem to merit particular attention: one relating to an empowering of state institutions, and another to a thickening of hyperlocalized citizen engagement or micropolitics. Defining these concepts, the chapter sets up a framework for analyzing the double-faced dynamics of democratic and anti-democratic politics in the chapters that follow.

2010s Democratic Regression

Into the 2020s the state of play in global democracy has been a sobering one, after a decade of largely negative trends in political freedom and human rights. According to the Varieties of Democracy Institute, by the start of 2024, 71 percent of the world population was living under autocracy, an increase

Democratic Crossroads. Richard Youngs, Oxford University Press. © Oxford University Press 2024.
DOI: 10.1093/oso/9780197762417.003.0002

from 48 percent a decade earlier. The overall level of global democracy had fallen back to 1986 levels, and for the first time in over two decades, the number of closed autocracies exceeded the number of liberal democracies. Limited or electoral democracy was now the world's most common regime type. The world now had 91 (liberal plus electoral) democracies and 88 (electoral plus closed) autocracies, and the latter were the more populous states.[1]

In similar vein, Freedom House recorded the eighteenth consecutive year of decline in global democracy scores in 2023. By this stage, there were 83 "free" countries in the world, 56 "partly free" and 56 "not free," while over a third of the global population now lived in "not free" countries. Free countries made up 46 percent of the global population in 2005, and only 20 percent in 2023. The most dramatic increase was in partly free states, which rose from 18 to 42 percent of the global population between 2005 and 2023.[2]

Against this backdrop, most conceptual work in recent years has focused on explaining trends away from democracy. Analysis in the 2010s focused heavily on what was baptized as autocratization, a mutually exclusive antithesis to democratization.[3] The concept of democratic backsliding has become preeminent, encapsulating a focus on the incremental erosion of democratic quality, different from the more dramatic coups and episodic interruptions of constitutional processes that characterized previous decades. Most theoretical work to develop explanatory frameworks for democratic regression during the 2010s recognized that a combination of factors needed to be taken into consideration, including issues of political strategy and leadership in conjunction with more structural change.[4] Debates centered on the balance between these multiple factors.

The impact of economic recession, financial crisis, and widening socioeconomic inequality was a prominent concern through the decade. Many studies put their stress on *economic crisis* in the 2010s as a prime driver of democratic regression. Even if economic problems did not always have dramatic effects, the recession of these years hit fragile democracies hard and

---

[1] V-Dem Institute, *Democracy Report 2024, Democracy winning and losing at the ballot* (Gothenburg: V-Dem Institute at the University of Gothenburg, 2024).

[2] Freedom House, *Freedom in the World 2024 The Mounting Damage of Flawed Elections and Armed Conflict*, 2024, https://freedomhouse.org/report/freedom-world/2022/global-expansion-authoritarian-rule.

[3] V. Boese, S. Lindberg, and A. Lührmann, "Waves of Autocratization and Democratization: A Rejoinder," *Democratization* 28, no. 6 (2021): 1202–1210.

[4] L. Diamond, "Democratic Regression in Comparative Perspective: Scope, Methods, and Causes," *Democratization* 28, no. 1 (2020): 22–42.

12   DEMOCRATIC CROSSROADS

showed them to be most vulnerable to democratic deterioration.[5] There was strong consensus among analysts that negative economic trends in this period correlated with negative trends in democracy and democratization.[6] Many scholars marked the 2008 economic crisis as the beginning of the democratic decline and authoritarian rise that unfolded through the 2010s. While much of this focus was on the eurozone crisis in Europe and developments in the US, the economic prism had global relevance and economic drivers were evident elsewhere too. In many parts of the Global South, the deepening crisis of neoliberal economic paradigms played a major role in propelling political forces hostile to pluralist politics.

Other explanations put the stress on *shifts in identities*. This perspective emerged from the rise of authoritarian values among populations around the world and the sharpening of illiberal identity politics. Some authors detected an "authoritarian reflex" among groups in certain age cohorts feeling that their traditional values were under threat from a generally more liberal majority.[7] This was one powerful explanation for the rise in support for ethno-populist parties across Europe, for example. Citizens felt an increasingly strong sense of resentment toward politics and disempowerment. Since mainstream political parties and political institutions at the national level failed effectively to represent these voters, participation declined, parties and democracies hollowed out, and competition shifted to the realm of values and identity.

The rise in identity politics and polarization was seen strikingly in the US. One study found that 90 percent of US citizens would vote for their party even if it engaged in undemocratic action, rather than cross party lines.[8] Surveys in European countries have shown that even if not subject to US-style polarization, here too many voters have become more partisan on identity issues to the extent of overlooking their preferred party's disregard for some democratic norms, especially the abridgement of civil liberties. While the far-right has been more guilty of this than others, both center-right and even center-left voters also show such

---

[5] J. Møller, A. Schmotz, and S. Skaaning, "Economic Crisis and Democratic Breakdown in the Interwar Years: A Reassessment," *Historical Social Research* 40, no. 2 (2015): 301–318.

[6] C. Boix, "Development and Democratization," *Institut Barcelona d'Estudis Internacionals (IBEI)* (2009), https://www.jstor.org/stable/resrep14156.

[7] P. Norris and R. Inglehart, *Cultural Backlash: Trump, Brexit, and Authoritarian Populism* (Cambridge: Cambridge University Press, 2019).

[8] M. Graham and M. Svolik, "Democracy in America? Partisanship, Polarization, and the Robustness of Support for Democracy in the United States," *American Political Science Review* 114, no. 2 (May 2020): 392–409.

traits.[9] Data shows that much democratic backsliding from the early 2010s has come from reactionary nationalist parties, with identity shifts evolving hand in hand with anti-pluralist positions.[10]

Many writers have argued that mutually reinforcing interlinkages between these economic and values-based explanations added weight to anti-democratic trends. Economic crisis and the rise of illiberal identities fed off each other. It was also increasingly clear that the kind of spillover from economic to political liberalization that was predicted by modernization theory was failing to emerge in many countries. Social values were impeding, reversing, and slowing down political openings even where economic development was relatively healthy. Authoritarian values systems were preventing positive economic change and modernization from having pro-democratic effects. Economic modernization was in many places not matched by the kind of social modernization that was so important to democratic change.[11]

Analysts have also pointed to *international factors* as a key background factor whose importance grew during the 2010s. Chinese and Russian global actions and their use of more assertive power have become another source of authoritarian ascendency. This international dimension seemed to grow in significance as several trends unfolded together. China and some rising authoritarian powers gained more leverage and were better able to rebuff pressures for democratic opening. Western democratic powers' shares of global GDP, trade, investment, population, and military spending declined. By the end of the 2010s, around three-quarters of countries had China as their main trading partner, with China in most cases having supplanted the US or the EU since the turn of the century to attain this status.

On the back of such shifts in structural power balances, the Chinese regime adopted an increasingly confrontational foreign-policy posture as part of its tightening control over dissent domestically—with the internal and external elements of autocracy marching ever more closely hand in hand with each other.[12] This was compounded by an apparent weakening of Western commitments to democracy. Democratic nations appeared hesitant both in

---

[9] E. Avramovska, J. Lutz, F. Milačić, and M. Svolik, *Identity, Partisanship, Polarization: How Democratically Elected Politicians Get Away with Autocratizing Their Country* (Vienna: Friedrich Ebert Stiftung, 2022) https://library.fes.de/pdf-files/bueros/wien/19536-20220926.pdf.

[10] V-Dem *V-Party Dataset*, 2022, https://www.v-dem.net/data/v-party-dataset/.

[11] D. Silander, "Building Democracy: National and International Factors," in *Globalization*, ed. G. Wang (London: Intech Open, 2017), doi:10.5772/intechopen.71984.

[12] G. Wu, "For Xi Jinping, the Economy Is No Longer the Priority," *Journal of Democracy* (October 2022), https://www.journalofdemocracy.org/for-xi-jinping-the-economy-is-no-longer-the-priority/.

14   DEMOCRATIC CROSSROADS

their support for potential political openings around the world and in their defense against authoritarian powers' anti-democratic interventions. Many analysts saw this switch as the crucial explanatory change from the 1975–2005 third wave of democratic expansion.[13] In this way, exogenous threats to democracy added to the endogenous drivers of democratic malaise.[14]

As the 2010s progressed, debates over the role of *digital technology* and social media became more prominent. Broad agreement formed that these technological developments were an increasingly powerful driver of political trends and that their impact on democracy was largely negative. Analysis shifted from the initially supposed benefits of "liberation technology" to the digital sphere's deepening menace to democratic openness. Toward the end of the decade, indeed, much debate was dominated by concerns that digital surveillance and tech companies' business models were undermining democratic individual agency and facilitating illiberal and repressive forms of governance. The strategic misuse of embryonic artificial intelligence raised the prospect of further intimidation against democratic institutions.[15]

Fears accumulated about anti-democratic views spreading on social media. Social media were especially influential in the far-right's rise, with radical parties' presence online exceeding their vote shares in most countries. A parallel trend was the increasing use of digital surveillance as a prominent part of authoritarian regimes' toolbox for maintaining power and quashing democratic movements both within and beyond their own borders. Democracies and especially elections came under direct attack from so-called digital influence operations. In fact, even relatively democratic governments increasingly deployed these means of digital surveillance against their own citizens.[16]

A different emphasis has been on *country-specific tactics* adopted by leaders and governments in undermining democracy or holding pressure for democratic opening at bay, as opposed to underlying structural or economic factors. Notwithstanding the overall decline in global democracy during the 2010s, there was significant variation in democratic backsliding,

---

[13] L. Diamond, "Democracy's Arc: From Resurgent to Imperiled," *Journal of Democracy* 33, no. 1 (January 2022): 163–179.

[14] J. Gerschewski, "Erosion or Decay? Conceptualizing Causes and Mechanisms of Democratic Regression," *Democratization* 28, no. 1 (2021): 43–62.

[15] S. Zuboff, *The Age of Surveillance Capitalism: The Fight for a Human Future at the Frontier of Power* (London: Profile Books, 2019); M. Moore, *Democracy Hacked: How Technology is Destabilizing Global Politics* (London: Oneworld Publications, 2018).

[16] S. Feldstein, *The Rise of Digital Repression: How Technology is Reshaping Power, Politics, and Resistance* (Oxford: Oxford University Press, 2021).

DEMOCRACY'S ALTERED CONTEXT   15

and numerous cases disproved each of the standard explanations above. Democratic erosion in countries with a reasonably high level of democracy did not happen everywhere, but in around 30 states concentrated in Africa, the former Soviet Union, the Balkans, and Central and Eastern Europe, and also the United States.

Structural context factors, like overarching international shifts or digital technology or economic problems, cannot explain why some countries have been affected but others less so. There was not a strong correlation between democracies' level of economic crisis or trends in inequality and their respective degrees of backsliding. Prime backsliders like India, Poland, Tanzania, Serbia, the Philippines, and Turkey all recorded strong economic growth in the 2010s. There were not many former democracies in which material support from China and Russia has been that significant. And neither were degrees of democratic erosion strongly related to levels of dissatisfaction with democracy.[17]

Rather, analysts adopting this line argued that the key explanatory factor came from leaders' different tactics and strategies of power preservation. Some governments were more determined and effective than others in using and fueling grievances, and then moving in stages to neutralize checks and balances. The significant change from the early 2010s came from how in many countries elites slowly dismantled democracy to protect their own power, and how in some transition states nondemocratic actors like the military were able to regain power by stealth.[18] Rather than simply reacting to value shifts, leaders have fostered more illiberal identities by exaggerating threats, cultivating resentments, and fanning the flames of xenophobia.[19]

Social and economic modernization has pushed autocratic regimes to be more skillful in their tactics, and this has helped them prosper.[20] They have successfully used tactics of incrementalism, chipping away in subtle fashion at civil liberties and countervailing powers, helping to explain their populations' forbearance of autocratization. In many countries, elites drove democratic backsliding after they had won power through broadly democratic means. Significantly, this meant that it was democracy's winners, and

[17] T. Carothers and B. Press, "Understanding and Responding to Global Democratic Backsliding," *Carnegie Endowment for International Peace*, October 20, 2022, https://carnegieendowment.org/2022/10/20/understanding-and-responding-to-global-democratic-backsliding-pub-88173.

[18] Carothers and Press, "Understanding and Responding to Global Democratic Backsliding."

[19] L. Bartels, *Democracy Erodes from the Top* (Princeton, NJ: Princeton University Press, 2023).

[20] S. Guriev and D. Treisman, *Spin Dictators: The Changing Face of Tyranny in the 21st Century* (Princeton, NJ: Princeton University Press, 2022).

16 DEMOCRATIC CROSSROADS

not just its losers, as in socioeconomic theories, that drove backsliding. This was different from history's earlier democratic downfalls, which were driven by political actors who, unable to win electorally, overthrew the system via coups or insurrection.[21]

While different analysts brought different factors to the foreground, there was a relatively widespread agreement that multiple dynamics or *composite models* were gaining momentum and that it was the combination of so many factors that made the decade of the 2010s so challenging for democracy. The interplay of economic, identity, technological, international, and tactical factors was of crucial importance. Underlying social and other structural change conditioned moments of crisis and elite power strategies, while these latter in turn reshaped underlying economic and social conditions. Structure and agency combined with each other, accounting for the many ways in which democracy appeared to be menaced. Causal arrows ran in both directions between top-down and bottom-up dynamics as the decade unfolded, and it was often difficult to quantify the causal weight of each relative to the other.[22]

New Era, Altered Dynamics

These dynamics that gathered momentum during the 2010s are still relevant and continue to condition trends in autocratization. Many analysts, journalists, politicians, foundations, and research organizations continue to be concerned primarily with shifts in identities, illiberal populism, and autocratization strategies. It remains necessary to chart the still deepening challenges of authoritarian value systems, polarization, financial disruption, and the pernicious effects of social media platforms and surveillance capitalism. The sounding of democratic alarm bells in the 2010s has rumbled on into the 2020s.

At the same time, however, another layer of updated analytical perspectives and modified debate is also needed. Conceptual approaches need to adapt to an evolving context and incipient political trends. They need to widen their conceptual lens to remain fit for purpose. Epochal shifts have either

[21] J. Corrales, "Democratic Backsliding through Electoral Irregularities: The Case of Venezuela," *European Review of Latin American and Caribbean Studies*, no. 109 (2020): 41–65.

[22] M. Vachudova, "Ethnopopulism and Democratic Backsliding in Central Europe," *East European Politics* 36, no. 3 (2020): 318–340.

appeared or reached heightened levels of political impact. The determinants of democratic success and failure are shifting in far-reaching ways. Struggles for democracy are about different issues than those that both drove and inhibited democratic transitions in previous eras. They are being shaped by different kinds of actors than those that have previously played the most crucial roles in supporting and blocking democracy. As one prominent theorist suggests, new dynamics require analysis to move beyond "our grandparents' democratization literature."[23]

Frameworks for explaining the significant political-system trends of the 2020s and beyond need to include several features. They need to embrace and examine new *drivers* of political change, mixed *directions* of political trends, and a shift in the *levels* of democracy-related agency. Taken together these emerging features direct the analytical gaze toward a particular set of issues—these do not make up a theoretical template as such but are the kinds of factors that need to be part of any endeavor to update theories of democratization, de-democratization, and autocratization. They present the analytical challenges that the rest of this book seeks to address.

New Drivers

First, conceptual frameworks need fully to build in new drivers of political change. As previous crisis-clusters pushed political trends in new directions, they informed the analytical frameworks of their respective eras. The late 1960s and 1970s saw a combination of oil-price shocks, the Vietnam War, anti-system protests in Paris, the civil rights movement, and the breakdown of the Bretton Woods system, and reshaped conceptual approaches to democracy-building and democratization. The challenges of the 2020s have revealed new drivers of change and represent the most potent fusion of such transformative vectors for many decades.[24] Historians debate whether the current situation is relatively unique in the intensity of its turmoil or lies within the normal pattern of periodic crises.[25] While such

---

[23] *Democracy Rules: A Book Discussion with Jan Werner Muller and His Critics*, Central European University, Democracy Institute, online event 13 July 2021, https://www.youtube.com/watch?v=EpKyRWMNR60&list=PL_0phSnA7tyRLbTWOCpRA6poMQf4X20xm&index=37.

[24] E. Jones, "From the End of History to the Retreat of Liberalism," *Survival* 59, no. 6 (2017): 165–174

[25] See discussion between these respective views on "Democracy in the Age of Polycrisis with Adam Tooze," *World in 30 Minutes,* https://ecfr.eu/podcasts/episode/democracy-in-the-age-of-polycrisis-with-adam-tooze/.

18 DEMOCRATIC CROSSROADS

historical comparison lies outside this book's remit, the emergence of different kinds of political drivers is certainly significant enough to invite analytical adjustment.

The combination of multiple crises in recent years has generated what some have labeled a poly-crisis whose overall effect is greater than the sum of its parts and that opens the way toward qualitatively different and systemic forms of political change.[26] In particular, analytical frameworks need to build in three unfolding crises: the impact of ecological disruption, the devastating COVID-19 pandemic and its socioeconomic aftermath, and the violence of a visceral geopolitics. (Technological development might be considered a fourth axis of change, although this serves as a long-running structural factor and is addressed in this book as a cross-cutting influence that plays a role in each of the three areas of dramatic externally driven crisis).

The well-established analytical concept of "critical junctures" suggests that transformative crises open pathways of change in which individual and collective agency can repivot political patterns and lead to contrasting outcomes in different contexts.[27] This resonates with the specifically democracy-related impact of ecological, pandemic, and geopolitical crises. These three crises have given rise to forms of political agency that look different to those that informed the original democratization literature. Today's struggles are not quite the old-style battles against repressive regimes. They are mediated battles, as democratic agency is activated through the prism of other policy imperatives: a whole economic and international system buckling under ecological strain, a world reeling from global pandemic, a new and complex geopolitics. Emerging and stronger agency around these transformative crises enlivens and reshapes the meaning of democratic action and conversely of ongoing resistance to democratization too.

Conceptual work on democracy and democratization up to now has not adequately taken into account the potency of these momentous shifts. As outlined above, the explanatory focus in recent years has been more on internally rooted identity shifts or populist strategies and discourses, and on the

---

[26] A. Tooze, "Welcome to the World of the Polycrisis," *Financial Times*, October 28, 2022, https://www.ft.com/content/498398e7-11b1-494b-9cd3-6d669dc3de33.

[27] G. Capoccia and R. Kelemen, "The Study of Critical Junctures: Theory, Narrative, and Counterfactuals in Historical Institutionalism," *World Politics* 59, no. 3 (April 2007): 341–369; P. Hall and C. Taylor, "Political Science and the Three New Institutionalisms." *Political Studies* 44, no. 4 (1996): 936–957; P. Pierson, *Politics in Time* (Princeton, NJ: Princeton University Press, 2004); H. Soifer, "The Causal Logic of Critical Junctures," *Comparative Political Studies* 45, no. 2 (2012): 1572–1597; and M. Bernhard, "Chronic Instability and the Limits of Path Dependence," *Perspectives on Politics* 13, no. 4 (December 2015): 976–991.

balance of domestic forces reflecting these kinds of changes within particular countries. Perhaps the most prominent concern has been with unpacking the sequences through which leaders have dismantled democratic freedoms, rather than the larger outside factors that drive these political trends. In the 2020s global politics are subject to critical shifts that are now more dramatically overarching in their scale and impact. While many other variables of course retain their importance in determining regime legitimacy and stability, these major exogenous or systemic crises have become strikingly more powerful in shaping democracy's trajectory.

These major overarching shaping factors are not fully determinant in moving politics in one direction or another: they are mediated in contrasting ways through different actors. A pressing analytical challenge is to examine how these macro-level transformative crises create new forms of political agency and are played out through purposive actor engagement—in the form of either pro- or anti-democratic strategies, and either elite-managed or civic-oriented democratic politics. Democracy is being reshaped by these big structural and contextual shifts, but with intensified political agency solidifying in their shadow. Against this backdrop, there is a risk that debates about the state of democracy have in recent years leaned increasingly on democracy indices, when attention also needs to be directed at more qualitative trends in democratic and anti-democratic *agency*.

Decay and Renewal in Tandem

Second, in terms of the direction of political change, a conceptual framework is needed that can identify and accommodate both democratic decay and democratic improvements, and to see these as parts of an overarching whole. The tendency in recent years for accounts to foreground one singular, unidirectional set of democracy-related trends looks too cut-and-dried in the context of an increasingly diverse and varied set of political developments across the world. While democratic erosion continues in many countries, notable democratic advances have in the last several years occurred in places like Armenia, Ecuador, Honduras, Gambia, Malaysia, Moldova, North Macedonia, Slovenia, Sri Lanka, and Zambia. Most countries seem to have settled into a middle ground, neither suffering dramatic backsliding nor making steady, appreciable advances in democratic quality. Trends look increasingly mixed, with autocratic and democratic dynamics gaining force at

20   DEMOCRATIC CROSSROADS

one and the same time, often in the same political locality.[28] There are too many different patterns and challenges to democracy to generalize categorically across countries.[29]

After the sobering realization of the 2010s that democracy was no longer on a smooth path of expansion and improvement, the 2020s has witnessed some analytical rebalancing. Noted democracy experts stress that the emergence of more varied trends is now a defining feature of the current era, with some democratic dynamics unfolding even as the root causes of democratic regression remain powerful.[30] This rebalanced outlook is more attentive to and concerned with the coexistence of positive and negative trends in democratization—a trend captured in Table 2.1. More analysis has probed exactly how far populism is prime cause of democratic backsliding as opposed to its outcome, or simply not strongly correlated with overarching democratic trends. One emerging focus is on which kinds of institutional features have helped stop autocratization from gaining momentum. One notable volume maps structural and institutional attributes of states that began on the road to autocratization but then recovered their democracy.[31]

Other empirical studies suggest that by the early 2020s there remained a generally positive relationship between economic progress and the stability of democratic rule; the lack of any general breakdown of democratic rule in economically successful democracies has arguably been masked by many years of focus on illiberal identity issues.[32] Even those placing more stress on the gravity of authoritarian trends have also recognized strongly embedded institutional and civic features that have dampened anti-democratic swings in most places.[33] In addition, trends in satisfaction with democracy have become strikingly varied across countries.[34] Reflecting the variation in trends,

[28] C. Knutsen and S. Skaaning, "Chapter II: The Ups and Downs of Democracy, 1789–2018," in *Why Democracies Develop and Decline*, ed. M. Coppedge, A. Edgell, C. Knutsen, and S. Lindberg (Cambridge: Cambridge University Press, 2022), 29–54.

[29] N. Wunsch and P. Blanchard, "Patterns of Democratic Backsliding in Third-Wave Democracies: a Sequence Analysis Perspective," *Democratization* 30, no. 2 (2023): 278–301.

[30] T. Carothers, "Is the Global Tide Turning in Favor of Democracy?" (Washington, DC: Carnegie Endowment for International Peace, 2023).

[31] W. Merkel and A. Lührmann, "Resilience of Democracies: Responses to Illiberal and Authoritarian Challenges," *Democratization* 28, no. 5 (2021): 869–884.

[32] J. Brownlee and K. Miao, "Debate: Why Democracies Survive," *Journal of Democracy* 33, no. 4 (October 2022):133–149. But see responses in the same edition critiquing these findings.

[33] M. Coppedge, A. Edgell, C. Knutsen, and S. Lindberg, "Chapter I: V-Dem Reconsiders Democratization," in *Why Democracies Develop and Decline*, ed. M. Coppedge, A. Edgell, C. Knutsen, and S. Lindberg, (Cambridge: Cambridge University Press, 2022), 1–28.

[34] H. Schmitt and E. Scholz, *The Mannheim Eurobarometer Trend File, 1970–2002* (Europäische Sozialforschung, Mannheim: Mannheimer Zentrum für, 2005); L. Russo and M. Bräutigam, *Harmonized Eurobarometer 2004–2021* (GESIS Leibniz Institute for the Social Sciences, 2023).

Table 2.1 Variation in democratic trends

Country	Change in Score from 2021 to 2022
Thailand	+0.62
Angola	+0.59
Niger	+0.50
Montenegro	+0.43
Greece	+0.41
Iceland	+0.34
Sri Lanka	+0.33
Albania	+0.29
Chile	+0.29
Cambodia	+0.28
Hong Kong	−0.31
Mexico	−0.32
Jordan	−0.33
Iraq	−0.38
Belarus	−0.41
Tunisia	−0.48
El Salvador	−0.66
Haiti	−0.68
Burkina Faso	−0.76
Russia	−0.96

Ten countries with largest democratic improvements from 2021 to 2022, and 10 most dramatic declines, based on data from the 2022 Economist Intelligence Unit Democracy Index, https://www.eiu.com/n/campaigns/democracy-index-2022/. Quality of democracy in each country is scored on a scale of 10, with 10 being the best.

efforts have taken shape to measure and rank democratic resilience to balance the more widespread attention on democratic decay.[35]

More critical debate has taken shape about democracy indices, especially on what many see as their conjuring of one single narrative about democratic decline; critical assessment of these indices has itself become a whole area of inquiry.[36] Many writers increasingly contest the notion of an all-embracing

---

[35] GlobalFocus, *Democratic Resilience Index* (Bucharest: GlobalFocus Center, 2021), https://www.global-focus.eu/wp-content/uploads/2021/09/Democratic-Resilience-Index.pdf.
[36] J. Kempf, "Has Democracy Regressed Back to 1986?," *Democracy Paradox,* March 16, 2023.

22 DEMOCRATIC CROSSROADS

wave of autocratization. The notion that there is one clearly dominant direction of travel away from democracy toward autocracy shoehorns complex political dynamics into a one-way descriptor. In many places the dynamics of democratization and autocratization have become more "endogenously interlinked" in processes of "two directional regime transformation."[37] Similarly, there are ongoing methodological debates about what opinion polls really show, with much doubt that these reveal a clear-cut decline in the level of or support for democratic values.[38] Some writers suggest that in the 2010s debate swung too far from an almost uniform focus on the dynamics of democratization over to an equally monodirectional focus on the one overall trend of autocratization, and that a new analytical phase should now aim to correct this.[39]

All these variations and increasingly evident duality contain echoes of Karl Polanyi's classic "double movement" concept. He employed this concept to capture the way that the expansion of the market system simultaneously bred resistance to its own principles. Economic liberalism and restrictive interventions against that liberalism developed together, feeding off each other.[40] It is apt to explore whether the kind of dynamics that Polanyi identified in relation to market development might also illuminate the more political trends in democratization and autocratization in the current era. The concept seems highly relevant in turbulent and uncertain moments of "great transformation." Authors have applied it to help explain the gradual emergence over a decade and more of democratic crisis, as democratic deepening triggered the double movement of popular reaction against democracy's shortcomings.[41]

The concept might be considered especially useful in the contemporary context that is marked by different directions of movement in relation to democracy, democratization, and autocratization. The literature has commonly described democratization and autocratization as processes that occur in

---

[37] M. Nord, F. Angiolillo, M. Lundstedt, F. Wiebrecht, and S. Lindberg, *When Autrocatization is Reversed: Episodes of Democratic Turnaround since 1900*, V-Dem working paper, 2024, Gothenburg, V-Dem Institute at University of Gothenburg.

[38] C. Welzel, S. Kruse, and L. Brunkert, "Why the Future Is (Still) Democratic," *Journal of Democracy* 33, no. 1 (2022): 156–162.

[39] L. Tomini, "Don't Think of a Wave! A Research Note about the Current Autocratization Debate," *Democratization* 28, no. 6 (2021): 1191–1201.

[40] K. Polanyi, *The Great Transformation: The Political and Economic Origins of Our Time* (Boston, MA: Beacon Press, 1944).

[41] P. Ther, *How the West Lost the Peace: The Great Transformation since the Cold War* (Cambridge: Polity Press, 2023).

waves, which implies that particular moments in time are dominated in a commanding way by either one dynamic or the other.[42] A crucial question is whether this may look too absolute moving into an era in which powerful, transformative crises clearly pull politics in multiple directions. The following chapters examine the spread of double movements as pro- and anti-democratic dynamics condition each other around the ecological, pandemic, and geopolitical crises.

The Empowered State versus Micropolitics

Another such double movement is apparent in the *levels* of political action, as the center of political gravity appears to be moving upward and downward simultaneously. This is a duality that has emerged gradually over the last decade. Each part of the duality has been noted separately, but less so the congruence of the two dynamics. These are trends that are not only or even mainly about democracy and autocratization but reflect a range of other policy objectives and social trends. The analytical challenge is that they still need to be factored into explanatory frameworks for democratization and de-democratization.

Many analysts stressed the emergence during the 2010s of locally rooted mobilization and movements, a phenomenon of what can be termed micropolitics. They suggested that this calls for a shift in how democratization is theorized.[43] Empirical evidence reveals the thickening of informal social organization outside traditional political structures to be a strongly emergent trend around the world. This trend has begun to tilt the analytical balance back toward understanding democratic breakthroughs as the result of diffuse mobilization rather than smooth, structural modernization.[44] The new activism involves a new type of representational claim pursued through the collective action of local communities outside institutionalized channels of accountability. This flows from deep-rooted social shifts such as the loss of traditional authority and the disappearance of fixed, inherited identities.[45]

---

[42] J. Gerschewski, "II. Autocratization and Democratic Backsliding: Taking Stock of a Recent Debate," in *Democracy Promotion in Times of Uncertainty: Trends and Challenges* (Peace Research Institute Frankfurt, 2018), 6, http://www.jstor.com/stable/resrep20032.5.

[43] D. della Porta, *Mobilizing for Democracy: Comparing 1989 and 2011* (Oxford: Oxford University Press, 2014).

[44] D. Brancati, *Democracy Protests: Origins, Features, and Significance* (Cambridge: Cambridge University Press, 2016).

[45] S. Tormey, *The End of Representative Politics* (Cambridge: Polity Press, 2015).

24 DEMOCRATIC CROSSROADS

Crucially, this trend accords explanatory weight to local variations in social, political, and institutional environments—aligning with the double-movement concept's stress on how locally embedded differences deepen in response to common challenges.

An equally significant emerging analytical focus has been on a re-establishment of state power. The kinds of challenges that emerged in the 2010s began to shine a sharper spotlight on the need for effective state capacities of multiple kinds. Many leaders, politicians, and thinkers have called over a number of years for stronger state capacities across a range of policy areas. Analysts have begun to home in on how this would relate to democratic quality or conversely to trends in autocratization. Some key works of the decade pointed out that effective state institutions have been as crucial in upholding liberal democracy as strong political competition and accountability.[46] Noted historians stress that market-stewarding state power has often been crucial to the recuperation of democratic governance, rather than state intervention or challenges to globalism always having anti-democratic connotations.[47]

This denotes a shift in analytical thinking from a focus on democracy requiring robust control over states to it needing strong states working in tandem with strong societies—the "absent leviathan" being as damaging to democracy as the overweening state.[48] Other works more specifically have identified the presence or absence of central state-government power as crucial in explaining the success or failure of democratization in the 2000s and also in accounting for levels of commitment to the multilateral coordination needed to anchor liberal norms at the interstate level.[49] Recent empirical work finds strong evidence for a positive impact of state capacity on the probability of democracy's survival and on countries' general level of democracy.[50] Reworkings of liberalism have increasingly sought to reflect civic notions of national identity and belonging as vital to sustain liberal-democratic

---

[46] F. Fukuyama, *The Origins of Political Order: From Prehuman Times to the French Revolution* (New York: Farrar, Straus and Giroux, 2011).

[47] M. Mazower, "Keeping the World at Bay: Does Globalism Subvert Democracy or Strengthen It?," *Foreign Affairs*, May/June 2023.

[48] D. Acemoglu and J. Robinson, *The Narrow Corridor: How Nations Struggle for Liberty* (New York: Penguin, 2020).

[49] R. Pildes, "The Age of Political Fragmentation," *Journal of Democracy* 32, no. 4 (2021): 146–159.

[50] A. Hicken, S. Baltz, and F. Vasselai, "Chapter VI: Political Institutions and Democracy," in *Why Democracies Develop and Decline*, ed. M. Coppedge, A. Edgell, C. Knutsen, and S. Lindberg, (Cambridge: Cambridge University Press, 2020), 161–184.

politics.[51] Conversely, state authorities in many nondemocratic countries have also sought to rebuild or reclaim powers or establish new competences in the name of highly illiberal politics.

In the 2020s, these twin dynamics have clearly intensified in tandem with each other. Reflecting their significance, this book seeks to delve more systemically into both state-empowerment and fast-expanding micropolitics and assess how they have impacted on democracy and democratization in the midst of climate, health, and geopolitical crises. The chapters that follow show how an updated analytical framework of democratization needs to take these two factors more fully on board: the *empowered state*, defined as public authorities assuming enhanced powers of decision-making, more formal capacities, and more extensive resources in determined policy areas; and *micropolitics,* understood as organized collective action at grassroots or community level outside formalized structures of political representation.

A Framework

The book seeks to grasp these layers of change and the way they raise new considerations for democracy, democratization, and autocratization. It seeks to combine each of the layers of change into a comprehensive framework. Taking these different changes together means that the account systematically dissects the impact of major exogenous crises that have dominated recent global politics; that it assesses the coexistence of democratic and anti-democratic changes; and that it locates the source of key agency both in the state and in society.

To take on board the new *drivers* of political change, the book is structured around the three moments of critical change that result from ecological and climate crisis, the COVID-19 pandemic, and the Russian war on Ukraine, respectively. These are very different crises, of course, but each has profound and wide-reaching political implications. Other books covering one or two of these crises have tended to focus on what they mean for relations between states, with some analysts believing the magnitude of the pandemic and the climate crisis together are likely to push major powers toward more

---

[51] I. Dunt, *How to be a Liberal: The Story of Freedom and the Fight for Its Survival* (Kingston-upon Thames: Canbury Press, 2022).

26   DEMOCRATIC CROSSROADS

problem-solving cooperation.[52] This book looks more specifically at their impact on democratization, that is, how they open pathways toward a potentially new balance between democratization and autocratization dynamics.

To reflect a nuanced perspective on the *direction* of political change, the book uncovers both increasingly severe threats to democracy and the unfolding of stronger pro-democratic commitments. There is mounting evidence that these opposite trends or double-faced movements are both potent and both gaining momentum. Dissecting the simultaneous strengthening of democratic and undemocratic dynamics in response to climate change, COVID-19, and geopolitical conflict shows with extra clarity how analytical frameworks need to pay more attention to such mixed trends, and their double movements toward and away from democratic renewal.

And to reflect shifts in the *level* of political action, the book's chapters examine the impact on democracy of both state-empowerment and micropolitics. If analysts have alluded to these twin trends in general terms, in this book the focus is more tightly on their implications for democracy, democratization, and autocratization. State-empowerment is examined as the process by which states have gained additional roles and competences in relation to climate action, the pandemic, and security crises, covering both national and international policies. Micropolitics is highlighted as citizen engagement and self-organization have spread at a highly localized level pursuing collective aims related to the three crises. The emergent focus on democratic resilience, noted above, has focused mainly on countries' structural or institutional safeguards against authoritarian creep. This book instead focuses on how particular actors are responding in detail and through new ideas and models of democratic renewal.

The chapters examine whether the emergent state-empowerment and micropolitics are positive or detrimental to democratization. They show how each can have democratic or undemocratic impact. From this, a four-way categorization of political change can be elaborated. It distinguishes a *trustee statism* that sits uneasily with positive democratic change from a *liberal statism* that sees public authorities playing a more proactive role in protecting and enhancing democracy. And it differentiates a democracy-deepening *civic micropolitics* from a less liberal *rejectionist micropolitics*. An analytical framework can be usefully structured around these different categories of change. These categories denote whether ongoing change involves more

---

[52] I. Bremer, *The Power of Crisis: How Three Threats—and Our Response—will Change the World* (New York: Simon & Schuster, 2022).

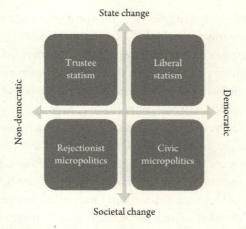

Figure 2.1 Analytical categories
The x axis represents the degree of democracy, the y axis denotes the level at which changes has occurred.

or less democratic change and, in addition, the level at which the change is taking place. This can be represented graphically, as in Figure 2.1.

This generates four categories of change:

Trustee statism: the emergence of empowered states that act in top-down, technocratic, or overtly repressive ways such that diminish levels of democraticness.

Liberal statism: the shaping of empowered states that facilitate wider democratic change and have positive impacts on democratic quality.

Rejectionist micropolitics: the emergence of micropolitics that tends to reject the salience of adjustments related to climate change, COVID-19, and geopolitics and that as such has negative implications for liberal democracy.

Civic micropolitics: the growth of a more liberal form of micropolitics that is concerned with community engagement and mobilization in ways that enhance democratic quality.

This framework guides the chapters that follow as these examine each crisis' impact on democracy. As democracy is pushed and pulled in different directions by epoch-defining macro-level crises, the new context invites a reconsideration of the factors driving both democratization and authoritarian or illiberal trends. The current era has reopened the "existential politics" of democracy, sharpening struggles over the most profound meanings of different political systems and values.[53] A core contention running through this book is that an updated conceptual explanatory framework is necessary to understand the factors and strategies that will determine political outcomes as governments and societies grapple with the three crises of climate change, the fallout from COVID-19 and geopolitical conflict.

This chapter has proffered categories around which this reworked conceptualization might be fashioned. One of these is a focus on new causal drivers that flow from the major exogenous crises as these have dominated global affairs in the last several years. Another is a more balanced focus on the increasingly evident multidirectional nature of changes in democracy. Finally, there is the shift of crucial political action simultaneously upward toward state-empowerment and downward to micropolitics. Double movement is a core theme through the book, both in the sense of positive and negative trends for democracy and in the form of upward and downward shifts in the levels of political agency. Guided by this framework, the book seeks to inject analytical order into the era of political restructuring that is now underway—an era that brings more open-ended implications for democracy and changed explanatory drivers of political trends.

---

[53] S. Hamid, *The Problem of Democracy* (Oxford: Oxford University Press, 2022), 3.

3

Democracy and Climate Crisis

As the effects of climate change and broader ecological crisis reach a crunch point, this opens the path toward profound economic, social, and political change. Quite apart from their direct physical consequences, ecological stresses are starting to reshape politics. In some ways the climate and ecological crisis is acting to increase government powers and state control over societies, fueling an era of empowered states. In many countries, the green empowered state is helping to make democracy more resilient to climate change. Yet in others it is intensifying authoritarian dynamics or powering a trend toward narrowed forms of elitist-trustee democracy.

At the same time, climate change has also become a powerful driver of the micropolitics that run as a unifying thread through this book. The climate crisis is increasingly a prompt to popular mobilization, calls for deeper democracy, community organization, climate assemblies, and new political-party engagement. Even if this civic micropolitics is partially offset by more rejectionist forms of mobilization that have problematic implications for liberal politics, it is striking how strongly the climate emergency increasingly stimulates demand for democratic renewal. The analytical framework's categories of different kinds of statism and micropolitics help distinguish these different political dynamics in this fast changing and fluid policy area. Reflecting different layers of double-faced movement, ecological concerns are driving vibrant and original forms of democratic organization and accountability, but also illiberal dynamics at both state and societal level. Several layers and forms of more far-reaching democratic transformation will be needed if democracy is to show itself the regime-type most attuned to the imperatives of ecological transition.

Ecological Authoritarianism

A conceptual debate has run for many years over which kind of political system is best placed to deal with climate change and ecological crisis.

Democratic Crossroads. Richard Youngs, Oxford University Press. © Oxford University Press 2024.
DOI: 10.1093/oso/9780197762417.003.0003

30 DEMOCRATIC CROSSROADS

Democracy is often said to have several advantages in this sense as democratic systems generate better quality information, create stronger incentives to deliver technological solutions, have accountability mechanisms to help ensure climate commitments are kept, and enable more open debate to arrive at optimal decisions. Recent research finds that countries with higher levels of political freedom have made stronger environmental commitments.[1] In the Climate Change Performance Index, the best performers are democracies, and no authoritarian state is among the high-ranking states, except Morocco; autocracies like Russia and Iran are notable laggards on climate action.[2]

Still, academics have compared data on this question for decades and conclusions differ. The relationship between climate change and politics is complex and indirect. Democracies have in recent years made more ambitious climate commitments but are also responsible for disproportionately high amounts of pollution. Levels of carbon emissions reflect levels of development more than political regime type. Although democracies tend to have made stronger commitments to reduce carbon emissions than nondemocracies, some suggest this is largely because they are wealthy and more postindustrial than other societies. These wealthy democracies outsource much of their dirty energy consumption by importing high-polluting goods from other countries. When these factors are considered, democracies are no more beneficial to the environment than autocracies.[3] The Climate Action Tracker ranks the climate action of many countries lacking full democracy as equal to or above those of democracies; its highest category of "almost sufficient" climate action contains more hybrid regimes than democracies (see Table 3.1).

Proponents of so-called eco-authoritarianism have long argued that climate change is such a severe challenge that it requires strong government that is unencumbered by public opinion and able to push through difficult change in the name of energy transition. Within academic debate, doubts have been present and growing for some time that liberal democracy is the political system most capable of implementing effective policies to curb

---

[1] E. Carayannis, D. Campbell, and E. Grigoroudis, "Democracy and the Environment: How Political Freedom Is Linked with Environmental Sustainability," *Sustainability* 13, no. 10 (2021): 5522. https://www.mdpi.com/2071-1050/13/10/5522.

[2] J. Burck et al., "Climate Change Performance Index 2023," *CCPI*, 2022, https://ccpi.org/wp-content/uploads/CCPI-2023-Results-3.pdf.

[3] V-Dem Institute, "The Case for Democracy Week: Combating climate change," webinar, March 25, 2021, https://www.youtube.com/watch?v=Mcew0ahVO9E&t=3857s.

DEMOCRACY AND CLIMATE CRISIS   31

Table 3.1 Climate action by political regime type

Country	Climate Action Sufficiency	Political Regime Type
Australia	Insufficient	Full democracy
Brazil	Insufficient	Flawed democracy
Chile	Insufficient	Flawed democracy
Colombia	Insufficient	Flawed democracy
Costa Rica	Almost sufficient	Full democracy
Ethiopia	Almost sufficient	Authoritarian regime
EU	Insufficient	Mix of full and flawed democracies
Germany	Insufficient	Full democracy
Japan	Insufficient	Full democracy
Kazakhstan	Insufficient	Authoritarian regime
Kenya	Almost sufficient	Hybrid regime
Morocco	Almost sufficient	Hybrid regime
Nepal	Almost sufficient	Hybrid regime
Nigeria	Almost sufficient	Hybrid regime
Norway	Almost sufficient	Full democracy
Peru	Insufficient	Flawed democracy
South Africa	Insufficient	Flawed democracy
Switzerland	Insufficient	Full democracy
The Gambia	Almost sufficient	Hybrid regime
United Kingdom	Almost sufficient	Full democracy
USA	Insufficient	Flawed democracy

All countries ranked within the Climate Action Tracker's three categories: "1.5 Paris Agreement compatible" (0); "almost sufficient" (9); and "insufficient" (12). Regime types defined by 2021 Economist Index.

climate change.[4] Some influential environmentalists have insisted that democracy has shown itself structurally unable to deal with the ecological crisis as governments in need of re-election cannot take unpopular actions to address climate and environmental challenges.[5]

The less examined question is the reverse one of what impact the climate crisis is having on political systems. On this matter, many observers suggest that recent trends are not entirely positive for democracy. This book's

[4] D. Shearman and J. Smith, *The Climate Change Challenge and the Failure of Democracy* (Westport, CT: Praeger, 2007).
[5] L. Hickman, "James Lovelock: Humans Are too Stupid to Prevent Climate Change," *The Guardian*, March 29, 2010.

32 DEMOCRATIC CROSSROADS

concern is not so much with whether democratic or nondemocratic systems in the abstract possess the strongest attributes to tackle the climate crisis. Rather, it is concerned with the impact that climate and ecological challenges are having on these different kinds of politics. A sobering starting point in this regard is that some authoritarian regimes seem to have positioned themselves to benefit from the energy transition. Some writers see trends pushing strongly toward a Climate Leviathan, a more authoritarian capitalism governed by strong states that manage the climate challenge through technologies and market mechanisms.[6]

The climate agenda is in some instances further empowering authoritarian states. Even if climate change is not the cause of this authoritarianism, in some countries incumbent regimes are pursuing climate action in a way that clearly deepens anti-democratic dynamics. A general sense of unmanageable ecological crisis tends to play into the hands of those calling for control and order. It also tends to feed the kind of nationalism and fear of the outside world more associated with autocracy than democracy. In some localities, climate disasters are fueling oppression and the growth of "storm autocracy" under the guise of emergency responses.[7] As climate change spurs the movement of people across borders this has contributed to political illiberalism in both receiving and sending countries.[8] Even if there is no obvious and direct trace between climate challenges and a generalized decline in democratic rights, ecological crisis is in some cases reinforcing anti-democratic dynamics.

The clearest and most cited case of this is China. China has pioneered "authoritarianism in green clothing" as an environmentalism engineered through state activism, coercion, and an undemocratic style of technopolitical governance. The Chinese government has taken on more control to force through hydroelectric dams and other green infrastructure.[9] China seems to be a textbook case in how autocracy can plan for the long term, take on vested interests and deal with complexity. The government's commitment

[6] G. Mann and J. Wainwright, *Climate Leviathan: A Political Theory of Our Planetary Future* (London: Verso, 2018).

[7] M. Rahman, N. Anbarci, and M. Ulubasoglu, "'Storm Autocracies': Islands as Natural Experiments," *Journal of Development Economics* 159 (November 2022), https://doi.org/10.1016/j.jdeveco.2022.102982.

[8] G. Vince, *Nomad Century: How Climate Migration Will Reshape Our World* (London: Penguin, 2022).

[9] Y. Li and J. Shapiro, *China Goes Green: Coercive Environmentalism for a Troubled Planet* (Cambridge: Polity, 2020).

to be carbon neutral "before 2060" seems to have reinforced the power of the state and its authoritarian model of political economy. The Communist Party has used China's lead role in renewable energy technologies to mobilize state and society behind a common national purpose. China's successive Five-Year-Plans have increasingly placed renewable energy at their heart as energy transition has become a pillar of the regime's legitimacy. Internationally, China's reinforced authoritarian regime has stood aside from many multilateral climate accords, although it has engaged in cooperation on renewable-transition issues with other states, including Western powers.

Other authoritarian regimes have also begun to instrumentalize the energy transition for their own political standing. As Persian Gulf regimes have recognized the need to move away from high dependency on hydrocarbons, they have taken on powers to pilot economic transformation strategies. These states are set to be leading exporters of green hydrogen and thus continue the rentier underpinnings of their autocracy.[10] For some years, Arab autocratic regimes have received a twin boost: as prices and demand for hydrocarbons rise, petro-autocracies' core power base has remained robust, even as they start gaining additional revenues from solar, hydrogen, and other sources.

Critical minerals are also providing rentier revenue for many autocratic regimes around the world. China holds the bulk of global supply for large numbers of critical materials. Other authoritarian states have large deposits too. Vietnam has the second largest deposits of rare earths in the world after China. The Democratic Republic of the Congo has the world's largest cobalt supplies. Russia has large deposits of critical minerals, and in 2022 sizeable rare-earth deposits were discovered in Turkey. Burundi and Myanmar are other nondemocratic states with large mining operations for critical minerals and rare earths, generating sizeable revenues for their regimes as global demand rises.[11] In the Persian Gulf, critical minerals are providing another strand to the emergent authoritarian eco-rentierism. Table 3.2 shows the concentration of critical minerals in nondemocratic regimes.

[10] J. Bordoff and M. O'Sullivan, "Green Upheaval: The New Geopolitics of Energy," *Foreign Affairs*, November 30, 2021, https://www.foreignaffairs.com/articles/world/2021-11-30/geopolitics-energy-green-upheaval.

[11] N. LePan, "Rare Earth Elements: Where in the World Are They?," *Visual Capitalist*, November 23, 2021, https://www.visualcapitalist.com/rare-earth-elements-where-in-the-world-are-they/.

34 DEMOCRATIC CROSSROADS

Table 3.2 Countries with most critical minerals, by regime type

Country	Regime Type	Critical Mineral	Description
China	Authoritarian	Cobalt	Highest share of global processing (at 85,000 mt)
DR Congo	Authoritarian	Cobalt	Highest share of global reserves (at 3,600,000 mt)
Australia	Full democracy	Cobalt	Second highest share of global reserves (at 1,400,000 mt)
China	Authoritarian	Copper	Highest share of global refining (at 9,447 kt)
Chile	Full democracy	Copper	Highest share of global reserves (at 200,000 kt)
Peru	Hybrid regime	Copper	Second highest share of global reserves (at 92,000 kt)
China	Authoritarian	Lithium	Highest share of global processing (at 202,295 mt)
Chile	Full democracy	Lithium	Highest share of global reserves (at 9,200,000 mt)
Australia	Full democracy	Lithium	Second highest share of global reserves (at 4,700,000 mt)
China	Authoritarian	Nickel	Highest share of global refining (at 852 kt)
Indonesia	Flawed democracy	Nickel	Highest share of global reserves (at 21,000 kt)
Australia	Full democracy	Nickel	Second highest share of global reserves (at 20,000 kt)
China	Authoritarian	Rare earths	Highest share of global magnet rare earth oxides-refining (at 40,165 mt)
China	Authoritarian	Rare earths	Highest share of global rare earth reserves (at 44,000,000 mt)
Vietnam	Authoritarian	Rare earths	Second highest share of global rare earth reserves (at 22,000,000 mt)

This table includes countries with the highest global shares of critical minerals. Regime types are based on the EIU Democracy Index 2022. Descriptions for each critical mineral are based on data from the Wilson Center's report *The Mosaic Approach*, which tracks global distribution of critical mineral processing and reserves as of 2020 (as of 2019 for rare earth refining). See https://www.wilso ncenter.org/article/critical-mineral-maps.

Buttressing authoritarian regimes' international leverage, importing states around the world have increasingly sought both renewable energy and critical minerals from nondemocratic countries. In 2022, European countries signed new deals either for access to critical minerals or renewable energy exports from autocratic regimes in the Persian Gulf, Egypt, Iran, and Azerbaijan. European governments conspicuously excluded critical minerals from their sanctions against Russia after the invasion of Ukraine. In many countries, Western democracies are pushing for access to critical minerals expressly against local citizen opposition to mining projects, further feeding anti-democratic repression.

While some autocracies seem empowered, many democracies have increasingly struggled to address the transition's relative costs and benefits of climate transition, especially who pays for what and how these decisions are to be made within democratic political systems. The strains of energy transition have made democracies' internal politics more fractious and harder to govern effectively. Energy transition upends the whole social contract upon which liberal democratic rights have been premised. Political rights have historically gone hand in hand with freedoms in consumption and lifestyle choices whose continuation is incompatible with energy transition. With governments less able to promise or pursue economic growth as their main deliverable to voters in the same way as before, this has implications for the sustainability of welfare states and hence for the social legitimacy of democratic institutions.

All this became increasingly apparent in the turbulent politics of the energy crisis unleashed by Russia's invasion of Ukraine. In many countries, 2022 was dominated by rising energy prices and the political tensions these caused. Democratic governments promised to accelerate the transition away from hydrocarbons, yet also sought increased supplies for oil and gas as alternatives to Russian supplies. As energy prices rose, nearly all democratic governments offered some form of de facto subsidization of gas consumption for their citizens, incentivizing higher levels of carbon consumption than would otherwise have been the case and putting themselves at odds with the climate agenda. In 2022 and 2023, the highest subsidies for oil and gas consumption were given by Western democratic governments that scrambled to allay citizen discontent.

Such fraught politics demonstrate that democratic systems have yet to fortify themselves for the energy transition. The energy crisis has deepened a growing debt crisis around the globe and put particular strain on many fragile democracies.[12] Green issues have unsettled and cut across the

---

[12] L. Jensen, "Avoiding 'Too Little Too Late' on International Debt Relief," *United Nations Development Programme*, October 11, 2022, https://www.undp.org/publications/dfs-avoiding-too-little-too-late-international-debt-relief.

36   DEMOCRATIC CROSSROADS

traditional dividing lines between political parties, causing further governance challenges.[13] Surveys suggest that even those European citizens supportive of ambitious climate targets are still not willing to incur significant personal costs to meet these.[14] The thorny political dilemmas flowing from these considerations are dragging democracy into a period of turbulence and uncertainty. Some observers point to an ingrained structural flaw in democracy: because democracy works by building governing alliances across different opinions and interests, it guarantees there will be some climate action but also that this will be modest only, in a kind of split-the-difference strategy with resistors.[15]

Green Trustee-Democracy

These vulnerabilities have elicited responses from democratic governments that have implications for the depth and quality of democracy. A view has gained ground that in democratic states the key lies in strong and effective institutional capacities and not open, competitive politics as such.[16] Governments have begun to take a more hands-on lead role in advancing supposed technological solutions to the climate crisis—a combination of electrification, hydrogen, renewables, and carbon capture.[17] They have increasingly sought to short-circuit planning issues to make it more difficult for citizens to block ecological projects like wind farms.

Governments in many democracies have adopted more top-down policy styles. Although there is little sign that democratic systems have become overtly authoritarian in the pursuit of climate action, a more subtle trend is unfolding. Many democracies have started to close off climate-related decisions from open democratic debate. Climate and ecological challenges are driving political trends toward a more managed form of democracy. Some commentators argue that so-called expert-guided democracy is

[13] For discussion of some of these issues, see D. Lindvall, *Democracy and the Challenge of Climate Change* (Stockholm: International IDEA, 2021).

[14] Counterpoint and OSEPI, *Green Wedge? Mapping Dissent Against Climate Policy in Europe*, Counterpoint, 2021, https://counterpoint.uk.com/projects/climate-policy-in-a-post-covid-19-europe/.

[15] C. Abadi, "What if Democracy and Climate Mitigation Are Incompatible?," *Foreign Policy*, January 7, 2022, https://foreignpolicy.com/2022/01/07/climate-change-democracy/.

[16] M. Povitkina, "The Limits of Democracy in Tackling Climate Change," *Environmental Politics* 27, no. 3 (2018): 411–432.

[17] I. Azevedo et al., "The Paths to Net Zero," *Foreign Affairs* 99, no. 3 (2020): 18–27.

needed to design and implement an effective ecological transition. A key argument is that technocratic governance led by experts may be able to focus on the long-term imperatives of change beyond electoral cycles.

Many environmentalists increasingly advocate this kind of more controlled decision-making.[18] Support remains strong among policymakers in the advanced democracies for the long-standing call for "planetary stewardship," the notion that enlightened experts are best equipped to oversee crucial processes of ecological transition and societal adaptation.[19] The notion of such stewardship is integrally linked to the international dimension: the imperative of succeeding in intricate and technocratic multilateral negotiations underpins the push toward such eco-technocracy at the national level too. This draws from polls showing that policymakers remain more committed to climate action than citizens.[20] A related concern is that climate change will require migration of such mass scale that this will need to be planned and overseen by experts and technocrats—running and pushing forward all-encompassing relocation schemes that will plan where new cities are to be built and how many people shall be moved around between different places in the world.[21]

Some trends are returning to an old and previously influential notion of "ecological mandarins" taking more control to steer necessary environmental policies. Nearly 50 countries have now set up some kind of expert climate and ecological crisis body. Empirical research shows these have helped governments lift their climate-policy ambitions and to deliver a credible message to the public that action is needed.[22] The first of these was created in the UK. In a notable addition, the EU climate law of 2021 comes with an expert council to drive its implementation. Politicians from Africa and Indonesia note that policymaking in their democracies has become more top-down and expert-oriented in response to climate and environmental concerns.[23]

---

[18] Counterpoint and OSEPI, *Green Wedge?*

[19] J. Rockström et al., "A Safe Operating Space for Humanity," *Nature* 461 (September 2009): 472–475.

[20] L. Rapeli and V. Koskimaa, "Concerned and Willing to Pay? Comparing Policymaker and Citizen Attitudes towards Climate Change," *Environmental Politics* 31, no. 3 (2022): 542–551.

[21] Vince, *Nomad Century*.

[22] H. Dudley, A. Jordan, and I. Lorenzoni, "Independent Expert Advisory Bodies Facilitate Ambitious Climate Policy Responses," *Science Brief Review* (March 2021).

[23] A. Averchenkova, O. Plyska, and J. Wahlgren, *Addressing the Climate and Environmental Crises through Better Governance: The Environmental Democracy Approach in Development Cooperation* (London: Westminster Foundation for Democracy, 2022), 19.

38 DEMOCRATIC CROSSROADS

Ecological policies are embedded in the increasingly numerous environmental and climate agencies that wield influence now in most democracies. These proffer measures to advance climate action, supposedly circumventing partisan blockages and vested interests that lobby democratic institutions against change. While prompting advances, their approach tends to be incremental and positioned within existing economic and social models.[24] While some of these agencies offer environmental rights like access to information over climate crises, many have had less positive democratic effects as they "cordon off some aspects of the law from conventional processes of popular amendment."[25]

This kind of depoliticization is beginning to feature in the politics of climate change as more environmental issues are being insulated from competitive day-to-day politics. It is apparent in multiple aspects of many governments' approaches to climate change.[26] Climate targets have been ring-fenced in constitutions especially in the Indo-Pacific and in Asian states like Bhutan and Mongolia. Most European governments have also enshrined climate-related commitments in constitutional provisions or enacted carbon targets in climate laws. The new provisions have helped governments as they expropriate land for solar parks and the like with increasing frequency and with less scope than previously for public redress. Even where governments have made commitments to greater transparency in releasing environmental data and reporting on the progress they have made toward emissions targets, this is still a top-down process of informing at the behest of public authorities' control.

In several countries—such as Germany and the Netherlands—courts have ruled that governments' climate plans are not commensurate with these constitutional promises. The increasing use of so-called climate litigation has spread, including to places like Colombia, France, and the UK. The European Court of Human Rights has also begun to oblige governments to answer for the shortcomings in their environmental policies in cases brought by activists. Welcomed by many as a possible guarantor of climate commitments, this legal route also sees courts playing a more significant role

---

[24] A. Machin, "Democracy, Disagreement, Disruption: Agonism and the Environmental State," *Environmental Politics* 29, no. 1 (2020): 155–172.

[25] J. Pickering, K. Bäckstrand, and D. Schlosberg, "Between Environmental and Ecological Democracy: Theory and Practice at the Democracy-Environment Nexus," *Journal of Environmental Policy & Planning* 22, no. 1 (2020): 9.

[26] D. Sherman and J. Smith, *The Climate Change Challenge and the Failure of Democracy* (London: Praeger, 2007).

relative to democratic actors like parliaments and political parties and risks leaving social input and engagement aside. Indeed, it is expressly aimed at taking decisions out of democracy's uncertain and fluctuating political arena.

Even more clearly, the increasingly frequent practice of governments and local authorities declaring climate emergencies involves exceptional measures that abridge normal democratic rights. By 2022, over 2000 jurisdictions, housing over one billion citizens, had declared a climate emergency that gave authorities potentially extraordinary powers. These were declared mainly by regional and local entities within democratic countries to give these authorities enhanced powers. The list also included 18 national climate emergency declarations in broadly democratic states—European states plus Argentina, Australia, Canada, Japan, New Zealand, Peru, and South Korea, as shown in Table 3.3.[27] As of 2023, over four hundred local UK authorities had declared a climate emergency, covering around 90 percent of the population.[28] In democracies, these emergency laws have rights-protection safeguards, but allow executives to short circuit many normal democratic processes and checks and balances.

The energy crisis of 2022 accentuated these trends in most democracies. Many democratic governments tackled this crisis in strikingly top-down ways. Environmentalists criticized many governments for simply instructing people to use less energy rather than including them in a deeper conversation about how the politics of energy transitions should be managed.[29] The European Union used emergency powers to speed up renewables amid the deepening energy crisis and sought to use express procedures in allocating large amounts of funding related to ecological transition—this case is examined in detail in Chapter 6. In late 2023, the German government contemplated using emergency measures to circumvent a constitutional court ruling against its climate financing programs. Alongside the nearly two hundred US jurisdictions that have invoked emergency measures, in July 2022 President Biden proposed a national-level US climate-emergency act; while differences in Congress held this back, the idea remained on the agenda.

---

[27] "Climate Emergency Declarations in 2,327 Jurisdictions and Local Governments Cover 1 Billion Citizens," *ClimateEmergencyDeclaration.org*, April 17, 2023, https://climateemergencydecl aration.org/climate-emergency-declarations-cover-15-million-citizens/.

[28] See data at CAPE, https://cape.mysociety.org/councils/ (accessed February 19, 2024).

[29] V. Jack, "Ukraine War Heats up Energy Poverty Debate," *Politico*, May 17, 2022.

40   DEMOCRATIC CROSSROADS

Table 3.3 Countries that have declared climate emergencies

National or Supra-national Government	Date Climate Emergency Declared
Scotland (Scottish Government)	April 2019
Wales (Welsh Government)	April 2019
United Kingdom (House of Commons)	May 2019
Republic of Ireland (Parliament)	May 2019
Portugal (Parliament)	June 2019
Vatican City (Holy See)	June 2019
Canada (Parliament)	June 2019
Argentina (Senate)	July 2019
Spain (Congress of Deputies)	September 2019
Austria (National Council Lower House)	September 2019
France (Parliament)	September 2019
Malta (Parliament)	October 2019
Bangladesh (Parliament)	November 2019
European Union (Parliament—27 member states)	November 2019
Italy (Chamber of Deputies)	December 2019
Northern Ireland (National Assembly)	February 2020
Spain (National Government/Cabinet)	January 2020
Andorra (General Council)	January 2020
Northern Ireland (Assembly)	February 2020
The Maldives (Parliament)	February 2020
South Korea (National Assembly)	September 2020
Japan (Parliament)	November 2020
New Zealand (Parliament)	December 2020
Singapore (Parliament)	February 2021
Fiji	July 2022
Peru	January 2022
Vanuatu (Parliament)	May 2022

Based on data from Climate Emergency Declaration and Mobilization in Action (https://www.ceda
mia.org/fact-sheets/), as well as from (https://climateemergencydeclaration.org/climate-emerge
ncy-declarations-cover-15-million-citizens/, this table shows countries that have declared climate
emergencies at the national level).

While such moves are not undemocratic—governments with democratic legitimacy promote them and opposition parties often support
them too—they have narrowed the boundaries of democratic pluralism.
They give the impression that climate action is a matter of ensuring that

objectively correct measures are implemented and accelerated, as technocratic imperatives beyond the cut and thrust of ordinary politics. The 2022 IPCC (Intergovernmental Panel on Climate Change) report lamented that this trend was moving in the wrong direction: it insisted that climate resilient development needs inclusive and rights-based processes and noted that governments around the world have so far limited their actions to changing physical infrastructure rather than the social infrastructure needed for "transformational change."[30]

The Micropolitics of Climate Action

In the flipside double-movement offsetting the dynamics of eco-authoritarianism and trustee-democracy, the rise of bottom-up climate action points toward a different scenario of ecological crisis acting as catalyst for deeper democratic engagement. In a powerful trend and example of civic micropolitics—as defined in the analytical framework—the climate and ecological crisis is leading to different forms and levels of pro-democratic mobilization and initiatives. Local community micropolitics, mass protests, and formally organized climate assemblies are three levels of citizen engagement helping either sustain democratic politics or creating openings for citizen engagement.

Environmental civil society activism has undergone a particularly notable evolution in relation to democracy. For many years environmental civil society organizations (CSOs) and movements were often criticized for advocating more far-reaching progress on climate action without democratic consent. Indeed, many of the early generation of environmental activists were openly impatient with democracy and skeptical that it could deliver ambitious environmental policies. Far from promoting a conjoining of democracy and climate activism, they insisted that ecological imperatives must be privileged even if this meant circumventing or limiting democratic checks and balances.

This situation has begun to change in recent years. A generation of civil society organizations has taken shape around the notion of "energy democracy," a concept that goes beyond standard activism to embrace the idea of community control over the use of energy resources. The trend is amplifying

---

[30] IPCC Sixth Assessment Report (IPCC, 2022), 23, 27.

42   DEMOCRATIC CROSSROADS

democratic input to difficult environmental decisions while also moving toward an "eco-co-operativism" model of energy consumption based around more localized resources and community decision-making over how these are distributed.[31] Decentralization of energy production is necessary to meet current emissions targets, and this is unlikely without locally rooted, inclusive decision-making at community level.

A thicker and more vibrant civil society has taken shape in reaction against the trends of eco-authoritarianism and technocratic depoliticization. Social movements based around environmental concerns have grown in number, size, and reach in all regions of the world.[32] Crucially, CSOs long focused on political rights have begun to redefine their activism as part of such green-democracy mobilization, tightening the fusion between environmental and democracy concerns. A commitment to grass roots democracy has become an increasingly defining and integral feature of many of these newer climate movements. Ecological crisis has been one of the most powerful catalysts for civil society growth globally. With relatively few countries around the world having green parties present in parliament, this civil society route to strengthening the democratic element of climate action has become especially significant.

This civic driven agenda of environmental democracy focuses on deep reform to current democratic practices and not just raising the profile of environmental issues.[33] There has been a notable trend in recent years toward a democracy of practical everyday living—a communitarianism built around more sustainable material practices. This is the focus adopted by many established CSOs, but it has also increasingly attracted citizens not part of the world of professionalized environmental activism. It is a thickened form of citizen engagement for an era in which the focus is on climate adaptation more than mitigation—that is, on communities adjusting to the effects of climate change more than on governments' overarching targets. It also fits an era in which liberal democracy at the macro-systemic level is in ill health generally and spaces for engagement need to be carved out through alternative routes.[34]

---

[31] K. Szulecki and I. Overland, "Energy Democracy as a Process, an Outcome and a Goal: A Conceptual Review," *Energy Research and Social Science* 69 (November 2020), https://doi.org/10.1016/j.erss.2020.101768.

[32] S. Staggenborg, *Grassroots Environmentalism* (Cambridge: Cambridge University Press, 2020).

[33] Pickering, Bäckstrand, and Schlosberg, "Between Environmental and Ecological Democracy."

[34] R. Eckersley, "Ecological Democracy and the Rise and Decline of Liberal Democracy: Looking Back, Looking Forward," *Environmental Politics* 29, no. 2 (2020): 214–234.

DEMOCRACY AND CLIMATE CRISIS   43

This is the case with many of the most prominent climate organizations to have emerged in the last decade or so. The 350.org movement, Extinction Rebellion (XR), the Climate Reality Project, Fridays for Future, and others portray grassroots democratization as an integral and essential part of solutions to the climate and ecological crisis.[35] XR has pressed for citizen assemblies to be core to climate action and has used participative measures in its own decisions. It set up a Future Democracy Hub with "empathy circles" in small-scale community settings and funded a Trust the People project to build locally participative communities. XR's stated aim has been to marry radical social-movement tactics with local community assemblies: the former to shift the political conversation around systemic change, the latter to bring citizens into more practical solutions.[36] Many civic groups focused on social justice have criticized current international policies on climate change for regressively placing higher costs on poorer sectors of society; these groups link such critiques to a call for radical democratic renewal.[37] Often environmental activists are now moving into politics on this agenda. A notable example was in Australia where activists from the Climate 200 organization were elected to parliament in May 2022 and played a role in defeating the climate-skeptic incumbent administration.

A major focus of the newer movements is on creating sustainable food systems managed by local communities in open and participative fashion. The aims are not about democracy in a national-systemic sense but rather about communities overseeing "local democratic and sustainable flows" based on practical popular engagement in new green localities and circular economic patterns. They also focus on how such models that function within "planetary boundaries" are themselves part of the quest to safeguard personal freedoms in the future. Indeed, they use this narrative of needing to respect planetary boundaries as a framework for preserving open politics, as democracy is unlikely to endure if physical conditions deteriorate beyond certain points.[38]

Such self-organized local communities have prospered and grown around local sustainability aims even in highly or partially authoritarian contexts.

---

[35] See 350.org website, https://350.org/; Extinction Rebellion website, https://rebellion.global/; Climate Reality Project website, https://www.climaterealityproject.org/; and Fridays for Future website, https://fridaysforfuture.org/ (all accessed April 27, 2023).

[36] See Extinction Rebellion UK website, https://www.xrdemocracy.uk/ (accessed April 27, 2023).

[37] D. Gabor, "The European Green Deal Will Bypass the Poor and Go Straight to the Rich," *The Guardian*, February 19, 2020.

[38] Pickering, Bäckstrand, and Schlosberg, "Between Environmental and Ecological Democracy."

44 DEMOCRATIC CROSSROADS

A notable example exists at village level in Thailand, where the uptake of eco-friendly methods has advanced through communal decision-making and shared microcredit schemes.[39] In Turkey, civil society organizations have engaged in new actions of local community resilience against government plans to take control of forests, build a huge canal project into the Black Sea, and other such schemes.[40] Even in China many community groups have played a role in monitoring local pollution and prompting government environmental commitments—these are concerned with making an authoritarian regime more open, transparent and responsive as part of the climate agenda.[41]

In democracies, these kinds of civic movements are highly critical of the trend toward eco-technocracy. They stress that the same proponents of the trustee state model are those immersed in the networks of vested interests that enable elites and public authorities to limit energy transition. They have increasingly challenged the numerous climate agencies and committees set up as guardians of the trustee-democracy model of climate action.[42] In the US many climate CSOs opposed President Biden's climate emergency law, in the name of safeguarding community democratic participation.

Many movements see climate democracy emerging as part of whole system change away from both "fossil capitalism" and the current official goal of "climate capitalism." Through a new Energy Democracy Alliance, their key focus is on local democratic participation to decide on resource issues and ensure fairer access to renewable energy generation.[43] Many civic groups have found an entry point to engage on this nexus through the many networks that have formed between city governments on climate action, like the C40 and Zero Cities initiatives. And many civil society organizations have fashioned agendas around a link between climate democracy and a nascent post-development agenda. Young activists from the Global South insist they are often more vocal in linking climate and democracy than their Western

[39] L. Delina, "Climate Mobilizations and Democracy: The Promise of Scaling Community Energy Transitions in a Deliberative System," *Journal of Environmental Policy and Planning* 22, no. 1 (2020): 30–42.

[40] F. Siccardi, "Will Green Activism Save Turkey's Democracy?," *Carnegie Europe*, June 30, 2022, https://carnegieeurope.eu/2022/06/30/will-green-activism-save-turkey-s-democracy-pub-87413.

[41] Averchenkova, Plyska, and Wahlgren, *Addressing the Climate and Environmental Crises Through Better Governance*, 16.

[42] G. Smith, *Can Democracy Safeguard the Future?* (Cambridge: Polity Press, 2021).

[43] W. Carroll, "Fossil Capitalism, Climate Capitalism, Energy Democracy: The Struggles for Hegemony in an Era of Climate Crisis," *Socialist Studies* 14, no. 1 (2020): 1–26. On the Energy Democracy Alliance, see https://socialiststudies.com/index.php/sss/article/view/27275/20189.

counterparts, not least because in poorer countries the prospect of degrowth does not entail voters giving up so much privilege and consumption.[44]

The Environmental Reporting Collective has coordinated collaboration across borders to report environmental crimes and damage, as the twin agendas of media freedom and climate emergency fuse into a single area of concern. Choked Up campaigns for clean air legislation through a rights perspective. Pass the Mic presses for community engagement specifically to take attention away from the high profile, media-present movements that focus on climate summits. Planet Patrol is based on local communities organizing democratically to improve their own immediate environments.[45] The MovementHub in Germany links work on local climate democracy to social justice issues, while the E3Zero initiative brings together youth activists across developing regions to merge climate, poverty, and democracy agendas with a slogan of "zero exclusion for zero emissions."

In the US, the League of Conservation Voters expanded from 2021, advancing environmental progress through democratic action on the grounds that "the long-term health of our planet is inextricably linked with the health of our democracy"; it has organized an increasingly wide range of participative policymaking on environmental issues.[46] The New York group Climate Mobilization similarly assists local communities to organize themselves to influence decision-making over climate change.[47] In Europe, the civic micropolitics trend intensified notably after Russia's invasion of Ukraine, as the energy crisis gave a strong boost to local energy communities across Europe. After a dramatic expansion, by 2022 around 2 million European citizens were involved in over 7000 local energy schemes, making their own renewable energy and sharing it on a community basis.[48]

This local civic spirit is beginning to filter into government policies linking the climate agenda and democracy-building. The EU has funded the

---

[44] SIPRI, "Addressing the Climate Crisis and Protecting the Future of Democracy," *YouTube*, May 23, 2022, https://www.youtube.com/watch?v=UQ1kyo0OxVk.

[45] W. Coldwell and K. Chaddah, "Beyond Extinction Rebellion: The Protest Groups Fighting on the Climate Frontline," *The Guardian*, October 30, 2021, https://www.theguardian.com/environment/2021/oct/30/beyond-extinction-rebellion-the-protest-groups-fighting-on-the-climate-frontline.

[46] League of Conservation Voters website, https://www.lcv.org/ (accessed April 27, 2023).

[47] Climate Mobilization website, https://www.theclimatemobilization.org/ (accessed April 27, 2023).

[48] J. Henley, "Energy Citizenship: Europe's Communities Forging a Low-Carbon Future," *The Guardian*, September 3, 2022, https://www.theguardian.com/environment/2022/sep/03/energy-citizenship-europes-communities-forging-a-low-carbon-future.

46 DEMOCRATIC CROSSROADS

so-called Greta project to develop "energy citizenship" across Europe.[49] The Dutch government has a program to ensure that 50 percent of energy production is community owned, while New Zealand has pioneered a model that brings citizens into dialogue with expert advisors.[50] In July 2022, the Biden administration made available 60 billion dollars for US community organizations to work on climate empowerment and justice projects.[51] The UN has created an Action for Climate Empowerment initiative to promote democratic engagement in policies related to multilateral carbon-reduction commitments.[52]

In Latin America, civic activism and the human rights potential of environmental issues is reflected in the landmark Escazú Treaty that entered into force in 2021. This treaty guarantees citizens' right to access environmental information and participate in environmental decision-making, and it requires states to prevent and investigate attacks against those who protect and defend environmental rights. It promises to give human rights CSOs fuller participation in climate action and promises wider civic participation in environmental matters. Then United Nations High Commissioner for Human Rights, Michelle Bachelet called it "a cornerstone for environmental democracy." Civic activists played a leading role in defining and negotiating the treaty alongside governments.[53]

Climate Protests

Alongside the thickening of this often practical and community level micropolitics, the climate crisis has also unleashed an increasingly dramatic and confrontational democratic engagement. Around the world, mass protests related in some form to the climate and ecological crisis have

---

[49] See GRETA, https://projectgreta.eu/project/ (accessed February 19, 2024).

[50] Dudley, Jordan, and Lorenzoni, "Independent Expert Advisory Bodies Facilitate Ambitious Climate Policy Responses."

[51] Averchenkova, Plyska, and Wahlgren, *Addressing the Climate and Environmental Crises Through Better Governance*, 34.

[52] United Nations Climate Change, "Action for Climate Empowerment," https://unfccc.int/topics/education-youth/the-big-picture/what-is-action-for-climate-empowerment#eq-3(accessed February 19, 2024).

[53] Z. Ali, "The Escazú Agreement: A Landmark Regional Treaty for Environmental Defenders," *Universal Rights Group*, February 10, 2021, https://www.universal-rights.org/contemporary-and-emerging-human-rights-issues/the-escazu-agreement-a-landmark-regional-treaty-for-environmental-defenders/.

become ubiquitous in recent years. These are relevant to global democracy in both an indirect and direct sense: indirectly because such large-scale mobilization denotes a general democratic vibrancy and capacity; and directly because many such protests have expressly linked environmental issues to citizens' grievances over the lack of or limitations to democracy. Figure 3.1 shows the spread of these protests, by regime type.

Different categories of climate- or environment-related protests have spread. In terms of the book's analytical framework, these exhibit differing degrees and combinations of civic and rejectionist micropolitics. One category is protest directly in favor of more ambitious climate action. These mobilizations have become more frequent, larger, and more geographically widespread in the last several years and have also been framed with a more fused climate-democracy narrative. A second category is protest more indirectly related to environmental issues. Revolts against food and water shortages are becoming more numerous, as are those critical of governments' mismanagement of climate-related disasters. These kinds of protests can be quite oblique in their climate messaging but have increasingly provided a trigger for democratic uprisings. A third category is protest more critical of climate and environmental policies, which points to a more complex and problematic relationship between democracy and ecological crisis.

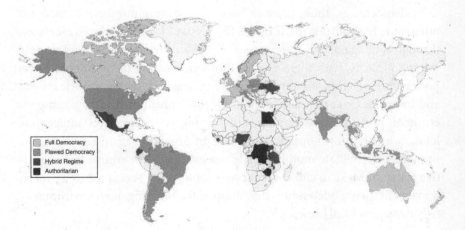

Figure 3.1 Map of climate protests by regime type

This map shows countries in which sizeable climate protests have occurred, with countries shaded according to regime type, as classified by the EIU Democracy Index 2022. Based on data from Carnegie's Climate Protest Tracker, https://carnegieendowment.org/publications/interactive/climate-protest-tracker.

48 DEMOCRATIC CROSSROADS

Direct Pressure for Climate Action

An increasing number of protests has focused on pushing governments for more ambitious climate action or to get more serious in meeting their emissions targets. Many groups have adopted more radical mobilization tactics as the climate emergency has worsened. In 2019, 6 million people mobilized in climate protests that formed part of the Global Week for Future—the largest ever climate protest. Many of the best-known protest organizers, like the Fridays for Future movement, have tended to focus on this level of objective. Other protests have pushed for a more far-reaching set of aims, asserting that the climate emergency requires a more fundamental change in economic policies and deeper democratization of existing power structures.

In authoritarian regimes, environmental protests have intensified as these regimes often show a disregard for the social impact of large infrastructure projects. Turkey is a good example, as from 2019 protests erupted against several such projects with serious environmental impacts. These protests attracted large numbers of citizens even as the regime made overtly political protests increasingly difficult to organize, meaning that the environment became a rallying point for general discontent with President Erdoğan and his tightening grip on power. In one notable case, opposition figures joined community-run protests against a gold-mining project in the forested mountains outside Istanbul as they realized these local events had wider political significance and potential.[54]

In democracies, these protests have also become more numerous and often more hard-hitting in the tactics they deploy. Protests in India increased through 2022 against the government's heavy-handed seizure of land for new mining projects, with these mobilizations connecting the administration's poor record on climate action with its general assault on democratic checks and balances. Over the same period, protests spread in Brazil against government plans to ease mining and logging restrictions on indigenous lands, while tens of thousands protested in Argentina against government proposals to facilitate multinationals' operations in environmentally sensitive areas. In Mexico, citizens' concerns about water access led to a protest movement then a referendum that stopped the building of an environmentally damaging local brewery.[55]

---

[54] Siccardi, "Will Green Activism Save Turkey's Democracy?"

[55] D. Agren, "Mexico Protesters Fear US-Owned Brewery Will Drain Their Land Dry," *The Guardian*, February 4, 2018, https://www.theguardian.com/world/2018/feb/04/mexico-water-brewery-mexicali-constellation-brands.

More globally spread events have equally become frequent and have mobilized increasing numbers of people. Fridays for Future resumed weekly in-person protests across the word in September 2021 after suspending these during the COVID-19 pandemic. Over a quarter of a million congregated to protest at the COP26 summit in Glasgow in autumn 2021. This was preceded and accompanied by multiple events in cities across the world; in one example, over 25,000 marched in Brussels against governments' failure to meet climate targets. Between April and May 2022, international scientists organized protests across 26 different countries against governments' limited progress toward meeting emissions targets.

Many movements reacted against government subsidies for oil and gas consumption after the Russian invasion of Ukraine. Some of the large climate groups like Extinction Rebellion, EcoAction, and Fridays for Future organized a stream of events in multiple cities through the spring and summer of 2022 to press governments for a more decisive cut in Russian oil and gas imports. In Europe, the XR offshoot Just Stop Oil gained a high profile and much notoriety with a series of protest events. Protests with tens of thousands of participants pushed for more ambitious climate action in France, the UK, and Germany, linked with pressure to hasten decoupling from Russian gas. A protest of over 15,000 people in Germany that lasted several months opposed plans to demolish a village so that a coal mine could expand. The wave of protests gained in intensity into 2023. Protests at the European Gas Conference called for an end to new gas and oil projects. In the Netherlands, a motorway blockade led by XR supporters opposed the government's handling of subsidies for fossil energy producers. Significantly, in these protests many climate movements framed their ecological demands in terms of the geopolitical implications of Russian actions—a link picked up in Chapter 7.[56]

Although the energy crisis most directly affected Europe, such protests took place globally. In several US cities, the Fight for our Future movement mobilized against the Biden administration's adoption of post-invasion measures that would take the US even further from emissions targets. A US senior citizens' protest pushed to make banks stop financing fossil fuels. Similar events were of notable scale and fervor in Israel too. In March 2023, Global Climate Strike protests took place across Africa, New Zealand, and

---

[56] Climate Protest Tracker, *Carnegie Endowment for International Peace*, https://carnegieendowm ent.org/publications/interactive/climate-protest-tracker(accessed February 19, 2024).

50   DEMOCRATIC CROSSROADS

elsewhere, calling for more ambitious climate action and less reliance on fossil fuels. At the World Economic Forum, protestors demanded a move away from profit-oriented capitalist growth. In December 2022, Mongolian citizens protested corruption behind government support for the country's coal industry, alongside skyrocketing inflation.[57] The gathering wave of protests targeting oil and gas exploration around the world fed into the COP28 summit in December 2023, at which states for the first time committed to reducing the production and use of fossil fuels.

These revolts clearly represent a fillip for democratic engagement and mark a notable change, as climate-related protests have become an entry-point for mobilizations concerned with political-systemic issues. While many of them focus on standard repertoires of climate campaigning, many have also developed an increasingly political edge to their mobilizations. Yet differences have arisen among activists over this democracy-ecology link. Frustrated with the modest progress being made on ecological change, many activists have in the last several years adopted more radical forms of civil disobedience and high-profile disruptive actions. These groups insist that patient democratic deliberation has failed the climate challenge and many of them question the very concept of democracy. A number of these more radical groups have formed an alliance, the A22 network, committed to an agenda of "mass civil disobedience."[58]

Climate Impacts as Protest Trigger

There have been an even larger number of mass protests triggered by the general or indirect effects of climate change and ecological devastation. This category of revolts is not directly concerned with advocating for climate action and is not focused expressly on governments' emissions reductions. Rather, these protests tend to center around ordinary people being affected by the secondary consequences of environmental stresses and resource limitations. The growth of this kind of protest is especially significant to this book as these kinds of mobilizations show a marked tendency to widen out into a focus on bad governance. Protests around a specific natural disaster or resource shortages can often become triggers for political change. It is here

[57] "Protesters in Mongolia Try to Storm State Palace," *Al Jazeera*, December 6, 2022, https://www.aljazeera.com/news/2022/12/6/protesters-in-mongolia-try-to-storm-state-palace.
[58] K. Mathieson, "Climate Activists Have a New Target: Civilians," *Politico*, May 2, 2023

that the interface between environmental problems and poor political governance has been most directly felt—and given most tangible expression.

Protests in authoritarian regimes in response to climate disasters have become a frequent trigger for political change. Food shortages indirectly linked to climate change have been a factor in many protests that morph into calls for democratization. One example was the Arab spring, as various environmental events fed into the social discontent behind democracy protests across the Middle East and North Africa in 2011 and 2012 and for some years after. Poor harvests in many Arab states forced large scale movements of people into cites; here, unemployed and rootless, they joined a swell of frustration against authoritarian regimes. While there are contrasting views about how much of a direct causal role these climate factors played in the Arab protests, the events certainly showed how climate factors have begun to have a cascade of indirect consequences with political ramifications.

The earthquake that shook Nepal in 2015 led to greater social pressure on the political elite to prepare the country better for natural disasters and pushed forward an incipient democratization process. Many thousands protested in Iran in late 2021 against water shortages, in criticism of both environmental mismanagement and authoritarian patterns of governance in the regime. Although initially connected to a ban on chemical fertilizers, the uprising in Sri Lanka in 2022 over time focused more on government environmental mismanagement and climate activists played a leading role in pushing for democratic reform and ousting the incumbent president. In September 2022, protests erupted in Cuba in reaction to Hurricane Ian's worsening of already poor living conditions.[59]

As these protests and activism have become more widespread and powerful, so governments have sought to clampdown on them, precisely because of the connection with political reform issues. A less benign side of the protest equation is that many regimes' responses to these mobilizations have been highly draconian. Many governments have clamped down hard, using environmental activism as a pretext for a turbo-charged authoritarian control. In many countries, this has left political freedoms in a worse position, at least in the immediate short term. Authoritarian regimes have made climate protests harder in many countries. The same trend is apparent in many

---

[59] C. Acosta and M. Abi-Habib, "Protests Erupt in Cuba Over Government Response to Hurricane Ian," *New York Times*, September 30, 2022, https://www.nytimes.com/2022/09/30/world/americas/cuba-hurricane-ian-protests.html.

52   DEMOCRATIC CROSSROADS

democracies too: most European governments have increased police powers to circumscribe protests in general, and this affects those events related to environmental concerns. In June 2023, the French government moved to close direct-action group Les Soulèvements de la Terre. Climate related civic micropolitics has often engendered illiberal statism in its wake.

The rights organization, Front Line Defenders reports that over two-thirds of civic activist killings now target those working on environmental and land rights.[60] Global Witness reports a rising number of lethal attacks on climate activists around the world, especially in places like Colombia, Mexico, and the Philippines. Most deaths are related to activists' opposition to the local environmental impacts of mining, logging, or dam-building projects. Indigenous peoples are disproportionately a target of attacks, accounting for over a third of the deaths. State, business, and crime-related actors have played a part in the worsening situation, often in collusion with each other.[61] The UN reports that activists involved in environmental protests have become especially vulnerable and now account for over half of all reported killings related to human rights civil society initiatives.[62] Large renewables multinationals have gained more intrusive access to local land and resources for projects that export green energy out of developing areas to advanced economies; in recent years an increasing number of attacks and restrictions on activists have been associated with their opposition to such green projects.[63]

Rejectionist Protest

A final group of protests show a more complex and difficult relationship between climate factors and democracy. This covers a very broad range of mobilizations that are in some fashion critical or questioning of climate action. Citizens around the world have become perhaps most directly concerned with the cost of energy and have increasingly taken to the streets to

[60] Frontline, *Annual Report 2021*, March 17, 2022, https://www.frontlineplc.cy/annual-report-2021/.

[61] Global Witness, *Last Line of Defence*, 2021, https://www.globalwitness.org/en/campaigns/environmental-activists/last-line-defence/.

[62] M. Lawlor, *Final Warning: Death Threats and Killings of Human Rights Defenders: Report of the Special Rapporteur on the Situation of Human Rights Defenders* (Geneva: United Nations, 2021).

[63] N. Lakhani, "A Just Transition Depends on Energy Systems That Work for Everyone," *The Guardian*, November 13, 2022, https://www.theguardian.com/environment/2022/nov/12/cop27-dash-for-gas-africa-energy-colonialism.

press governments for cheaper access oil and gas supplies. In some cases, more political activists have harnessed such concerns to organize protests that are explicitly against ambitious environmental policies. These protests may be unhelpful for climate policies, while their impact on democratization is uncertain. This group of protests suggests that positive climate and democracy activism are not straightforwardly synonymous with each other.

These kinds of revolts have come to represent one of the main sources of citizen activism in authoritarian regimes. In one of the most dramatic cases, tens of thousands took to the streets in Kazakhstan at the beginning of 2022 to protest the removal of a price cap on gas. These protests were primarily for lower gas prices but also took on a pro-democracy dimension against the government's general corruption, nepotism, and lack of transparency. Russian intervention quelled the uprising, but pressure for governance reforms continued and had some impact. Large scale protests also rocked Ecuador in 2022 as indigenous groups pressed the government to take measures to bring down rising fuel prices, and similar revolts took place in Morocco.

In advanced democracies too, such concerns have ignited critical citizen engagement. While extreme weather events and the Ukraine war increased public support for climate action in 2022, protests also spread against rising energy prices. In summer 2022, 50,000 Dutch farmers protested the government's new emissions-reduction target enshrined in a law that would require a drastic reduction in livestock farming; in part they complained at the lack of consultation and openness in the process. The protestors morphed into a political party, the Farmer Citizen Movement that unexpectedly won provincial elections in March 2023 and became the largest party in the national upper chamber. Farmers in New Zealand mobilized on and off through 2021 and 2022 for similar reasons.

Protests multiplied in European states after the Russian invasion of Ukraine to press governments to limit the rise in oil and gas prices. Even if many of these events were not expressly against the climate agenda, their core case was that the fast-spiraling cost of living crisis was now a more urgent priority. In the summer of 2022, over 10,000 citizens took to the streets of Athens to push the government to intervene to bring down gas prices and rocketing electricity bills. Large mobilizations occurred in Germany, the Czech Republic, and other European countries, with a line that European governments were wrong to be putting support for Ukraine and sanctions against Russia ahead of domestic energy priorities. Most dramatically, a wave

54   DEMOCRATIC CROSSROADS

of farmers' protests across Europe in early 2024 pushed the EU to dilute environmental targets for the agricultural sector.

In a notable emerging trend, protests multiplied against mining projects involving so-called critical minerals. A notable case was in Serbia where protests ran on and off against a Rio Tinto lithium mine, with some effect as the government revoked its license. Civil society organizations and citizen groups have increasingly mobilized against the environmental impact of mining projects for critical minerals in Europe, just as governments and the EU institutions have stepped up funding for these initiatives.[64] These cases are complicated, as protestors have organized against harmful environmental impacts but in doing so push back against the use of materials that governments present as integral to ecological transition. Some of the same logic can be seen in protests against other nominally green energy projects. In Georgia, the Rioni Valley Defenders movement and protests in 2021 got a hydroelectric project stopped after government authorities sold village land to a private company without local peoples' involvement—the group's demand was for citizen participation in any decision to go ahead with future projects linked to energy transition.

Many conservative movements have organized protests that present *resistance* to climate policies as essential for defending and renewing democracy. They have built a narrative that governments' heavy-handed implementation of climate policies is restricting democratic freedoms. In the US particularly, many local community groups have invoked the language of democratic rights to stop green projects. Such groups insist that democratic systems have not been open or participative enough for citizens to challenge elite views on climate policy. They have effectively turned the language of democratic rights against ambitious climate policy.[65] Some participants in these events are hardcore climate-change deniers, while others are mainly concerned with what they see as the unfair and opaque ways in which governments have advanced the climate agenda. They often argue that national democratic renewal is needed as a means to counter opaque and technocratic multilateral climate accords. Those participating in activism against fuel tax rises are not necessarily inveterate climate skeptics, but they dislike the political processes through which transitions are being taken forward.[66] The

---

[64] O. Granados, "Las minas españolas resucitan," *El Pais*, August 21, 2021, https://elpais.com/economia/2021-08-22/las-minas-espanolas-resucitan.html.

[65] Counterpoint and OSEPI, *Green Wedge?*

[66] J. Kulin, I. J. Sevä, and R. E. Dunlap, "Nationalist Ideology, Right-Wing Populism, and Public Views about Climate Change in Europe," *Environmental Politics* 30, no. 7 (2021): 1111–1134.

large environmental movements have often failed to involve marginalized communities in rural locations, leaving these parts of the population drawn more to skeptical hard-right agendas.

So, the spread of these protests raises uncomfortable questions about the environment-democracy nexus. In many cases, climate-skeptics' appeals to a spirit of democratic renewal are insincere and opportunistic—a strand of rejectionist micropolitics. Many hard-right groups have deployed violent tactics and their political programs are clearly incompatible with basic democratic norms. Anti-climate protestors who claim they are rescuing democracy from environmental authoritarianism often then vote for political parties with highly illiberal agendas and questionable commitment to democracy. Mirroring the way that decisions to take key aspects of economic policy out of the political sphere fueled populism in the 2010s, citizens' frustration with the top-down nature of climate decisions has more recently begun to cause more serious challenges for democratic governments.

Still, in many senses these protests represent a legitimate quest for democratic voice and a counterreaction to the rise of trustee technocracy and elite-controlled multilateral commitments. One large research project looked closely at the relationship between these skeptical protests and broader trends in anti-democratic populism and found this link to be varied: they had clearly negative spillover for democratic quality in some instances, but more positive implications in others.[67] This does leave the uneasy prospect that a push for democratic renovation may be associated with anti-climate as much as pro-environment agendas. Some hard-right activists even position themselves as architects of a kind of anti-globalism, anti-modernism based around local community and resource management. Even if many of these same groups clearly menace democracy in other ways, at least it might be said that the fraught politics of energy transition is driving heightened democratic engagement on both sides of these debates.

The Era of Climate Assemblies

In parallel to civil society organizations and protests, a more formal and structured kind of citizen participation in climate issues has taken root in

---

[67] F. Reusswig, interview, Strom Forschung, January 7, 2021, https://www.strom-forschung.de/int erviews/interview-with-dr-fritz-reusswig.

56 DEMOCRATIC CROSSROADS

the last several years. Climate assemblies are a fast-spreading and different way in which the climate crisis has triggered efforts to improve and extend democratic engagement. This is a more top-down trend, generally led by state bodies—a form of liberal statism in the climate sphere. Increasing numbers of public authorities at the national, regional, and municipal levels have convened citizen assemblies to debate the climate crisis. The distinctive feature of these initiatives is that ordinary citizens are selected on a random basis by lot to draw up policy recommendations. Climate assemblies are one part of a broader trend toward the use of so-called selection-based mini-publics. Many analysts see this latest wave of deliberative forums as the leading edge of democratic renewal and climate change has been the most frequently covered subject of these assemblies.

By 2024, national climate assemblies had been run in Austria, Belgium, Denmark, Finland, France, Germany, Ireland, Luxembourg, Spain, and the UK. They have been especially numerous at city and regional level. Climate assemblies have run in hundreds of local administrations across European countries, including in democratic-backsliding Hungary and Poland, and in countries like Brazil, Colombia, India, the Maldives, New Zealand, and South Korea. Many of these subnational assemblies were not mandated to address overarching climate policy directly but related issues like urban redesign plans and water management.[68] In 2022, Milan and Brussels city councils set up permanent climate assemblies. The first of its kind to take place in the US, a Washington climate assembly convened virtually in 2021. Also in 2021 the European Climate Foundation set up a Knowledge Network on Climate Assemblies to exchange best practice in their design and methodology.

Several of these citizen assemblies have pushed their governments to make new climate commitments. Climate assemblies have spread to such a degree that many see them set to become standard practice within local, subnational administrations. Governments tend to respond supportively, giving an opening for organized groups to push for change and link climate issues to political rights. These assemblies are an increasingly important democratic process that has resulted directly from the climate challenge. Supporters stress that assemblies have made proposals relevant to the most sensitive costs of climate change—like the need for higher taxes on carbon—and that

---

[68] For overview of all climate assemblies worldwide, see Bürgerrat, https://www.buergerrat.de/en/citizens-assemblies/citizens-assemblies-worldwide/ (accessed February 19, 2024).

ordinary citizens have shown that they will support radical changes if they have the issues explained to them and if they are obliged to make proposals themselves.[69]

Increasingly, climate assemblies have established a formal and regular place within institutional decision-making processes. Ireland's net-zero commitment came at the end of a long process involving a citizen assembly that fed into a parliamentary committee and wider civic engagement too. The Irish assembly made far-sighted recommendations on climate that went beyond the initial government agenda, and it helped produce a new climate law.[70] In some French municipalities processes are going beyond standard, authority-controlled climate assemblies to combine lot-based selection with politicians and social movements within formal deliberation on the local green transition agenda.[71]

Other varieties of participation around climate issues have borrowed from these initiatives while fashioning their own distinctive modes of green democracy. In many experiments, citizen forums on climate change have adopted more open forms of participation. Many examples could be given from around the world. In the Green Human City in Skopje, civil society organizations, citizens, social movements, and local councilors have engaged in coordinated fashion all around sustainable city plans. Village parliaments and social audits have spread in India with ecological issues among their main concerns. In the UK, a coalition of environmental groups initiated a Nature Assembly around a core of open citizen conversations, with a view to drawing up a People's Plan for Nature.[72] Participatory budgeting has been used to widen citizens' engagement over climate action and has led to environmental improvements in African and Latin American states.[73] The C40 Cities Climate Leadership Group has sought to develop such innovations within municipal administrations across the world.

---

[69] R. Willis, *Too Hot to Handle? The Democratic Challenge of Climate Change* (Bristol: Bristol University Press, 2020).

[70] D. Torney, "Deliberative Mini-Publics and the European Green Deal in Turbulent Times: The Irish and French Climate Assemblies," *Politics and Governance* 9, no. 3 (2021), https://www.cogitat iopress.com/politicsandgovernance/article/view/4382.

[71] I. Babelon, N. Nickel, and P. Pierri, "A Novel Approach to Local Climate Action in France," *Carnegie Europe*, April 22, 2021, https://carnegieeurope.eu/2021/04/22/novel-approach-to-local-climate-action-in-france-pub-84363.

[72] See People's Plan for Nature, https://peoplesplanfornature.org/sites/default/files/2022-09/Peo ple%27s-Plan-for-Nature-Conversation-guide_1.pdf(accessed February 19, 2024).

[73] Lindvall, *Democracy and the Challenge of Climate Change*, 38.

58 DEMOCRATIC CROSSROADS

Of course, there are limitations to these climate assemblies and other forms of publicly run engagement. They are still not that numerous and rarely established on a permanent basis. The number of local authorities declaring climate emergencies increasing their own executive powers is far greater than the number that have run climate assemblies, trustee statism outweighing liberal statism on this measure. Most of them have been held in Europe and have dealt with low-hanging fruit, changes to which almost all citizens can acquiesce without game-changing consequences to their lives. The most common pattern is that climate assemblies are held at city or local level to take forward climate targets pre-imposed by national governments—targets not open to being questioned by those with climate-skeptic concerns. Most assemblies tend to present long-term aspirations without measures to deal with short-term energy crises or costs of energy transition. Participants tend to call for measures likely to offer general societal benefits like investments in energy efficiency and recycling but overlook more controversial and far-reaching aspects of change. They risk giving legitimacy to governments that are committed to only partial ecological transitions. Deliberative theorists generally concur that recent climate assemblies have helped foster some wider debate on environmental issues but fall short in connecting with other parts of the democratic system.[74]

Indeed, many climate movements and activist groups have become increasingly frustrated that climate assemblies are too slow and timid, and simply legitimize a broken system. Such frustration was behind the Just Stop Oil group breaking away from XR to pursue more radical protest tactics. This impatience resulted especially from developments in France where a high-profile national climate assembly set the gold standard for direct democratic engagement but led to a 2021 climate and resilience bill that watered down the assembly's recommendations. Reports from these assemblies commonly read like a shopping list of all the ideal and general features of a green transition. They typically say little about the tensions between policy goals—like that between speeding up the green transition and redressing fuel poverty. The data shows that climate action has been more ambitious not where more assemblies are held but where overall levels of democracy are stronger.[75]

---

[74] N. Curato, J. Vrydagh, and A. Bächtiger, "Democracy without Shortcuts: Introduction to the Special Issue," *Journal of Deliberative Democracy* 16, no. 2 (2020): 1–9.

[75] V-Dem Institute, "The Case for Democracy Week: Combating Climate Change," *YouTube*, https://www.youtube.com/watch?v=Mcew0ahVO9E (accessed February 19, 2024).

Assessment: Top-Down versus Bottom-Up Climate Action

The relationship between democracy and climate change will be one of the most crucial for the future of humanity and the international system. Analysts have been running correlations for many years to ascertain whether democratic or authoritarian systems are best suited to advance transitions to low carbon economies. However, political systems are not simply a fixed variable. The interaction of environmental crisis and politics is more symbiotic, as ecological challenges begin to reshape political systems as much as different kinds of political systems affect environmental policy. Indeed, in recent years this has clearly become one of the most potent shapers of political processes. The ecological emergency is a long-burn challenge that will unfold over many years into the future, but it has also begun to generate dramatic-crisis tipping points. Crucially, these political impacts are now an integral part of the divide and balance between democracy and autocracy across the world.

Some trends point toward the climate crisis having a prejudicial impact on democracy and the prospects for democratization. Many authoritarian regimes have appropriated the climate change agenda in ways that have further empowered their anti-democratic politics and tightened their grip on the levers of power. Crises of all kinds that take politics out of business-as-usual mode can easily be used to justify centralized decision-making and this tendency is certainly evident in many of the countries undergoing either authoritarian consolidation or democratic backsliding in recent years. Many regimes are clamping down against environmental activism as a core part of their strategies for power-preservation, with such societal pressures resulting in more draconian authoritarianism.

One trend in democracies is toward a form of eco-technocracy—a notable and specific variant of the trustee statism analytical category—that is enshrined in the creation of multiple agencies, expert committees, and legal processes. The need to make progress through carefully crafted multilateral accords reinforces this trend toward abridged forms of trustee green democracy, with eco-technocracy at the international and national levels feeding off each other—showing how within-state and between-state political trends are mutually constitutive. Many argue that the climate agenda is less about citizen-led environmental movements and community engagement than it is about a combination of strong, realist-based nation-state

60 DEMOCRATIC CROSSROADS

action and elite-mediated multilateral negotiations.[76] These measures might be formally democratic and widely deemed as entirely positive and necessary for climate action; they often reflect bipartisan consensus on climate priorities and can in principle be reversed by democratic decisions. Yet the eco-technocracy trend entails important ecological commitments being inoculated from democratic cut and thrust and the uncertainties of citizen preferences. Whatever the virtues of this depoliticization in terms of policy output, citizens have often been left frustrated and feeling disenfranchised by such dynamics, and this has added to the appeal of illiberal populist parties.

At the same time, in a striking double movement, other trends are afoot that offer more positive democratic potential. Indeed, against a backdrop of much democratic pessimism, it is this strand of civic engagement that is in many ways most noteworthy. Academic inquiry on the democracy-environment nexus has mostly been pursued by environmental experts looking for ways in which different kinds of democratic practice might help advance climate action; this book is instead concerned with the reverse question of how the mounting climate and ecological crisis impacts on democracy and democratization. In this regard, a significant political trend is that climate protests and energy activism are reclaiming influence over energy systems and contributing to a wider reshaping of democracy. Energy transition is acting as a catalyst for democratic renewal. Climate activism is becoming an increasingly powerful antidote to rising authoritarianism and a fillip to democratic dynamics.

In a parallel dual movement, this civic micropolitics is often emerging hand in hand with a more liberal statism. After years of debate around the notion of energy justice, this is now being supplemented with a deeper concept of energy democracy. Many different forms of democratic engagement have begun to change political approaches to climate and ecological challenges. In some quarters of government, it is increasingly recognized that difficult decisions related to energy transition need social legitimation and that societies are mobilizing more around these questions. Where climate specialists and policymakers previously tended to be rather dismissive of the need for democratic buy-in, or indeed even explicitly insistent on closed-door top-down regulatory approaches, some have now begun to acknowledge the political dimensions of ecological change.[77] Some insist it is

---

[76] A. Lieven, *Climate Change and the Nation State: The Realist Case* (London: Allen Lane, 2020).
[77] Szulecki and Overland, "Energy Democracy as a Process, an Outcome and a Goal."

this societal mobilization that has ensured democracies are belatedly making more ambitious emission reductions.[78]

One dynamic is that democratic engagement is playing a more powerful advocacy role for climate action, while another is that more democratic engagement is developing as part of the practical changes associated with energy transition itself. The first reflects new, direct democratic agency, the second is a structural change in socioeconomic relations that offers potential as a driver of localized democratization. The climate movement has begun to take on some of the features and significance of previous historical social struggles, such as those for postcolonial independence, and root its aims in wider political notions of self-governance.[79] Climate scientists and practitioners have begun to realize that political processes and alliances need to be factored into their modeling, as these processes shift in response to climate agendas and recondition the pattern of interests in favor of more climate action.[80]

A crucial and yet unanswered question is whether eco-technocracy and eco-democracy can somehow be combined in positive fusion. Expert-led deliberations and multilateral summits on climate change still lack means of legitimization with ordinary citizens. There are huge numbers of local level democratic engagement initiatives, but big technocratic multilateral forums still overshadow these and often draw out their lifeforce. If climate goals are to be enshrined in commitments that are immune to the push and pull of everyday politics, indicators are needed to ensure such depoliticization is rooted in prior democratic consensus building. Current approaches to climate change have not yet taken this wider democratic imperative into account. Select parts of the ecological challenge are being cordoned off from the political arena, with some being entrusted to technocratic agencies or legally enshrined in constitutional commitments while others are being ensconced in small-scale forums for public deliberation: neither are sufficient for an inclusive climate democracy.

Moreover, trends on the democratic side of the equation have different and still unresolved implications for the future of democracy. Increasingly, two separate forms of democratic engagement are pitted against each other: mass

---

[78] R. Pacheco-Vega and A. Murdie, "When Do Environmental NGOs Work? A Test of the Conditional Effectiveness of Environmental Advocacy," *Environmental Politics* 30, no. 2 (2020): 1–22.

[79] L. Delina, *Emancipatory Climate Actions: Strategies from Histories* (New York: Palgrave Pivot, 2019), 11.

[80] F. Moore et al., "Determinants of Emissions Pathways in the Coupled Climate-social System," *Nature* (2022), 103–111.

62 DEMOCRATIC CROSSROADS

mobilization, on the one hand, and mini-public deliberative forums, on the other hand. Often, the proponents of an environmental democracy rooted in mass societal engagement dismiss climate assemblies as an overly controlled version of democracy. Indeed, these assemblies have some overlap with expert-led governance, as experts play a pivotal role in "tutoring" nonexpert citizens—and indeed some feel these experts have rather too much influence in pushing citizens in a certain direction in these deliberative processes. This might be seen as a virtue as assemblies become a venue where experts and citizens co-decide—a welcome fusion from a trustee-democracy perspective. But this is a very different dynamic to the kind of radical reforms for which advocates of environmental democracy habitually call.

Climate assemblies are certainly a necessary and exciting innovation, but other reforms to democratic practices are also needed to broach the macro-level politics of who pays for the transition and how societies can push beyond the superficial focus on technological fixes toward full-scale adjustments to economic and political models. There is still not full democratic buy-in to far-reaching climate action, especially from those set to lose their jobs or pay disproportionately for measures related to the transition. The empowered-state, technocratic approach has taken the focus away from a broader framework of inclusion required for the fair sharing of costs and the containment of vested interests. As state capacities increase to inject the necessary funding for the transition, new and strengthened means of democratic control are not yet fully keeping pace. Energy communities have made much progress on a local level, but less progress is evident at democracy's more systemic level.

Environmental and democracy activism have come partially into line with each other, but there are still differences between their respective priorities. Democratic activists focus on open, plural process which may or may not produce more climate action: the freedom of choice is what is a priori. For many ecologists, the point is to reform democracy so that it guarantees or ringfences certain environmental outcomes. It is these outcomes that are a priori rather than the pluralistic quality of political processes as such—even if many activists insist that widening citizen engagement through such processes will in general tend to push forward climate action and take influence away from vested interests that have curtailed energy transition.[81] Energy democracy is still often framed in terms of public consent being

---

[81] Eckersley, "Ecological Democracy and the Rise and Decline of Liberal Democracy."

needed for necessary climate and environmental measures. This is different from open-ended democracy as an end in itself: many assemblies and other initiatives can often sound like they are setting citizens an exam test in which they must reach the right answers.

Moreover, climate rejectionism is driving much new mobilization. Protests against the removal of fuel subsidies and the like are difficult to interpret, politically. These protestors commonly use a democratic narrative. They are a form of democratic engagement, but also an "energy populism" that is commonly linked to movements that have an illiberal stance on political rights. These movements are in part a response to the way in which climate action has been pursued nationally and internationally. Many suspect expert-driven degrowth ideas to be the next stage of neoliberalism, a new disciplining tool, pushed by an already comfortable middle class to deny poorer sectors the right to improve their material conditions.[82]

Notwithstanding the importance and dynamism of the emerging civic engagement, a more vibrant, open ended democratic politics is still needed, with more plural debate between clearly different pathways forward. This would push beyond expert-driven solutions around green growth that foreclose the cut and thrust of democracy.[83] How governments can achieve social order without endless growth—or even with degrowth—is still uncertain and the role of democracy in this adds another layer of dilemmas. Democracies have so far eschewed any kind of democracy-enhancing national conference-style approach that involves all stakeholders and multiple perspectives on the energy transition, including political parties, state bodies, organized civil society, experts, local administrations, and climate activists. Social contracts for the climate transition have not emerged from within fully inclusive forms of democratic process.

For now, the trends of both democracy-narrowing and democracy-widening climate action are unfolding and the balance between them fluctuates across time and different countries. The analytical framework outlined in the previous chapter helps identify the different kinds and levels of dynamic at play: these involve trustee statism and liberal statism, as well as civic and rejectionist micropolitics. Climate issues are increasingly the terrain upon which struggles take place between democratic reformers and

---

[82] M. Huber, *Climate Change as Class War: Building Socialism on a Warming Planet* (London: Verso, 2022).
[83] Machin, "Democracy, Disagreement, Disruption."

64   DEMOCRATIC CROSSROADS

those resisting democratization. In an era of concern over authoritarian threats, it is perhaps natural to focus on the additional strains on open politics. Yet the extent of new democratic participation around the climate and ecological crisis is striking and its importance not to be dismissed. The challenge is that this democratic renewal and reform are for now not far-reaching enough to show that open politics can thrive and prosper in the era of climate crisis. If democracy cannot in this fashion deal with climate change, then climate change will ensure there is no future for democracy anyway.

4

Snapshot: A Global Climate Assembly

One specific example of democratic renewal around the climate agenda usefully illustrates the vital debates now at play: the organization of a first global climate assembly in 2021 and 2022. This represented an important innovation in moving citizen participation from the local to the international level, to match the global scale of the climate crisis. The formally entitled Global Assembly on the Climate and Ecological Crisis ran with some success and may become a permanent forum from 2024. The experiment sheds light on the balance between the different categories of political action identified in the book's analytical framework. The Global Assembly's successes and shortcomings speak to the relationship between governmental and civic action in the area of climate change. How far the initiative can help advance democratic engagement and accountability depends on whether in a next phase it can gain a higher profile, become more widely known, involve more global citizens and attract buy-in from democratic institutions.[1]

Shortfalls in Climate Global Governance

The structures of international governance on environmental issues challenge democratic accountability. Critics argue that an opaque and top-down set of multilateral negotiations over climate change have allowed little space for fair democratic engagement. The structures and patterns of global governance have become particularly well-developed in relation to climate change and other aspects of ecological crisis. As they have thickened, so concerns have deepened about their effect on democracy. Over two decades, governments and scientific experts have incrementally ratcheted up their

---

[1] The chapter draws from extended interviews and exchanges with two of the Global Assembly's main organizers, Claire Mellier and Rich Wilson.

Democratic Crossroads. Richard Youngs, Oxford University Press. © Oxford University Press 2024.
DOI: 10.1093/oso/9780197762417.003.0004

66 DEMOCRATIC CROSSROADS

multilateral negotiations and commitments. While these have made some progress on climate commitments, they constitute an eco-technocracy that sits uneasily with open, democratic engagement.

International climate governance has increasingly centered around the COP (Conference of the Parties) process. Under the COP rubric, governments gather each year for high level summits with the aim of making commitments to a range of climate action. The COP process has gained momentum as the primary venue for key decisions on climate policy, especially when the summit held in Paris in 2015 seemed to make decisive breakthroughs in garnering more ambitious promises from national governments. For many, the COP process is the epitome of a highly top-down and expert-dominated process.

The politics of multilateral climate agreements reveal the acute difficulty of combining progress on climate action with fairly organized democratic representation. Defenders of the COP and United Nations Framework Convention on Climate Change (UNFCCC) processes point out that expert-led work and intricate deals between governments are necessary to make progress on the climate agenda. They insist that these processes have begun to secure meaningful advances on both mitigation and adaptation: the climate crisis is so pressing that the priority is to get governments signed up to carbon emissions reductions and other measures, on the basis of robust scientific influences. While this may indeed be the case, however, as the COP process has increasingly faltered and failed to secure ambitious enough climate action to keep global warming on track for the crucial 1.5 degrees Celsius limit, so interest has grown in more democratically open forms of decision-making process.

The COP process has become a focus for civil society engagement, as the summits have come to attract thousands of civil society organizations, activists, and private sector representatives. Some efforts at global coordination among civil society have taken shape around the summit: for example, the Climate Action Network mobilizes 1,500 CSOs worldwide to influence the agenda. Despite all this input, however, by the 2020s this process was clearly struggling to deliver far-reaching climate action, fast enough. In the last several years, many climate organizations have begun to disengage from the process, seeing its inclusion of civil society as little more than cosmetic. Moreover, the voice gained by large environmental CSOs or high-profile individual activists has not necessarily reflected the concerns of ordinary citizens or civic movements from the developing world. At the COP27 meeting in Egypt in 2022, many CSOs stepped away from engagement out of concern that the summit process was "greenwashing" the Egyptian regime's human rights abuses. As multilateral talks deal with increasingly life determining decisions, the lack of adequate channels of democratic influence over these has become a glaring omission.

The main avenues of climate-related democratic engagement have developed at a local or subnational, and to some extent, national scale. As outlined in the previous chapter, climate assemblies have proliferated in recent years at the subnational level. These have made an impact but suffer from a weakness: climate change is a transnational challenge and cannot be tackled by initiatives within the borders of single states. There is a mismatch between the way that these deliberative processes are rooted in local communities or in national polities, on the one hand, and the transnational nature of ecological impacts, on the other hand. As climate issues become the defining political issue, this mismatch has come to represent a profound structural challenge for global democracy.

Global Democratic Deliberation?

Civil society groups raised the need for some kind of global level citizens' forum as far back as the early 2000s. Yet while dozens of climate assemblies were run at municipal and national level, no global equivalent emerged in the 2010s. In an effort to unlock progress, a group of civil society organizations and participation experts launched plans for what became the Global Assembly on the Climate and Ecological Crisis in 2020. Three main bodies came together to steer the initiative—the Spanish Deliberativa, the pan-African Innovation for Policy Foundation, and a UK-based group made up of people from the Iswe Foundation—and these were joined by other civic organizations too. The assembly's core delivery team comprised people from 34 different countries, while two advisory committees of experts led on its governance.[2]

The initiative was an attempt to fashion a global interface between deepening ecological crisis and citizen participation. The logic behind the

---

[2] Global Assembly, *Report of the 2021 Global Assembly on the Climate and Ecological Crisis: Giving Everyone a Seat at the Global Governance Table*, 2022, https://globalassembly.org/resources/downloads/GlobalAssembly2021-FullReport.pdf.

68   DEMOCRATIC CROSSROADS

Global Assembly was that the international politics of climate transitions were especially thorny and prone to tensions and distrust. Difficult decisions would be required about sharing the costs of climate commitments between very different regions of the world—citizens in developing states feeling they had not contributed as much to the problem as those in richer states, the latter anxious that all parts of the globe play a part in climate transition. If city-level assemblies had demonstrated that the politics of transition were difficult even in one single location, then these difficulties were many times more challenging at a global level. The need to narrow these differences made a global deliberative and trust-building exercise especially important and pressing. If understanding and democratic debate could not be fostered across borders, then international progress on climate commitments would remain limited.

The organizers framed the initiative not just as the world's first global citizens' assembly, but an attempt to provide the blueprint for a new piece of global governance infrastructure. The Global Assembly was codesigned with communities, institutions, scientists, citizens, and social movements from around the world and built from the ground up. Initiated from within civil society in this way, it was "docked" into formal United Nations COP governance arrangements with the guidance of representatives from the UN Secretariat, the UNFCCC, the UK as COP26 host government, the COP Champions Network, and the Scottish Government. It was endorsed by UN secretary general António Guterres who acknowledged that "people power" was needed to unlock bolder climate action, as well as by several national ministers.

Three core activities defined the Global Assembly: a Core Assembly, Community Assemblies, and a Cultural Wave. The Core Assembly consisted of 100 citizens randomly selected from around the world. The novel factor was that this selection was run by a global lottery process, never before carried out. Sortition software was used to select 100 points around the world which were weighted toward high density population centers (shown in Figure 4.1). At each of these locations, a Community Host organization was recruited to select people through random door-knocking and on-street engagement to join an initial pool of potential assembly members (in practice these Hosts often drew from their personal networks). This pool was then stratified to create a globally descriptive sample by age, gender, education, and views on climate. Putting all this together, over one hundred civic organizations were involved in these different levels of democratic

Figure 4.1 Global Assembly participation.
Global Assembly, *Report of the Global Assembly on the Climate and Ecological Crisis, 2022.*
https://globalassembly.org/resources/downloads/GlobalAssembly2021-FullReport.pdf.

engagement and deliberations. A central team was supported by several layers of facilitators in the countries and local communities involved.

The selected representatives came from 49 countries. These included nondemocratic states, where the exercise gave citizens a unique chance for engagement that they lacked in their domestic politics. Reflecting what some see as a shortcoming of randomized selection, the 49 states did not include the small states most affected by climate change. The members met through the autumn of 2021 in 20 sessions that totaled nearly 70 hours of deliberative debate. Organizers worked at the overarching level to run the assembly and facilitate debates, while Community Hosts ran meetings in particular localities. The assembly members divided into blocks to cover diagnosis of the challenge, developing principles of action, writing recommendations, organizing the assemblies' interventions at COP26 and planning follow-up actions. The assembly collectively produced the People's Declaration for the Sustainable Future of Planet Earth that was presented to the COP26 summit in Glasgow in November 2021.[3]

---

[3] Global Assembly, "People's Declaration for the Sustainable Future of Planet Earth," last updated December 18, 2021, https://globalassembly.org/declaration.

70　DEMOCRATIC CROSSROADS

Alongside the randomly selected core assembly, Community Assemblies were self-organized events, guided by a "do-it-yourself" toolkit.[4] They were presented as a way of ensuring that anyone who wasn't selected for the Core Assembly could still get involved. The Community Assemblies ran concurrently and beyond the core process. They had no formal connection to the Core Assembly but provided a parallel track to expand the numbers who participated and to increase the associated benefits such as activation, solidarity, data generation, and political momentum. In the 2021 pilot year, 408 organizations registered to run a Community Assembly and 1,300 people participated from at least 41 countries. Some unregistered events also took place, taking activity beyond these formal numbers. Their rationale was to give the initiative a decentralized structure and stronger local ownership of the various countries involved.

As a third element, the Cultural Wave brought in artists to develop poetry, street art, and other forms of expression with the aim of getting the Global Assembly known to a large audience. This artistic work helped generate a wider public debate around the assembly and to raise the profile of its main recommendations. A large team was needed to run the three strands of the Global Assembly, with a core delivery team, around 50 staff to oversee the core meetings and the partner organizations helping prepare materials and collating results. The initiative cost around 1 million dollars and was funded by several donors including the European Climate Foundation, the Climate Emergency Collaboration group, and the Scottish government.

The assembly's People's Declaration for the Sustainable Future of Planet Earth insisted that the principle of equity must be central in the energy transition, in terms of how much different countries should contribute to emissions reductions. It also called for the global transition to be managed in ways that are fully participative and involve citizens in the crucial decisions and trade-offs ahead—and in particular ensure that citizens from developing countries have a more influential role than hitherto. The participants stressed that climate action should be approached and treated as a core human rights issue, and that democratic participation must be a core element of a "just and fair transition."

The members presented their proposals to the COP26 and gained significant attention there in November 2021. The full final report[5] was formally

---

[4] Global Assembly, "Community Assembly Toolkit," https://globalassembly.org/resources/brand-imagery/GA_DIY-Toolkit_v5.1.pdf(accessed February 19, 2024).
[5] Global Assembly, *Report of the 2021 Global Assembly on the Climate and Ecological Crisis*, 2022, https://globalassembly.org/report.

published one year later, during COP27. After the assembly concluded, its organizers began to develop long-term plans, working with the UN Foundation to set up a permanent global assembly, with the aim of involving one million participants by 2030. They sought to improve selection techniques to enable larger forums and more initiatives in local community settings and to run many more community assemblies to give the process stronger grounding. The focus was on giving the future assembly formal institutional docking through the 2024 UN Summit for the Future. The strategy was both to embed the assembly within the United Nations process, but also function more as an outside advocacy group to generate publicity and push more far-reaching climate ambition.

Assessment: Democracy Without Borders

Doubts have long existed about the feasibility of organizing sortition based democracy at the international level. Even champions of deliberative mini-publics often caution that selection-based forums work best at a local level, and many have remained skeptical about the practicalities or indeed political desirability of trying to scale them up to the international level. The Global Assembly on the Climate and Ecological Crisis was run with enough constructive input to allay some of these doubts. The experience demonstrated that citizens can be selected from vastly different societies and backgrounds across the world and that they are then keen to engage in constructive democratic debate.

An evaluation of the assembly found that participants felt empowered and that levels of empathy between participants increased. Unsurprisingly, there were teething problems with some detailed organizational issues, in the first such attempt at running sortition based democratic deliberation at a global scale and all the complexities this entailed. Yet in general the exercise was a success in allowing local voices from developing countries to gain prominence in transborder civic discussions.[6]

Some have criticized the many national or subnational climate assemblies run in recent years for entailing an overly sanitized and managerial form of

---

[6] W. Conway-Lamb, N. Curato, K. de Pryck, S. Elstub, A. Morán, M. Ross, E. Sanchez, N. Sari, S. Tiliteke, L. Veloso, and H. Werner, June 2023, *Global Assembly on the Climate and Ecological Crisis: Evaluation Report*, chrome-extension://efaidnbmnnnibpcajpcglclefindmkaj/https://researchprofiles.canberra.edu.au/files/82182314/Global_Assembly_Evaluation_Report.pdf.

72 DEMOCRATIC CROSSROADS

debate over ecological crises—as detailed in Chapter 3. These initiatives have struggled to exert critical pressure over the deep-seated power imbalances and political interests that inhibit more far-reaching progress on climate action and the wider ecological crisis. The Global Assembly sought to address these concerns. It had more of an "outsider" identity than the city-level assemblies called by official bodies. The agenda was more open-ended, and participants invited to consider issues well beyond the scope of existing intergovernmental, multilateral negotiations. It did not work at the behest of formal authorities and aimed at a wider agenda-setting role than other assemblies have typically enjoyed. In effect, it sought to work in the democratic space between institutionally run engagement and critical civil society activism.

The Community Assemblies were seen as a way to bring in critical voices and encourage local communities to set their own terms for debate over the changes required for energy transition. The organizers sought to maximize this outsider strategy to overcome the significant gap between policies and real action that has persisted despite the spread of climate assemblies.[7] The local forums could help address a recurrent problem of climate assemblies leading to formal policy changes that are then not implemented on the ground. Critically engaged networks of citizens that engage on their own terms are likely to be more attentive to these kinds of practical, community-level actions. Despite these innovations and the critical democratic engagement, however, the assembly's final report did not in practice propose really radical alternatives that would entail a major push toward degrowth in advanced economies.[8]

Indeed, the Global Assembly focused less on detailed policy recommendations than on using its global representativeness to get the guiding principles of justice and inclusiveness more prominently onto the multilateral climate agenda. The impact was perhaps most notable locally, as many participants started climate action initiatives in their communities after the assembly concluded—participants generally wanted to build on their experience though continued democratic engagement. The organizers acknowledged that the assembly has not yet had a major, tangible impact on

---

[7] D. Naatujuna, "Bridging the Gap Between Policy and Action," *UNDP Strategic Innovation*, March 10, 2022, https://medium.com/@undp.innovation/bridging-the-gap-between-policy-and-action-84335c48041; G. Teddy, "Policy and Implementation Gap: A Multi-Country Perspective," *International Journal of Advanced Research* 7 (2019): 678–704.

[8] Conway-Lamb et al., *Global Assembly on the Climate and Ecological Crisis*.

COP decisions, and that the challenge is to give a future permanent forum more of a formal institutional role. Governments have not indicated that they would be willing to accord a citizen assembly formal power within future COP summits, so more oblique routes to influence will be needed, for example though alliances with other civic initiatives on the ecological crisis.[9]

In terms of the book's analytical framework, the Global Assembly was an original attempt to marry the ethos of civic micropolitics with expert-driven dynamics within the international bodies that have gained powers in relation to climate action in recent years. It sought to foster a more positive interplay between democratic participation and effective climate multilateralism, and to counter the view that these two agendas are intrinsically at odds with each other. The Global Assembly was, of course, only one modest experiment and unlikely in itself to make a major difference to the international politics of climate change. Yet it does show how global ecological crisis has begun to spur ambitious ways of strengthening democratic processes. The sternest test is whether global-level direct citizen engagement can be developed far enough to bring the spatial organization of democracy fully into line with the transnational nature of ecological threats. The Global Assembly represents a modest but innovative first step in this direction.

---

[9] C. Mellier and R. Wilson, *A Global Citizens' Assembly on the Climate and Ecological Crisis* (Brussels: Carnegie Europe, 2023).

5

COVID-19, Democracy, and Post-Neoliberalism

The COVID-19 experience has fed into debates about different types of political system worldwide. The pandemic was a world-historic moment of crisis that shook democracies across the world. Many democratic governments implemented emergency measures that abridged democratic rights. Those countries in the midst of democratic transition saw reforms stall and even unwind, while some authoritarian regimes seemed to gain new power as they battled to contain the pandemic. At the same time, COVID-19 also intensified efforts at many levels to improve and defend democracy. In addition to the direct impact of the pandemic itself, COVID-19's indirect effects have left a severe impact on social and economic conditions, and the period since COVID-19 first appeared has seen a tentative shift in economic models away from neoliberal orthodoxy. This shift in economic thinking has important implications for the quality of democracy and the broader balance between democratic and autocratic dynamics.

While the COVID-19 crisis has now more fully run its course than the other two crises covered in this book, its longer-term legacy is profound and still playing itself out. Taken together, the pandemic and its associated shift in economic models represent a closely entwined set of factors now driving political restructuring. This chapter examines both the direct impacts of the COVID-19 emergency and these more indirect economic changes; it groups these together as they have both begun to shift the relationship between societies and states, and in this way have implications for democracy and democratization.

While COVID-19's impact initially seemed severely detrimental to open politics and another spur to global democratic regression, the pandemic tragedy has also given rise to new layers of citizen engagement, new demands for political reform and more empowered states potentially better equipped to undergird democracy. In terms of the book's analytical framework, the political dynamics of the pandemic and its socioeconomic aftermath have been

Democratic Crossroads. Richard Youngs, Oxford University Press. © Oxford University Press 2024.
DOI: 10.1093/oso/9780197762417.003.0005

Pandemic versus Democracy

associated with and partly driven by new forms of micropolitics and more empowered state functions—as this double-faced change deepens at both these levels in tandem. While the pandemic has left clearly authoritarian impacts, new concerns with and initiatives for democratic renewal have also appeared in its wake.

Pandemic versus Democracy

The pandemic's outbreak in late 2019 and early 2020 had clearly prejudicial effects on democracy around the world. COVID-19 related developments meshed with broader trends in global democracy that predated the pandemic. While it would be difficult to isolate COVID-19's impact on any particular political development, the pandemic generally served to intensify pre-existing democratic shortcomings. COVID-19 generated different kinds of dynamics detrimental to global democracy. One was that governments used restrictive legal or emergency measures in their genuine attempts to mitigate the COVID-19 emergency, laying aside democratic rights within the limits of the law. Another was that governments took advantage of the virus by using emergency measures in disingenuous fashion to tighten their hold on power and hollow out democratic checks-and balances. And finally, the wider impact was that COVID-19's ravages rendered more difficult the effective exercise of democratic rights and functioning of formal democratic institutions. These three dynamics elided and shaded into each other in many countries.

According to the Economist Intelligence Unit, in the pandemic's first year of 2020 over half the countries in the world saw declines in their democracy scores due to government measures adopted. The situation got even worse in 2021. The global democracy score fell from 5.37 to 5.28, a sharper decline even than in 2020 and the lowest score since the index started in 2006. The pandemic resulted in a narrowing of civil liberties in developed democracies and authoritarian regimes alike. Even if many developments were not directly caused by the pandemic, there were major violations of rights norms in 44 countries that were linked specifically to the pandemic and moderate violations in 57 states.[1] In 2022, political rights stabilized but

---

[1] Economist Intelligence Unit, *Democracy Index 2021: The China Challenge*, 2022, https://www.eiu.com/n/campaigns/democracy-index-2021/.

76 DEMOCRATIC CROSSROADS

still without rebounding to their pre-pandemic levels at an aggregate global level.[2]

The pandemic was perhaps the most dramatic development of recent years that required an empowered state. In some cases, this empowered state became a threat to democracy and advantage to authoritarian governance—in different variants of the trustee or illiberal statism framework-category. Most commonly, governments used COVID-19 measures for wider political ends beyond steps related strictly to the pandemic. Examples can be drawn from around the world, and different types of political regime.

After the pandemic struck, the Chinese government became even more repressive and restrictive of rights. Initially, there was much criticism from Chinese society of the regime's response, and the Communist Party met this with a wave of draconian repression, stifling local level mobilizations. A prevalent view in 2020 and 2021 was that China's initially strong containment of COVID-19 showed the need to sacrifice liberal freedoms for the sake of good societal outcomes.[3] As much of the world relaxed emergency measures, in China harsh lockdowns continued to the end of 2022 with even more complete state control. After these unleashed protests—covered below—the government reacted with a mix of tougher repression and moves to loosen lockdown measures and testing requirements. As a spike in cases and deaths followed, it appeared that the Chinese regime had moved to deflect criticism against its own empowerment at the cost of thousands of lives. Even if President Xi emerged personally discredited, the regime more broadly had taken on stronger powers to crush dissent.

Similarly, governments in Cambodia, Malaysia, the Philippines, Singapore, and Vietnam arrested hundreds of people alleging their criticisms of COVID-19 management to be fake news. Singapore's well-functioning state was initially able to control the virus without imposing a full lockdown, but as infection rates increased in late 2021 the government resorted to more repressive measures, opening judicial proceedings against thousands of those it charged with damaging trust in the government and "public tranquillity." In Myanmar, the military junta used pandemic measures as a means of suppressing opposition; civilians that were suspected to be a part

---

[2] Economist Intelligence Unit, *Democracy Index 2022: Frontline Democracy and the Battle for Ukraine*, 2023, https://www.eiu.com/n/campaigns/democracy-index-2022/.

[3] E. Li, "Eric Li on the Failure of Liberal Democracy and the Rise of China's Way," *The Economist*, December 8, 2021, https://www.economist.com/by-invitation/2021/12/08/eric-li-on-the-failure-of-liberal-democracy-and-the-rise-of-chinas-way.

of the pro-democracy movement were refused treatment in hospitals and vaccines were withheld from the junta's political opponents.

Political restrictions multiplied across Asia's more open polities too. In India, the central government assumed more power and police began intervening on the streets with striking brutality, using emergency laws as cover for violent crackdowns on Muslim and Dalit leaders. The Sri Lankan government dissolved parliament then postponed elections; the lack of a functioning parliament meant that there was no institution to ensure transparency and oversee the pandemic response which allowed for assistance plans to be structured to favor groups loyal to the prime minister. In Malaysia, a declaration of emergency was used to suspend meetings of parliament, while the pandemic pushed Indonesian politics further in an illiberal direction.

In Egypt, many doctors were arrested during the pandemic for publicly criticizing the government's response. In Turkey, state repression increased against journalists after news reports challenged official causality figures, and hundreds of reporters were charged with provoking the public and inciting public fear and panic. In Algeria, authorities used the pandemic to suppress the opposition and move against the on-going Hirak protest movement. In Iran, thousands of citizens were arrested as the army was given control of the pandemic response.

In Brazil, far-right president Jair Bolsonaro deliberately stoked polarization, publicly attacking government officials that implemented social distancing policies. Bolsonaro mobilized his political base, which led to many pro-government protests taking place against "left-wing" ideas of social distancing. The Chilean government postponed votes on constitutional reform and in Colombia the government stirred unrest by taking powers from regional and municipal authorities. Even in well performing democracies like Australia and Uruguay concerns were raised in parliament about excessive use of force by police forces in imposing emergency restrictions. In Canada, the government used emergency laws and heavy police intervention to end the so-called Truckers Convoy anti-vax protests as hostility rose against state emergency measures.

In Russia, activists were targeted for drawing public attention to the government's inadequate supplies of medical equipment. In Azerbaijan, the government took advantage of the opportunity to arrest opposition politicians for alleged quarantine violations. The Polish government tightened restrictions on civil liberties, dismissed healthcare workers who

78 DEMOCRATIC CROSSROADS

had spoken out about bad conditions in their institutions, and sought to limit civil society access to foreign funds. In Serbia, the government self-servingly lifted restrictions just before an election, tightening its grip on power. In Zimbabwe, the deployment of soldiers to conduct policing duties in townships helped the regime's autocratic consolidation, as troops detained many opposition figures under health-emergency pretexts.

Across the world, restrictions on civil society organizations became more severe, with the pandemic adding to a trend that had been present and gathering force for at least a decade. Well over a hundred governments enacted constrictions on civil society organizations related to COVID-19—or at least justified by reference to the health emergency. The international civil society organization, Civicus showed deepening problems especially in authoritarian states but in democracies too. It uncovered rising concerns over state surveillance, an increase in the coercive capacities of law enforcement agencies to enforce lockdowns and restrictions on human rights defenders. Attacks were especially severe against those seeking to protect the rights of the politically, economically, and socially excluded particularly in remote locations.[4] An American Bar Association report corroborated the finding that human rights defenders had been disproportionately restricted by governments' COVID-19 measures.[5]

In addition, COVID-19 turbo-charged the prevalence of disinformation and demonstrated even more clearly its damaging effects on democracy. Authoritarian regimes like that in Russia also used counterdisinformation in a disingenuous manner, introducing new measures and fines against those spreading COVID-19 "disinformation" that were then used against political opponents. The pandemic revealed how a lack of transparency can have tragic consequences. In equal measure it stirred anger against corruption where this effected access to and the quality of medical supplies. COVID-19 related apps and welfare and health programs were rolled out hand in hand with more intrusive surveillance of citizens, in democratic and nondemocratic states alike.[6]

---

[4] CIVICUS, *2021 State of Civil Society Report*, https://civicus.org/state-of-civil-society-report-2021/(accessed February 19, 2024).

[5] American Bar Association, "COVID-19 Related State of Emergency Measures: Impact and Responses," February 8, 2022, https://www.americanbar.org/groups/human_rights/reports/covid-19-related-state-of-emergency-measures-impact-and-response/.

[6] S. Feldstein et al., "The Global Struggle over AI Surveillance," *National Endowment for Democracy*, 2022, https://www.ned.org/wp-content/uploads/2022/06/Global-Struggle-Over-AI-Surveillance-Emerging-Trends-Democratic-Responses.pdf.

More indirectly, COVID-19 compounded problems of governability in many countries. Concerns have been mounting for years over democracies' ability to provide effective governance. In many democracies, parties have struggled to form stable governing coalitions, and they have been less willing or able to compromise around practical problem-solving agendas—this being one element of a much-discussed widening of political polarization. This trend deepened during the early phases of the pandemic and democracies' basic decision-making effectiveness was seriously compromised. In Japan, for example, public anger with government crisis responses contributed to the resignation of two prime ministers and in-fighting within the ruling Liberal party, while regional authorities rejected many central government measures. Many governments sought to improve governance efficiency by handing more powers to scientific experts during the pandemic; while this might have been medically justified, it raised concerns over democratic accountability.[7]

Mixed Trends

While the early phase of the pandemic was dominated by concerns that governments' emergency measures would leave democratic rights and institutional checks severely depleted, as the crisis unfolded and many governments' measures moved through several phases of response, ultimately the end effect on democracy was not as dramatic across the board as many initially feared. In many places, democratic institutions were resilient and did not collapse in the way that many predicted when the pandemic first appeared. Governments that managed the crisis in an open and inclusive way gained legitimacy. Many authoritarian regimes suffered more and saw their legitimacy undercut far more dramatically than these resilient democracies.

Data from the Varieties of Democracy institute show a differentiated pattern. In summer 2021, only 13 states out of the 144 countries measured recorded no rights violations at all—with nondemocratic or partially democratic states experiencing the most serious deterioration in political rights. By mid-2022, the situation had changed significantly, with 83 states recording either no or only minor democratic-rights violations.[8] In the Blavatnik

---

[7] Economist Intelligence Unit, *Democracy Index 2021*, 30.
[8] V-Dem, "Pandemic Backsliding: Democracy During COVID-19," March 2020 to June 2021, https://www.v-dem.net/pandem.html.

80 DEMOCRATIC CROSSROADS

Table 5.1 Regime type and stringency of emergency measures

Country	Regime Type	Stringency of Pandemic Emergency Measures on December 17, 2021
Fiji	Hybrid regime	96.30 Most stringent 10
Azerbaijan	Authoritarian	82.41
Myanmar	Authoritarian	80.56
Greece	Flawed democracy	79.17
Guyana	Flawed democracy	78.70
Jamaica	Flawed democracy	75.93
Saudi Arabia	Authoritarian	75.93
Suriname	Flawed democracy	75.00
Italy	Flawed democracy	73.15
Peru	Hybrid regime	73.15
…	…	…
Sweden	Full democracy	19.44 Least stringent 10
Belarus	Authoritarian	19.44
Afghanistan	Authoritarian	19.44
Niger	Authoritarian	16.67
Burundi	Authoritarian	16.67
Gambia	Hybrid regime	13.89
Burkina Faso	Authoritarian	13.89
Mauritania	Hybrid regime	12.04
Tanzania	Hybrid regime	8.33
Nicaragua	Authoritarian	8.33
Cote d'Ivoire	Hybrid regime	6.48

The COVID-19 Stringency Index, developed by the Blavatnik School's Coronavirus Government Response Tracker, assigns each country a score between 0 and 100, with a higher score indicating a stricter response (i.e., 100 = strictest response). This table shows the countries with the most and least stringent pandemic emergency measures at the end of 2021 and their regime type as classified by the EIU Democracy Index 2022.

School's Coronavirus Government Response Tracker it was notable that the "stringency" of government responses fluctuated back and forth over time and did not leave any clear pattern in terms of impacts on different regime types (as shown in Table 5.1).[9]

[9] E. Mathieu et al., "Policy Responses to the Coronavirus Pandemic," *Our World in Data*, https://ourworldindata.org/policy-responses-covid(accessed February 19, 2024).

COVID-19, DEMOCRACY, AND POST-NEOLIBERALISM   81

Democratic resilience came from different sources. In many democracies, courts and parliaments pushed back against executives' use of emergency measures and watered them down. Democratic processes adjusted to hold increasingly influential expert bodies to account; changes have been incorporated into some countries' constitutions with the next crisis in mind, more firmly in line with democratic rights and open to the involvement of nongovernmental and other societal actors.[10] In some cases, courts even forced governments to retract some quarantine and testing rules. Different levels of courts limited some such measures even in strongly de-liberalizing India. Freedoms were often defended arguably at the cost of health imperatives. In many democratic states, the courts limited both discriminatory measures against the unvaccinated and government controls over the media reporting false information about the pandemic. Surveys suggest that citizens' distrust in democratic governments evolved in very different ways across different countries due to COVID-19, decreasing in some places but increasing in others.[11]

The multilateral organization, International IDEA tracked COVID-19's impact on democratic freedoms from early 2020 into 2022. By 2022, most countries with "concerning developments" according to its tracker did not include Western liberal democracies, with the notable exception of the United States. Drawing just a few select and illustrative examples from this dataset suffices to show that democratic freedoms did not fold easily.[12] South Korea's 2020 elections garnered the country's highest turnout since 1992, even as the country had emergency restrictions in place well into 2022 after a late spike in infections. The ruling party's COVID-19 response boosted its approval rating leading up to the election that handed it a landslide victory.[13] In Japan, public concern over the Tokyo Olympics and general handling of

---

[10] On this issue, see new projects: International IDEA, "Taking Stock of Global Democratic Trends Before and During the Covid-19 Pandemic," December 9, 2020, https://www.idea.int/publications/catalogue/global-democratic-trends-before-and-during-covid19; Club of Madrid, *Democracy & Emergencies: Lessons from the Covid-19 Pandemic for Democratic Resilience*, 2021, https://clubmadrid.org/global-commission-on-democracy-and-emergencies/.

[11] *2021 Edelman Trust Barometer*, https://www.edelman.com/trust/2021-trust-barometer(accessed February 19, 2024).

[12] International IDEA, *The Global State of Democracy Indices*, accessed April 28, 2023, https://www.idea.int/gsod-indices/covid19globalmonitor.

[13] J. Hollingsworth and J. Kwon, "South Korea Sees the Largest Turnout in Almost 30 Years in Election Held During Coronavirus Outbreak," *CNN*, April 16, 2020, https://www.cnn.com/2020/04/15/asia/south-korea-election-intl-hnk/index.html.

82   DEMOCRATIC CROSSROADS

the health emergency contributed to October 2021 elections ushering in a new government, giving citizens a chance for more effective accountability during the pandemic. In Taiwan, civic activists were able to push through a successful municipal recall vote in June 2020. Despite the country's international reputation for handling the crisis well, internally there was a lively democratic debate and scope for robust criticism of the government.

New Zealand held an inquiry into crisis management that was headed by the leader of the opposition. Australia was categorized as experiencing only very minor limitations on democratic rights. In Canada a "civil liberties caucus" formed in parliament across party lines and provided accountability on rights-based aspects of crisis management. Uruguay was widely seen as a case of light-touch pandemic management as the emergency was handled without major restrictions or infringements on democratic rights, with limits on protests removed by mid 2021, and local elections attracting a 90 percent turnout.

Populism and polarization were in some places held in check. Empirical research suggests that COVID-19 management had different impacts on polarization: the actions of highly partisan governments intensified political and social tensions, whereas in countries with more inclusive crisis management the pandemic served to dampen polarization.[14] Many populist leaders fared badly in elections during the acute phase of the pandemic.[15] Polls showed that American citizens' lack of trust in President Trump's handling of the pandemic directly contributed to support for Joe Biden in the 2020 election.[16] In Europe, hard-right populists softened some of their positions and coordinated across borders around an effort to get the EU to support local communities' health priorities.[17] Polling suggested that in some countries

[14] A. Flores et al., "Politicians Polarize and Experts Depolarize Public Support for COVID-19 Management Policies Across Countries," *PNAS* (2022), https://www.pnas.org/doi/10.1073/pnas.211 7543119.

[15] B. Meyer, "Populist-led Governments Are More Likely To Be Punished by the Electorate for Rising Covid-19 Deaths," *LSE* (2022), https://blogs.lse.ac.uk/europpblog/2022/01/28/populist-led-governments-are-more-likely-to-be-punished-by-the-electorate-for-rising-covid-19-deaths/; R Foa et al., "The Great Reset: Public Opinion, Populism, and the Pandemic," *Centre for the Future of Democracy* (2022), https://www.bennettinstitute.cam.ac.uk/publications/great-reset/.

[16] G. Langer, "Pandemic Surge Damages Trump, Boosting Biden's White House Bid: POLL," *ABC News,* July 19, 2020, https://abcnews.go.com/Politics/pandemic-surge-damages-trump-boosting-bidens-white-house/story?id=71779431.

[17] C. Lamour and P. Carls, "When COVID-19 Circulates in Right-Wing Populist Discourse: The Contribution of a Global Crisis to European Meta-Populism at the Cross-Border Regional Scale," *Journal of Contemporary European Studies* (2022), https://www.tandfonline.com/doi/full/10.1080/14782804.2022.2051001.

societies came out of COVID-19 less polarized and with more effort to band together against such a major threat.[18]

In at least some countries, cross-party cooperation helped governability and democratic stability. In Malaysia, negotiations opened between the ruling and opposition parties on combatting the pandemic. These negotiations led to the signing of an agreement in September 2021 that ushered in improvements to the state's COVID-19 response as well as judicial, administrative, and parliamentary reforms; after November 2022 elections, long-time opposition leader (and previously jailed) Anwar Ibrahim became prime minister. In Thailand, there was some lowering of hostilities between the Red Shirts and Yellow Shirts factions, with both supporting a new pro-democracy Milk Tea Alliance, spearheaded by younger activists; the pro-regime Yellow Shirts did so because the pandemic revealed weaknesses in the junta's decision-making.

In South Africa, political parties also showed an unprecedented amount of unity in their response to COVID-19. In these cases, differences generally reappeared as the pandemic receded, but the attempts at cooperation did leave a more positive mark on the state of democratic politics. In a later and perhaps even more significant case, Brazil's November 2022 elections ousted Jair Bolsonaro in part because of his mismanagement of the pandemic. This mismanagement spurred a broad-based opposition alliance that drove the hard-right populist from power expressly around a project of democratic renewal.[19] Incoming President Lula's first speech promised deep democratic reform, after the pandemic's chastening impact on Brazil—although the Bolsonaro-backed uprising of January 8, 2023, showed the risk of a new phase in polarization.

Democratic Outreach

Even as governments centralized powers and curtailed some political freedoms, the very gravity of the crisis prompted them to find ways of reaching out to their citizens. COVID-19 drove a dynamic of liberal statism in the

---

[18] ESO, *Future Energy Scenarios 2022*, https://www.nationalgrideso.com/future-energy/future-energy-scenarios.

[19] O. Stuenkel, "How Brazil's Democracy Stepped Back from the Cliff," *The Globe and Mail*, October 31, 2022, https://www.theglobeandmail.com/opinion/article-how-brazils-democracy-stepped-back-from-the-cliff/.

84 DEMOCRATIC CROSSROADS

form of greater democratic-outreach programs involving governments and citizens working together. Most major cities around the world either widened existing or created new participative platforms to engage local populations in COVID-19 recovery plans. A large number of local administrations ran participative forums, rediscovering "the value of listening to communities" and generating a new "co-productive" relationship between citizens and public authorities.[20]

Governments reached out to citizens to provide information, solicit input, allay fears, involve citizens in disaster response strategies, help in the design of digital solutions, and target emergency help for vulnerable communities. An Open Government Partnership dataset listed a huge number of joint dialogues run between public authorities and tech platforms to provide information to citizens and invite them to offer input during the crisis.[21] This became a standard format across capital cities, with notable programs in Buenos Aires, Lima, Santiago de Chile, Sao Paulo, Sofia, Rome, and Ulaanbaatar, and particularly participative versions in cities like Milan and Madrid. These also ran at a national level in some cases, for example those launched through government authorities in Haiti, Latvia, Lithuania, Mexico, Nepal, and in the case of Norway, including through a novel People's Question Time. An especially notable new process of 50 open, participatory "binding dialogues" was run by Colombia's new government in 2022, not only related to COVID-19 issues but partly so.[22]

The Taiwanese government gained international reputation as it reached out to citizens for their input and ideas, encouraging more open availability of data and a sharing-societal rather than technocratic approach to the pandemic. South Korea also implemented a celebrated and successful program of outreach and collaboration between public authorities and a coalition of over five hundred civil society organizations under what was baptized the Civil Society Countermeasure Committee to the COVID-19 Societal and Economic Crisis. This aimed to protect economically vulnerable citizens as well as transform and increase the sustainability of the existing economic

---

[20] D. Hall, S. Kaye, and C. Morgan, "How the Pandemic Has Accelerated the Shift Towards Participatory Public Authorities," *Democracy in a Pandemic: Participation in Response to Crisis*, ed. T. Hughes and G. Smith (University of Westminster Press, 2021), 145.

[21] Open Government Partnership, "Collecting Open Government Approaches to COVID-19," https://www.opengovpartnership.org/collecting-open-government-approaches-to-covid-19/(accessed February 19, 2024).

[22] C. Osorio, "Francia Márquez visita una Buenaventura que espera su nueva oportunidad," *El Pais*, October 22, 2022, https://elpais.com/america-colombia/2022-10-22/francia-marquez-busca-una-segunda-oportunidad-para-buenaventura.html.

system. Korean state agencies provided opportunities for citizens to meet with representatives and provide input on pandemic policies. In Kenya, the senate committee responsible for pandemic responses invited the public to send in their opinions which were then taken into consideration during the drafting of the state's pandemic management bill.

In Europe around 60 cities and numerous regional authorities ran assemblies for selected citizens to provide recommendations on COVID-19 responses. Examples included the West Midlands in the UK, Haute-Garonne in France, and Thuringia in Germany. Barcelona city council even reached down to schoolchildren about participation.[23] The French parliament hosted a virtual public forum for citizens to give their recommendations for post-pandemic policy; approximately 15,000 people engaged in this. The Basque regional administration undertook an especially far-reaching and collaborative outreach scheme.

The pandemic inspired public authorities to experiment with new digital democratic innovations, as COVID-19 disrupted existing patterns of engagement and forced public officials, their staff, and citizens to adapt to a world where face-to-face meetings were impossible. This spurred democratic innovations to serve the pandemic's most pressing needs: generating verified information and reliable data; mobilizing resources to address the health emergency; connecting volunteers and service organizations with people who needed help; and monitoring public policies.[24] Finland's Dialogue Academy and Timeout Foundation organized a series of lockdown dialogues. Scotland's government launched a digital platform for citizens to provide their input on decisions and held an online consultation on COVID-19 responses. In Madrid, authorities used the Decide Madrid platform to allow citizens to connect with local businesses, submit ideas for solidarity and ask municipal experts about the pandemic directly. The Brazilian senate used proposals submitted by citizens through an e-Citizenship Portal in deliberations about COVID-19 response policy. In Ecuador, a two-day post-crisis hackathon gave citizens an opportunity to discuss the future of the state after the pandemic with officials.

[23] These examples are outlined in R. Falanga, *Citizen Participation during the Covid-19 Pandemic* (Bonn: Friedrich Ebert Stiftung, 2020). https://repositorio.ul.pt/bitstream/10451/45726/1/ICS_RFalanga_Ctizen.pdf.
[24] T. Pogrebinschi, *30 Years of Democratic Innovation in Latin America* (Berlin: WZB Berlin Social Science Center, 2021).

86 DEMOCRATIC CROSSROADS

Notably, even the most authoritarian governments felt the need to reach out to societies in this way, as the pandemic created a new demand among fearful citizens for information and transparency from authorities. Various formats of popular, village, and neighborhood assemblies and councils multiplied in nondemocratic contexts like Cuba and Venezuela, albeit heavily controlled by regimes. In Azerbaijan, the government hosted a hackathon to join tech platforms and citizens to devise ways of managing the health crisis. Bahraini authorities set up a portal to allow citizens to make requests of government leaders about the pandemic, and launched another initiative where public bodies teamed up with volunteers to provide food and other services to vulnerable communities. In Serbia and Singapore too, authorities not noted for democratic openness reached out to citizens for transparency and dialogue on the pandemic. Even in China, authorities tentatively sought to engineer citizen forums to help smooth management of the pandemic response.[25]

COVID-19 and Community Mutualism

In more bottom-up fashion and outside formal authorities, the pandemic also gave rise to a flourishing realm of—in the analytical frameworks' terms—civic micropolitics. One of the most striking trends was the spread of self-organization aimed at practical problem-solving related to the pandemic. Since the coronavirus first broke out in 2020, many civic organizations have formed and organized themselves around practical types of community action. This wave of community mutualism has continued beyond the acute phase of the pandemic emergency, building a new kind of legitimacy for civic activities rooted in issues of direct concern to local communities.

These kinds of civic initiatives played a major role in mitigating the pandemic's severity, countering government failings, and pushing official authorities into better health and social responses. They involved citizens seeking to take on more responsibility from both long-established CSOs and the state. The general ethos was that of "hyperlocal DIY" organization and decision-making. A horizontal spirit of self-organization among social

[25] M. Ross et al., "Resisting Colonisation, Avoiding Tropicalisation: Deliberative Wave in the Global South," *Deliberative Democracy Digest*, May 3, 2022, https://www.publicdeliberation.net/resisting-colonisation-avoiding-tropicalisation-deliberative-wave-in-the-global-south/.

COVID-19, DEMOCRACY, AND POST-NEOLIBERALISM   87

movements gained ground. The Emergency Governance Initiative charted such trends around the world and noted a rising presence of "the collective" through multiple forms of mobilization. This spirit has continued to expand as the emergency has given way to COVID-19's longer-term aftermath. The trend points toward an extended form of horizontal experimentalism that increases the number of citizens involved in democratic participation and resistance.[26]

New forms of civic engagement have come to the fore as populations seek a different kind of politics after the shock of the pandemic. More mutual societies and cooperatives have taken control of local housing, for example, through common purchasing. Accelerating a new lexicon of mutualism, new activist techniques linked to COVID-19 include community wealth building initiatives, so-called public commons partnerships, movements for citizen-led candidates for city elections, and housing democracy movements. Many larger CSOs that for a long time were top-down, hierarchical organizations have become flatter and more participation-oriented to give members more scope to deliberate and engage. More companies began to give workers participation in decision-making and offer customers a voice in decisions too—especially app-based businesses, in a trend of "platform co-operativism."[27] This was not all directly linked to or a result of COVID-19, but the pandemic dramatically deepened and accelerated such trends, with intensified engagement taking on COVID-specific elements.

A multitude of examples illustrate this trend—the sheer ubiquity of the new mutualism standing as striking testament to the depth of societal mobilization.[28] Citizen-organized task forces formed in villages across Indonesia. In Malaysia, Myanmar, Thailand, and Vietnam civil society groups were set up to raise funds to buy medical supplies and food for slum dwellers, disabled people and migrant workers. In the Philippines, so-called community pantries spread. Even in highly closed Laos, collaborative community assemblies formed. In India, village initiatives proliferated, and such civic mutualism was paramount in helping feed the poor in the early phases of the lockdown. In addition, young volunteers on Instagram and Twitter helped

[26] R. Suss, "Horizontal Experimentalism: Rethinking Democratic Resistance," *Philosophy and Social Criticism* 48, no. 8 (2021), doi: 10.1177/01914537211033016.

[27] J. Alexander, *Citizens: Why the Key to Fixing Everything Is All of Us* (London: Canbury Press, 2021)

[28] These examples draw from the Open Government Partnership database, https://www.opengovpartnership.org/collecting-open-government-approaches-to-covid-19/ (accessed February 19, 2024).

88 DEMOCRATIC CROSSROADS

people look for hospital beds and oxygen cylinders, replacing government helplines and becoming new collectives in the process.

The Innovate for Africa program, run out of Nigeria, aimed to bring people together at local community level to share practical solutions for pandemic related challenges. In Botswana, local communities organized through a rejigged traditional *kgotla* consultation system to focus debates on the pandemic. There was a dramatic increase in community level anti-corruption initiatives in Ghana during the pandemic. In Zimbabwe, civil society groups focused on health rights at the community level became more visible in response to the pandemic. One study on Mozambique, Nigeria, and Pakistan uncovered a growing number of very locally rooted citizen oversight mechanisms related to pandemic relief and support.[29]

In South Africa, one civic initiative developed 40 coronavirus testing teams to make up for government failures to develop a comprehensive testing program. South Africa's Choosing All Together platform allowed citizens to make decisions about what policies should be prioritized, including with budgetary implications and trade-offs between issues. The C19 People's Coalition tracked mismanagement of relief resources.[30] In Kenya, Shining Hope for Communities, a local service provision and microcredit organization, repurposed to COVID-19 work and expanded dramatically to reach two million people. African "pavement radio" stations spread to bring communities together around management of the emergency.

In Ukraine, the new civil society movements that formed in the 2014 Euromaidan uprising expanded operations to provide hospitals with critical equipment, as well as various services for healthcare staff, like transportation and free meals. One of the most popular new volunteer initiatives at the community level across Ukraine was Give a Medic a Lift that helped healthcare workers get to their workplaces when public transportation was suspended. A new online platform called Solidarity connected volunteers and people in need. A rich array of new civic organizations also appeared in Georgia, like the civic initiative Help Elders and the Knowledge Café that provided internet access and laptops to underprivileged high school students in rural areas.

In Belarus a new group ByCovid19 organized a crowdfunding campaign to buy and distribute medical and protective equipment for health

---

[29] L. Posse and E. Chaimite, "Perceptions of Covid-19 in Mozambique and the Influence of 'Intermediaries,'" *Institute of Development Studies*, November 12, 2020.

[30] C19 People's Coalition website, accessed April 28, 2023, https://c19peoplescoalition.org.za/.

professionals; this and other self-reliance initiatives then fed into the political protests against President Lukashenko. Similar movements formed in Russia, like Covid Solidarity, as public donations to such civic groups increased. In Azerbaijan, decentralized communities formed on Facebook to provide mutual aid to evade state repression. In Serbia, a new network of local organizations ran an awareness raising campaign to educate citizens on the public health and societal benefits of vaccination, winning a degree of legitimacy as the government narrowed democratic space.

In Tunisia, CSOs mobilized their members and resources for campaigns to raise awareness about the virus and help distribute medical equipment. In Turkey, they quickly mobilized to provide basic needs to furloughed workers and others who had lost their income, and new civic initiatives emerged to connect those in need directly with potential donors. One group of activists launched the Citizen Solidarity Network to map public support and volunteer networks, organizations, and initiatives across Turkey. In Jordan, many citizen-led initiatives gained traction, including one through a prominent tribal network in the city of Mafraq to coordinate local medical and emergency supplies, another involving the national teachers' association working with the army to manage local supplies, and several local civic initiatives to deliver bread to vulnerable families. In highly restrictive Egypt, where formal CSO activity has become prohibitively difficult, citizens started their own informal initiatives to voice complaints about the public health sector during the crisis. In Algeria, several local organizations worked to distribute food and support the health sector.

In Latin America, an already existing base of democratic innovations helped foster an increased number of COVID-related local initiatives. These were notable for being problem-oriented and civil society driven, for connecting citizen participation to wider agendas of democratic renewal more than in earlier deliberative experiments, and also for taking on a different, more mass-appeal format than participatory initiatives in Western countries. They made more visible and impactful the undercurrent of citizen innovations that had been slowly laying down roots but that had often gone unnoticed due to the dramatic negative trends for democracy at the level of political elites and macro-level politics. The new initiatives partially reversed the trend in some Latin American countries of authorities' top-down executive aggrandizement having had a chilling effect of local citizen participation in the late 2010s.[31]

---

[31] T. Pogrebinschi, *Innovating Democracy? The Means and Ends of Citizen Participation in Latin America* (Cambridge: Cambridge University Press, 2023), especially Chapter 1 and pp. 84–86

90 DEMOCRATIC CROSSROADS

In Chile, the civil society networks originally created to mobilize protestors and organize anti-government rallies in 2019 were transformed into networks of solidarity to help communities mitigate the social and economic impacts of COVID-19. Valparaiso in Chile created a Democracy for Life initiative to allow local communities in the city to decide on how emergency resources were allocated. Chile saw a notable wave of mutual aid societies, while similar solidarity networks took root in Mexico. Brazil saw the launch of nearly a thousand new civic initiatives, especially in poor communities to pay for medical supplies. Brazilian social movements mobilized to help distribute respirators to landless movements and to combat the government's denialism and misinformation over the pandemic. In Argentina, the Poder Cuidadano network monitored corruption in public contracts for COVID-related services. In Latin America, the new wave of grassroots activism is credited with pushing many governments in the region toward more inclusive models of democracy and protection of minority rights.[32]

In the UK, over four thousand local mutual aid groups were created. A so-called Big Local program coordinating 150 neighborhood initiatives that predated the pandemic was mobilized to help in the emergency. A whole host of local community development initiatives in cities like Birmingham redirected their work to tackle the pandemic. Not all areas saw this rise of mutual aid initiatives and those that did not tended to fare worse in the crisis. A "hyperlocal social infrastructure" put down roots and more formal CSOs also shifted their traditional ways of working to help foster this informal localism.[33] The pandemic also kickstarted many deliberative processes in workplaces across the UK.[34] Not all these initiatives were solely or directly linked to the pandemic but gained new relevance and grew as they worked in response to the health emergency.[35]

The #PourEux initiative in France fostered neighborhood cooperation. The Spanish Frena la Curva initiative worked as a clearing house for volunteers, information and community bartering, and spread from Spain to other European countries and Latin America. A "maker community" emerged in the Basque country. In Romania, the Red Cross Society oversaw

---

[32] O. Encarnación, "Latin America's Abortion Rights Breakthrough," *Journal of Democracy* 33, no. 4 (2022): 89–103.

[33] M. Lech, "Mutual Aid and Self-Organisation: What We Can Learn from the Rise of DIY Responses to the Pandemic," in *Democracy in a Pandemic: Participation in Response to Crisis*, ed. T. Hughes and G. Smith (University of Westminster Press, 2021), 124–132.

[34] Democratizing Work website, accessed April 28, 2023, https://democratizingwork.org/.

[35] Alexander, *Citizens*.

COVID-19, DEMOCRACY, AND POST-NEOLIBERALISM 91

a network of self-help for the pandemic. In France, the Power to Live Pact, comprising 55 different civil society organizations, devised a program to aid vulnerable populations. Even as the overall state of US democracy continued to slide, local mutual-help efforts emerged to manage very concrete health and social issues and delink these from the country's national-level impasse. Many new US donor projects began to bring different sides of the political spectrum together at a local level around pandemic challenges.[36] Across the US the nonprofit National Conference on Citizenship expanded its work and coordinated a host of pandemic related local engagement projects, while a new Centre for Democracy Innovation oversaw a battery of deliberative community forums.[37] In Chicago, the Tenants United movement self-organized among communities to run services during COVID-19 and prevent evictions of those unable to pay rent.[38]

Certain cross-cutting themes were prominent in new activism across all these countries and regions. Efforts increased to bridge the digital divide, and many civic movements have taken up a neighborhood-level agenda of shared internet access, which has become much more consequential since the pandemic began. Clusters of activism have also intensified around housing vulnerability and high rental costs. Violence against women also increased during the pandemic and became another issue commanding more attention from activists. For example, Tunisian women's groups formed to lobby courts to hear gender violence cases. A UK grassroots federation called Women's Aid pressed the government to fund services to mitigate domestic abuse at an early stage in the pandemic and secured emergency funding for its work. Activists in Turkey paid heightened attention to increased violence against women and femicide during the pandemic, in particular after the government withdrew from the Council of Europe's Istanbul Convention on preventing and combating violence against women. In Egypt, the quarantine-related lockdown sparked gender-rights campaigns as social media became a platform for women's testimonials of sexual assault and domestic violence.

---

[36] R. Kleinfeld, "Five Strategies to Support US Democracy" (Washington, DC: Carnegie Endowment for International Peace, 2022), 39.

[37] National Conference on Citizenship, *National Conference on Citizenship 2020 Report,* https://ncoc.org/national-conference-on-citizenship-2020-report/(accessed February 19, 2024). On the Centre for Democracy Innovation, see https://www.nationalcivicleague.org/center-for-democracy-innovation/(accessed February 19, 2024).

[38] M. McClure, "'Here for Each Other': How COVID-19 Has Changed Community Organizing," *The Chicago Maroon,* February 25, 2021, https://chicagomaroon.com/28315/grey-city/covid-19-changed-community-organizing/.

92 DEMOCRATIC CROSSROADS

In short, the pandemic story was not only about the dilution of civic freedoms but also about the opening of new civic spaces. Even as governments suppressed civil society on some issues, they became more receptive to this new civic activity on pandemic-related issues. Some governments began to realize that such a major challenge required societal involvement and could not be managed by top-down state injunctions alone. The pandemic gave civic groups an opportunity to demonstrate a direct relevance to citizens. These emergent civic spaces involved national and local authorities in some places facilitating cooperation with local groups on health, social, economic and community service provision issues. Some international aid donors shifted their priorities to support these kinds of grassroots movements, reflecting their growing importance.[39] This civic micropolitics appeared and multiplied in the depths of the health emergency and its dynamism has continued into the post-pandemic period.

Pandemic Protests

In a parallel dynamic of civic micropolitics, mass protests increased in number around the world during worst moments of the pandemic and in its aftermath. Not all such mobilizations were about democracy or even necessarily favorable for democratic reform, but many of them were. Citizens' skepticism kept a healthy critical pressure on governments and helped improve authorities' COVID-19 strategies. Democratic protests and activism have proven robust since early 2020; indeed, protest intensity has increased and has in many cases focused on calls for democratic reform. Far from displacing democracy protests, the COVID-19 pandemic in some countries added to the demands of protestors and intensified pressure for democratic change. The Carnegie Global Protest Tracker identified protests in over 40 countries linked directly to COVID-19 in the acute phase of the pandemic in 2020 and 2021 (see Figure 5.1). These fed into post-pandemic revolts that have intensified around calls for new types of "political space."[40] There has been a big rise in middle class involvement in protests, reflecting this sector's new opposition to failing economic models and political repression.[41]

[39] J. Hicks, *Donor Support for "Informal Social Movements,"* K4D Helpdesk Report 1140, *Institute of Development Studies* (2022), doi: 10.19088/K4D.2022.085.

[40] D. di Cesare, *The Time of Revolt* (Cambridge: Polity, 2022), 14.

[41] I. Ortiz, S. Burke, M. Barrada, and H. Cortes, *World Protests: A Study of Key Protest Issues in the 21st Century* (London: Palgrave Macmillan, 2021).

Figure 5.1 COVID-19 protests
This map shows where the largest protests broke out from the beginning of the pandemic through to late 2022, based on data from Carnegie's Global Protest Tracker, https://carnegieendowment.org/publications/interactive/protest-tracker.

In Hong Kong, the pandemic added fuel to the city's democratic protests. Following the initial COVID-19 outbreak in mainland China, Hong Kong's citizens pushed the government to impose border controls. In February 2020, thousands of medical workers launched a five-day strike to demand border closures and better medical protections. As the crisis unfolded, Hong Kong opposition politicians and activists initiated a number of protests against official measures such as the establishment of quarantine centers. At the core of these disputes was the fact that the Hong Kong government closely followed mainland practices without consulting local political and civic actors. Hong Kong's civil society actors politicized the health crisis to galvanize their pro-democracy campaigning.

In mainland China, as mentioned, severe lockdowns triggered protests in 2022. The tactics of passive resistance gained ground against COVID-19 restrictions. The New Citizens Movement founded in 2012 stepped up its activities and reoriented them toward the COVID-19 emergency with local activities, using the harsh management of the pandemic as a platform to reframe criticism of the authoritarian system—several of the group's leaders were detained and tried in 2022.[42] In November 2022, the biggest protests

---

[42] Amnesty International, "China: Unfair Trials of Prominent Activists an Attack of Freedom of Association," June 21, 2022, https://www.amnesty.org/en/latest/news/2022/06/china-unfair-trials-of-prominent-activists-an-attack-of-freedom-of-association/.

94 DEMOCRATIC CROSSROADS

since 1989 took place, especially in universities across China. In a new development, protestors called openly for democracy. These expressions of discontent hastened the regime's removal of "zero COVID" measures but also spurred a repressive crackdown and arrests of peaceful demonstrators.[43] In the 2010s, the regime's stability had increasingly depended on a process of "controlled inclusion" offering citizens local-level consultative input; this system emerged badly shaken by the COVID-19 experience of toughened repression, surveillance and popular protest.[44]

In Thailand, growing economic concerns due to COVID-19 measures fed into existing protests against the regime's increasingly repressive authoritarianism: several hundred protests took place during 2020, the most since Thailand's 2014 military coup. The main banned opposition party re-formed as a social movement organizing mobilization and supporting candidates on a platform of promising more local democracy to improve citizens' say over healthcare issues. In Indonesia, labor activists protested against President Joko Widodo's attempt to relax Indonesia's business, labor, and environmental laws. In India, protests spread, with the farmers' movement spinning off from multiple other revolts. In the Philippines, there were protests to demand livelihood support during the lockdown and the government's failure to provide this. In Myanmar, factory workers staged small-scale protests against the government's pandemic-related measures, resulting in the legal prosecution of some workers.

In Lebanon, protests against lockdowns became part of a wider campaign against the costs of elite corruption made even more evident by the pandemic; public anger at elites using COVID-19 aid to strengthen their clientelist networks led to pressure for democratic change. Independents from these movements won seats in parliament in the Lebanese elections of 2022. In Tunisia, protests spread in mid-2021 due to soaring COVID-19 death rates and the government's botched vaccine rollout. In this case, pandemic activism and political rivalries nourished each other to the point of the president sacking the prime minister and suspending parliament after protests in July 2021. In Algeria, the Hirak movement resumed its opposition to the incumbent regime, buoyed by pandemic-related frustrations. In Egypt

[43] K. Huang and M. Han, "Did China's Street Protests End Harsh COVID Policies?" *Council on Foreign Relations*, December 14, 2022, https://www.cfr.org/blog/did-chinas-street-protests-end-harsh-covid-policies.

[44] D. Gueorguiev, *Retrofitting Leninism: Participation Without Democracy in China* (Oxford: Oxford University Press, 2021).

there were regular protests and occasional strikes by doctors and healthcare workers over the government's lackluster emergency response. In Turkey, protests erupted against insufficient health measures in the workplace.

In the US, COVID-19 protests overlapped with those related to racial and ethnic violence and injustices, as minority groups faced disproportionately heavy health and economic effects of the pandemic. Belarusian President Alexander Lukashenko recommended vodka, the fresh air of a tractor ride and a steam in the sauna as coronavirus curatives: his dismissive response was among the factors that drew people to the streets in protest after the August 2020 presidential election. In Georgia, the Shame Movement led protests against the government's attempt to use the emergency to backtrack on an agreed electoral reform package. In Poland, innovative civic protests were strong enough to force the government to push back elections until these could be held properly and with genuine competition, helping to catalyze the pro-democratic opposition.

Some types of protest corresponded more to the rejectionist than civic micropolitics category. In many countries there were protests against authorities' plans to turn local hotels into isolation centers, against the cremation of COVID-19 victims in local cemeteries or temples, and against the arrival of outsiders suspected of spreading the virus. In Indonesia, hundreds of people held a demonstration against the arrival of around 500 Chinese workers. In Venezuela, protesters demanded the border be closed to prevent the arrival of migrant workers from neighboring countries. These kinds of fear-driven activism often took place when citizens had reason to doubt the veracity of government-provided information about the pandemic, as official incompetence generated uncertainties about the health emergency.

In another fast-emerging strand of political activism whose implications for democracy are still profoundly uncertain, the pandemic unleashed a potent type of libertarian activism that deployed the language of democratic rights but embodied a relatively disruptive and unrestrained hostility to authority and state rules. This trend has changed the policy equation over liberal rights as many countries have moved beyond the pandemic. In some countries, illiberal or radical groups took the firmest and loudest stands pushing for rights and freedoms to be restored. This was evident in protests held in Berlin, London, Madrid, and Paris, amongst many other cities, that were often associated with COVID-19 denialism. While in some countries the pandemic put populists on the back foot, it has also bequeathed a legacy of often belligerent activism against top-down executive governance and the

96 DEMOCRATIC CROSSROADS

influence of experts—an ethos that has continued into many countries' post-pandemic phase.

This protest activity suggests that illiberal-populism changed shape in the COVID-19 crisis. Some populist parties lost appeal during COVID-19 but many retain significant levels of support, and a few have even gained ground. Perhaps most significantly, some variants of populism have adjusted. Some illiberal leaders used top-down powers to speed up vaccines and bear down on new variants, whereas others used the pandemic to advance a more libertarian agenda against state powers. If populists in power tended to increase executive power, populist-leaning parts of the population reacted against just this and called for radical reform to take power away from a feckless, power-hoarding elite.[45] In some regions like Latin America, populists gained from a focus on COVID-19's accentuation of inequalities, while in other regions like North America or Europe they tapped into more of an anti-state feeling. In developed countries they tended to push governments to focus measures on their own populations rather than on international cooperation for vaccines and the like. In short, the pandemic generated divergent and even puzzling trends in populism, and some uncertainty in how these might affect democracy in the long-term aftermath of the health emergency.

Economic Shift: What Impact on Democracy?

A more indirect impact flows from the pandemic's effect on economic models. The financial crisis that began in 2008–2009 and the austerity that followed in its wake shook the credibility of neoliberal economics. COVID-19 provided a further prompt into a new era of economic policies. While many elements of globalist free-market economics remain in place, the center of gravity in economic belief systems has shifted. The degree of change should not be overstated, but meaningful political debate has reopened on the state's role in economic development.[46] COVID-19 is one factor among several that has reshaped how many governments think about the state.[47]

---

[45] N. Ringe and L. Renno, eds., *Populists and the Pandemic: How Populists Around the World Responded to COVID-19* (London: Routledge, 2022).

[46] A. Tooze, *Shutdown: How Covid Shook the World's Economy* (New York: Viking, 2021).

[47] D. Drezner, "Turns Out Covid-19 Didn't Reshape Global Politics," *Foreign Policy*, September 29, 2022.

The crisis revealed the tragic cost of states having cut back on health services and exposed the market's failure to provide reserve medical capacity.[48] Ideas for the state fulfilling functions previously discarded as impracticable are now part of policy agendas and discussions; even if these have are not been fully implemented, the terms of debate about political economy have shifted.[49] A "neo-statist politics of protection and control" has become a standard feature of policy debates in many countries and across regions.[50]

Around the world, new direct modes of welfare and central bank interventions were of unprecedented scale in response to the COVID-19 pandemic. Governments took a more active and direct role in the economy through buying shares in firms, providing loans, bailing out businesses and developing vaccines. State ownership of assets also increased in more indirect ways, through the use of sovereign wealth funds for government investment. The "new interventionism" is seen in state support and in new regulations, even if not in wholesale nationalizations.[51] The pandemic heightened the importance of competent state bodies and "put to rest" the neoliberal aversion to state action, with public authorities' role in relation to COVID-19 spilling over to more state action on other issues too.[52] Talk abounds of a new state capitalism and an ethos has taken root of the venture-capitalist state, aiding innovation.[53] One author summarizes: liberalism is moving from its laissez-faire to reformist strand in economic policy.[54]

The pandemic pushed public spending to record levels around the world, in diverse political systems—Table 5.2 gives a flavor of this trend. These rises were notable in China, Japan, and most Asian economies. Despite a decade of center-right government, by 2022 the British state was bigger than at any time since the end of World War II. In the US, President Biden passed the Inflation Reduction Act, with record levels of spending. Interventionist industrial strategy became an important part of Biden's external strategy

---

[48] Tooze, *Shutdown.*

[49] B. Macaes, *Geopolitics for the End Times: From the Pandemic to the Climate Crisis* (London: Hurst, 2021), 54–55.

[50] P. Gerbaudo, *The Great Recoil: Politics after Populism and Pandemic* (London: Verso, 2021), 4.

[51] The Economist, *The New Interventionism,* special report, January 15, 2022, https://www.economist.com/special-report/2022-01-15.

[52] F. Fukuyama, "The Pandemic and Political Order: It Takes a State," *Foreign Affairs* 99, no. 4 (July/August 2020): 26–30.

[53] M. Mazzucato, *Mission Economy: A Moonshot Guide to Changing Capitalism* (London: Allen Lane, 2021).

[54] I. Dunt, *How to be a Liberal: The Story of Freedom and the Fight for its Survival* (Kingston upon Thames: Canbury Press, 2022).

98 DEMOCRATIC CROSSROADS

Table 5.2 Neo-statism

Country	Government Expenditure as % of GDP, 2019	Government Expenditure as % of GDP, 2020	Government Expenditure as % of GDP, 2021	Government Expenditure as % of GDP, 2022
France	55.35	61.42	59.05	58.34
India	27.42	31.05	30.14	28.62
Italy	48.47	57	55.45	56.74
Japan	37.27	44.6	42.52	44.09
South Africa	31.46	34.64	32.98	32.47
Spain	42.32	51.76	50.6	47.11
Sweden	48.06	50.92	49.86	47.32
UK	38.25	48.92	44.87	44.3
US	35.73	45.3	42.36	36.26

This table shows the recent trend in public spending across countries, based on data from the IMF, https://www.imf.org/external/datamapper/exp@FPP/USA/FRA/JPN/GBR/SWE/ESP/ITA/ZAF/IND.

as a direct result of the pandemic experience.[55] The EU's post-pandemic Resilience and Recovery Facility made nearly 800 billion euros worth of stimulus available. Moreover, as the COVID-19 emergency elided into the energy crisis of 2022, so the EU agreed a further loosening of financial orthodoxy—the two crises acting together to deepen the change in economic policy (Chapter 6 looks in more detail at the EU's emerging political economy).

In parallel, most governments around the world now seek to manage and reshape globalization rather than extend or deepen it.[56] Many analysts detect a turn away from a 60-year era of globalization to one where deglobalization seems set to become a powerful trend. COVID-19 and many other challenges seem to show that global linkages are a source of threat. Even if many contest the notion that deglobalization is afoot, governments are stepping back from economic interdependence. Liberal internationalism is prizing itself apart from globalization.[57]

[55] "National Security Advisor Jake Sullivan on the Biden Administration's Foreign Policy," *C-Span*, https://www.c-span.org/video/?524890-2/national-security-adviser-jake-sullivan-discusses-biden-administrations-foreign-policy (accessed February 19, 2024).

[56] M. O' Sullivan, *The Levelling: What's Next After Globalization* (New York: PublicAffairs, 2019).

[57] J. Ikenberry, "The Next Liberal Order," *Foreign Affairs*, June 9, 2020, https://www.foreignaffairs.com/articles/united-states/2020-06-09/next-liberal-order.

Even if much talk of deglobalization risks being exaggerated, the dynamics of global political economy are clearly shifting in ways that will affect democracy and democratization. The shifts in economic paradigms are still incipient and partial; yet they do offer at least the possibility of a more benign context for global democracy. For many years, socioeconomic inequalities have undermined the effective functioning of democratic politics: economically underprivileged parts of societies increasingly isolated themselves from participating in democracy and struggling to exercise their political rights. The era of more empowered states offers the prospect of democracy being planted in firmer soil, as governments supposedly get more serious about action designed to reduce the inequalities that have comprised many citizens' de facto ability to exercise their democratic rights.

The emergent neo-statism goes hand in hand with a concern about local democratic control over economic resources and recovering this from impersonal global forces. The empowered state promises to act as an adjunct to popular sovereignty, while the more inward-looking caution about globalism entails a sense of place necessary to building communities of democratic belonging. While most strongly supported by leftist governments, these shifts have also been supported by a strand of conservatism that is returning to earlier traditions of communal solidarity and inclusion.[58] Even from fairly orthodox positions, a more competent and guiding state is now routinely posited as key to the combined reform of democracy and capitalism.[59]

Many of the ways in which states have become more empowered on the back of COVID-19 connect in positive ways to the exercise of political rights. Governments have begun to target resources more widely across the population in a way that helps more citizens exercise their democratic rights effectively. New initiatives have taken shape to include marginalized communities in economic decision-making. The Biden administration launched a battery of new participative citizen consultations and portals as part of its state capacity-building program, with projects under the Inflation Reduction Act including "community benefit plans."[60] In April 2023, US national security advisor Jake Sullivan gave what was widely seen as a seminal speech declaring the end of neoliberalism, and in this presentation explicitly

---

[58] C. Accetti, *What Is Christian Democracy? Politics, Religion and Ideology* (New York: Cambridge University Press, 2019).

[59] M. Wolf, *The Crisis of Democratic Capitalism* (New York: Penguin, 2023).

[60] K. Sabeel Rahman, "Statecraft and Policy Design in the New Political Economy," *Hewlett Foundation New Common Sense*, May 2023

100 DEMOCRATIC CROSSROADS

framed the building of state capacity as a means of ensuring stronger democratic inclusiveness.[61]

Recent academic research charts how state social protection correlates with populations' backing for democracy support internationally—with the emerging post-neoliberal era hence offering the prospect of restoring dynamism and credibility to global democratic order.[62] Many governments have belatedly moved to ensure stronger protection for the rights of gig workers like delivery riders; in some states, union rights have been reinstated; and many new, post-COVID regulations oblige companies to cut links to human rights abuses in their international supply chains. The reopening of debate about the state and economic doctrine widens the scope of democratic choice. A frequently expressed concern has been that an extremely narrow range of economic-policy options has been on offer to citizens and that this has eviscerated meaningful democratic choice.[63] Economic liberalism was de facto imposed in top-down fashion through a collusion of elites from different parts of the political spectrum.[64] In the wake of the pandemic, some governments have contemplated a wider range of policy choices and this opens the way to domestic democratic decisions becoming more meaningful once again, as opposed to economic policy being almost entirely pre-set by the regulatory molds of globalization.

In line with the book's framework-category of civic micropolitics, the democratic component of the new economic paradigm is seen most clearly in participative societal engagement playing an important role in this emerging agenda. The change in economic policy has in many countries been driven through grassroots, bottom-up dynamics. Data suggests that social movements, citizens, and NGOs have done a better job than elected politicians in reflecting populations' desire to see more open, balanced, and democratic forms of globalization and international order.[65] Across the

---

[61] The White House, "Remarks by National Security Advisor Jake Sullivan on Renewing American Economic Leadership at the Brookings Institution," April 27, 2023, https://www.whitehouse.gov/briefing-room/speeches-remarks/2023/04/27/remarks-by-national-security-advisor-jake-sullivan-on-renewing-american-economic-leadership-at-the-brookings-institution.

[62] P. Trubowitz and B. Burgoon, *Geopolitics and Democracy: The Western Liberal Order from Foundation to Fracture* (New York: Oxford University Press, 2023

[63] A. Tucker, *Democracy Against Liberalism* (Cambridge: Polity Press, 2020).

[64] M. Wilkinson, *Authoritarian Liberalism and the Transformation of Modern Europe* (New York: Oxford University Press, 2021).

[65] P. de Wilde, "The Quality of Representative Claims: Uncovering a Weakness in the Defence of the Liberal World Order," *Political Studies* 68, no. 2, (2019): 271–292.

COVID-19, DEMOCRACY, AND POST-NEOLIBERALISM   101

world, citizens' democratic engagement has worked as one dynamic among several pushing a new economic paradigm to the fore.

A range of varied examples demonstrates these different, overarching trends. In Turkey, the Deep Poverty Network was vocal during the pandemic in pushing though more protective policies. In Argentina, social movements and civic organizations close to the national governing coalition played a role in post-pandemic reconstruction built around new ideas and policies about state interventionism, taxes, and urban planning. In Asia, businesses and informal workers affected by the economic shutdown mobilized for government intervention. In India and Indonesia, unions and informal worker groups pushed back against new privatization laws in the pandemic. In Thailand, the group Wefair has emerged from the country's 2020 pro-democracy protests, linking the problem of economic inequality exacerbated by the pandemic with the concentration of political power in the hands of royalist elites. More broadly in Southeast Asia, social partners now talk more than they did before about the need for a reconsideration of the economic status quo.[66]

A dual movement in this policy domain is that moves toward empowered states do not have uniformly positive implications for democracy. In many countries, such moves hardly seem to address the primary root causes of autocratization. Indeed, in some cases an expansion of the state has been advanced in ways that sit uneasily with accountability, openness, and bottom-up pluralism. If the positive side is about democratic control over economic resources, a focus on relocalized national identities can also have less democratic implications. As one analyst concludes: "The return of the state does not necessarily herald a more democratic world and indeed might usher in new forms of oppression and exploitation."[67] Albeit with some exceptions, left and right now agree on the need for stronger and more extensive states; the real question lies in how newly empowered states exercise their competences. As president of Open Societies Foundations, Mark Malloch-Brown argues, the crucial debate is what form the "bigger, more active state" will take: "Will it be one that upholds individual rights . . . or one that hoards power and covets its own rights?"[68]

---

[66] For details on these and other examples, see R. Youngs et al., *Civil Society and Global Pandemic: Building Back Different* (Washington, DC: Carnegie Endowment for International Peace, 2021), https://carnegieendowment.org/2021/09/30/civil-society-and-global-pandemic-building-back-different-pub-85446

[67] Geraudo, *The Great Recoil*, 20.

[68] M. Malloch-Brown, "The Return of Conflict, the Retreat of Democracy," Speech at the Royal College of Defence Studies, London, June 26, 2023.

102   DEMOCRATIC CROSSROADS

A risk to democracy arises where the empowered state is not well enough constrained to be a boost to popular sovereignty. In some countries, the economic shift is serving to empower authoritarian states. Many new welfare programs have been delivered through a growth of state surveillance capabilities and digital tracking measures for contact tracing purposes. In countries like Brazil, India, the Philippines, Turkey, and Poland, moves away from free-market policies have gone hand in hand with more illiberal government programs. State intervention has in some places contributed to a rise in cronyism and corruption, with lucrative government contracts being given to companies that have personal or political connections with government officials. In many countries—Egypt is one clear example—regimes have distributed benefits expressly to undercut the pro-democratic middle classes. In some such places, empowered states have become something akin to family-run businesses. In Mexico, neo-statism has gone hand in hand with an authoritarian slide under President Andrés Manuel López Obrador. More intervention has in some countries been the handmaiden of a recrudescent nationalism that is not liberal or progressive and not concerned with better democratic accountability.

During the health emergency, China's stimulus package was extensive, the country registered record trade surpluses and its share of global GDP increased even faster than before the pandemic. China's government financed the production of medical equipment, unemployment insurance, tax relief and social security contributions, along with additional public investment. It issued 1 trillion yuan of government bonds for COVID-19 recovery and spent extensively on new medical facilities and monitoring equipment. All this was used by the Communist Party regime to mobilize society around a common national project of recovery. The Chinese government also insisted its empowered authoritarian capacities helped it provide more international support in the form of medical equipment and vaccines than Western democracies were willing or able to offer. Here the empowered state clearly empowered an authoritarianism that sought to push back against protests calling for political and social reforms. Many insisted that in this sense the pandemic dramatically accelerated the "great realignment" in favor of China and its vision of authoritarian power.[69]

Empowered states' heightened focus on economic security could have some negative consequences for democracy. Although stronger state agency

[69] Macaes, *Geopolitics for the End Times*, 75–77.

COVID-19, DEMOCRACY, AND POST-NEOLIBERALISM   103

has led to some efforts at recovery-related coordination across borders, in some ways the new statism sees governments turned inward to protect their own populations and internal balances to the detriment of interstate cooperation. This spillover from internal democratic protection to the multilateral sphere menaces the international rules and coordination needed to confront economic and health problems or to uphold liberal-democratic norms. Greater economic autarky would risk breaking the kind of cross-border networks and linkages that have often helped democratic transitions. If so-called decoupling or, alternatively, derisking are presented as ways of defending Western democracy, then by the same logic they might also serve to protect Chinese and other authoritarianism from democratic influences. If neoliberal globalization fueled the inequalities that led to democratic regression, its demise could widen the maneuverability of authoritarian state capitalism within more competitive forms of interdependence.[70] Suggesting a possible connection to current trends, noted historians have uncovered how previous periods of mass protests for more statist autarchy often had anti-democratic outcomes.[71]

Long-time critics of the liberal project insist the recent extension of state power in both democracies and autocracies is one part of liberalism's wider demise.[72] In many democracies, the emerging risk is of a more top-down and technocratic form of policymaking. Economic policy responses might be welcome in pointing beyond neoliberalism, but they have mostly been delivered top-down, in ad hoc crisis-management mode, rather than resulting from an openly debated shift to a coherently defined new model. In one notable example, Taiwan's technocratic approach to the pandemic left a mixed legacy: it proved effective but prioritized a collective right to health and life in a way that cut across individual democratic rights.[73] The technocratic trend was even more marked in Europe and is covered in more detail in the next chapter. After years of unhappiness with the prevailing economic

[70] M. Kutlay and Z. Onis, "Liberal Democracy on the Edge? Anxieties in a Shifting Global (Dis)order," *Alternatives: Global, Local, Political* 48, no. 1 (2022), https://doi.org/10.1177/0304375422 1096511.

[71] T. Zahra, *Against the World: Anti-Globalism and Mass Politics between the World Wars* (New York: Norton, 2023).

[72] J. Gray, *The New Leviathans: Thoughts after Liberalism* (London: Penguin, 2023)

[73] T. Lee, "The Rise of Technocracy and the COVID-19 Pandemic in Taiwan: Courts, Human Rights, and the Protection of Vulnerable Populations," *German Law Journal* 22, no. 6 (September 2021): 1115–1132.

104 DEMOCRATIC CROSSROADS

doctrine it was a virus not overwhelming, bottom-up political pressure that shook neoliberalism's foundations.[74]

The democratic opportunities offered by more empowered states are significant but not yet extensive enough to restore effective equality in rights or help democracy weather an era of multiple crises.[75] The economic shift in many countries comes with relatively weak democratic oversight specifically to retain the privileged position of private vested interests and to preserve the current system's core features.[76] Skeptics suggest that neoliberalism is not dying but rather mutating and maintaining its essential core of limiting real democracy. Poorer countries have had less capacity to spend big amounts for post-COVID recovery and have seen inequalities deepen despite new government programs.[77] Its most influential proponents acknowledge that neo-statism still has to build in more direct citizen participation in relation to big new public projects, so that it deepens democracy and avoids some of the top-down imbalances of previous statism.[78] If the key test is whether increased state resources and powers are accompanied by enhanced means of accountability over these, then democratic governments have so far fallen short in the post-pandemic era.

---

[74] Tooze, *Shutdown*.

[75] L. Savage, *The Dead Center* (New York: OR Books, 2022).

[76] L. Macfarlane, "Covid Has Forced a Neoliberal Retreat. But State Intervention Isn't Always Progressive," *University College London*, April 29, 2021, https://www.ucl.ac.uk/news/2021/apr/opinion-covid-has-forced-neoliberal-retreat-state-intervention-isnt-always-progressive; S. Borner, "Is the Coronavirus Going to Reshape the European Welfare State?," *Social Europe*, November 3, 2020, https://socialeurope.eu/is-the-coronavirus-going-to-reshape-the-european-welfare-state; J. Zielonka, "Has the Coronavirus Brought Back the Nation-State?," *Social Europe*, March 26, 2020, https://socialeurope.eu/has-the-coronavirus-brought-back-the-nation-state; J. Lent, "Coronavirus Spells the End of the Neoliberal Era. What's Next?," *Open Democracy*, April 12, 2020, https://www.opendemocracy.net/en/transformation/coronavirus-spells-the-end-of-the-neoliberal-era-whats-next/; V. Susova-Salminen and I. Svihlikova, eds., "The Covid-19 Pandemic: the End of Neoliberal Globalization?," *Transform Europe*, 2020, https://transform-network.net/wp-content/uploads/2023/05/ebook_the_covid-19_pandemic_en_version_final.pdf; J. Sandher and H. Kleider, "Coronavirus Has Brought the Welfare State Back, and It Might Be Here to Stay," *The Conversation*, June 24, 2020, https://theconversation.com/coronavirus-has-brought-the-welfare-state-back-and-it-might-be-here-to-stay-138564; A. Saad-Filho, "Coronavirus Crisis and the End of Neoliberalism," *Conter*, April 17, 2020, https://www.conter.scot/2020/4/17/coronavirus-crisis-and-the-end-of-neoliberalism/; J. Litobarski, "What Comes After Neoliberalism? A New Social Contract," *Friends of Europe*, January 25, 2022, https://www.friendsofeurope.org/insights/what-comes-after-neoliberalism-a-new-social-contract/; A. Tooze, "Has Covid Ended the Neoliberal Era?," *The Guardian*, September 2, 2021, https://www.theguardian.com/news/2021/sep/02/covid-and-the-crisis-of-neoliberalism.

[77] Tooze, *Shutdown*.

[78] P. Gerbaudo, "A Post-Neoliberal Paradigm Is Emerging: Conversation with Felicia Wong," *Agenda Publica*, November 4, 2022, https://agendapublica.elpais.com/noticia/18303/post-neoliberal-paradigm-is-emerging-conversation-with-felicia-wong.

Assessment: Empowered States and Micromobilization

The transformative crisis of the COVID-19 pandemic triggered major changes to political processes, societal organization, and economic policy across the world. These changes were both direct and indirect and awoke widespread concerns that the health emergency would add hugely to democracy's troubles and usher in more closed, technocratic, and overtly autocratic patterns of governance. An initial wave of direct restrictions on personal freedoms led into a subsequent series of indirect impacts on political systems as the pandemic evolved into a less acute phase. Even as the worst of the pandemic passed, some of these aftershocks have continued to buffet democratic systems and tilt in the direction of illiberal or even authoritarian dynamics.

However, ultimately COVID-19 did not force a decisive lurch against democracy and in favor of authoritarian control. In the early days of the emergency most observers believed or feared it was set to be a watershed with a clear undemocratic flavor and yet this did not transpire, at least not to the extent initially anticipated. Most democratic governments righted their political course as the pandemic retreated. The health emergency certainly placed new strains on democratic systems and empowered some authoritarian regimes, in some countries leaving a more closed and surveillance-oriented politics in its wake. But it proved not to be an all-encompassing or unidirectional inflection point in autocracy's favor. Given how dire the prognoses were in the first wave of the pandemic in 2020, this is a noteworthy outcome.

Indeed, over a longer sweep of time the pandemic has in some senses acted as catalyst for democratic actions and for policies that might in the long term have some positive implications for global democracy. As COVID-19 gradually ceased to be governments' highest priority or dominant concern, it left this democratic potential as a longer-term legacy. This was for several reasons. Most directly, many governments began to withdraw rights-restricting emergency measures, under pressure to do so from a rise in civic micropolitics in many cases. Then, as the tide of emergency receded it revealed a new infrastructure of civic organization that involved direct citizen engagement and more intense channels of democratic accountability. And, most indirectly, in a prospective hint of liberal statism, a post-pandemic adjustment in economic policies promised to correct neoliberalism's harmful effects on political rights.

The pandemic reinforced the need for engagement by highlighting the importance of connections and trust in society: how strongly people engaged with one another and with their institutions seemed to affect their willingness to wear masks, follow safe distancing practices, and get vaccines. Many people sought out engagement with one another in order to retain their connections and help each other with day-to-day needs during the crisis. While there was already a move toward these forms of engagement in the 2010s, the pandemic extended, deepened, and accelerated this trend. And these initiatives continued as the acute period of emergency passed and indeed, they extended into other functions and areas. Many of the community initiatives outlined in this chapter have begun to extend the dynamics of participative deliberation into democratic institutions. This bottom-up trend is making participation more far-reaching in its effect on improving democracy as it addresses stubbornly rooted problems and power imbalances. This "everyday democracy" has begun to seep into institutions, reflecting a different dynamic of democratic engagement.[79]

Alongside these social changes, new approaches to economic policy have brought further hope for democratic renewal. As the tectonic plates of economic doctrine have begun to shift, this has had powerful ramifications for democracy. Neoliberalism is not over, and nor is decoupling from economic globalism and interdependencies likely to be far-reaching in the short term. Yet new debates about an empowered role for states have become more dominant and this has fostered a different mindset in how many policymakers, politicians, activists, and citizens conceive the relationship between public power and effective democratic freedoms. If neoliberalism was rooted in an argument that state control tends to limit democracy, a contrasting political logic has become more predominant in the pandemic's wake: effective democratic choice needs to be rescued from impersonal market and globalist dynamics.

Some thinkers argue that in the post-pandemic world localized economics and localized politics are developing together.[80] Changes in social organization and in economic policy are tightly entwined, as the pandemic and its

---

[79] A. Bua and S. Bussu, "Reclaiming Participatory Governance: Social Movements and the Reinvention of Democratic Innovations," *Participatory and Deliberative Democracy*, May 3, 2022, https://deliberativehub.wordpress.com/2022/05/03/reclaiming-participatory-governance-social-movements-and-the-reinvention-of-democratic-innovations/.

[80] R. Foroohar, "After Neoliberalism: All Economics Is Local," *Foreign Affairs*, October 28, 2022, https://www.foreignaffairs.com/united-states/after-neoliberalism-all-economics-is-local-rana-foroohar.

economic effects have left fundamental changes in how citizens see the world and situate themselves in it, and causing them to question economic models and their social bases.[81] In terms of the book's analytical framework, this double movement shows a trend toward civic micropolitics and empowered states unfolding in tandem with each other. The pandemic and its socioeconomic impacts have together contributed to changes in the types, potency, and levels of democratic agency.

Skeptics might stress that these positive democratic impacts are of minor significance, that participative micropolitics are too small-scale to correct structural injustices or international power imbalances, and that economic policies have not adjusted nearly enough to replenish de facto democratic rights. At least some governments see neo-statism as being about the state becoming more determinant as arbiter of the public interest rather than more responsive to public engagement—a republican rather than liberal notion of the empowered state.[82] Domestic-international read-overs have become more varied and complex: internal state-empowerment does not necessarily go hand in hand with external state agency committed to the deepened multilateralism that binds liberal rules-based order. In the emerging link between geopolitics, COVID-19, and the economic paradigm shift, some analysts point out that shoring up democracy in a more autocratic world requires making democracy more just and less oligarchic, well beyond the potential of the modest economic changes witnessed to date.[83]

Still, for all these well-noted limitations, in the context of firmly rooted anti-democratic expectation, the fact that the pandemic has opened pathways of economic reform and democratic potential must be seen as analytically significant. The almost uniform pessimism of the pandemic's early phase that autocracy would emerge a clear victor, has given way to outcomes that offer a possible fillip to democracy and democratization in the longer term. Even if no longer at the forefront of global debate, the pandemic and its socioeconomic legacy have left an imprint on patterns of governance and on the way that many citizens relate to and engage with their political systems.

---

[81] B. Latour, *After Lockdown: A Metamorphosis* (Cambridge: Polity, 2021).

[82] C. Benoit and C. Hay, "The Antinomies of Sovereigntism, Statism and Liberalism in European Democratic Responses to the COVID-19 Crisis: A Comparison of Britain and France," *Comparative European Politics* 20 (2022): 390–410.

[83] P. Mason, "Ukraine: The Politics of Dying," *Medium*, February 25, 2022, https://medium.com/mosquito-ridge/ukraine-the-politics-of-dying-a37f9f1fe6e9.

108   DEMOCRATIC CROSSROADS

Although these changes have brought new difficulties for democratic systems and democratic reform, they also reflect a heightened demand for more open, accountable, citizen-responsive, and inclusive politics. As they open up new avenues for political transformation, these elements of democratic reworking still need to gel fully together if they are to enable democracy to deal effectively with the kind of global shocks experienced in the last several years.

6

Snapshot: Europe's New
Political Economy

While the re-examination of economic policies has had global reach, it has taken on particularly interesting dimensions in Europe. The COVID-19 pandemic prompted the European Union and its member states to deploy innovative forms of crisis management and then to introduce far-reaching policy changes to their economic policies. The global health emergency combined with parallel concerns relating to the energy transition and the bloc's general economic performance to drive a reassessment of economic strategies in the early 2020s. In the case of EU political economy, the COVID-19 and climate crises have acted in unison to produce more interventionist economic and social policies and a reshaping of governance processes.

In the last several years, the EU has pioneered some of the boldest shifts in economic policy anywhere in the world and has done so in a context of widespread democratic malaise across the European continent. As such, this case is especially useful in demonstrating the interplay between a rebalanced economic paradigm, on the one hand, and the quality of democratic governance, on the other hand. The way that European countries managed the pandemic and the related economic policy shifts has begun to have significant implications for democracy. The emergent post-pandemic political economy promises to reconnect citizens with the EU and restore the union's democratic credibility. Yet it also constitutes an especially notable example of trustee statism—one of the four analytical categories identified in Chapter 2.

Benign Rethinking

In the years preceding the pandemic, EU economic policies were dominated by the bitter tensions of the euro crisis. As is well known, economic orthodoxy was associated with a decade of painful austerity across most of the continent. The EU policy response to the COVID-19 pandemic was

Democratic Crossroads. Richard Youngs, Oxford University Press. © Oxford University Press 2024.
DOI: 10.1093/oso/9780197762417.003.0006

fundamentally different. The health emergency was a deeper and qualitatively different crisis, but initially reopened the just-healing wounds of the euro crisis as many feared a repeat of unbending austerity. However, after much internal debate, the EU's model of political economy adapted to the new circumstances. Debt and state-aid restrictions were quickly laid aside. Economic policy appeared to move into a new era as the EU agreed a mammoth 750 billion euro spending package to address the effects of the pandemic. Crucially, this Recovery and Resilience Facility (RRF) would provide grants and loans funded by pooled EU-level borrowing. What became known as the Next Generation EU package seemed to herald a more interventionist, more citizen-oriented and more inclusive process of European cooperation.

Most European governments also fashioned large-scale post-COVID packages of state funding at the national level. The French government introduced a package that promised 30 billion euros of support up to 2030; when elected in 2017, President Macron had promised to cut public spending but now increased it to 60 percent of GDP. These were not only high levels of spending, but the packages also came with rules designed to give states more scope to favor domestic production of health equipment and renewable technologies and more power to impose local content requirements.

The RRF represented not just major funding but a change of gear in the whole process of European integration. This was because the new measures broke several longstanding taboos. As common EU-level debt would be accumulated, the EU raised the likelihood of common taxes—especially digital and carbon levies—to pay back the debt over the longer term. The prospect took shape that something approaching a common fiscal policy might just be emerging from the shadows to match the EU's 20-year-old common currency and monetary policy. After many years in the doldrums, the EU project appeared to take on a new lease of life. Debate re-emerged about political union. Many policymakers in the EU and member states pushed for the major leap forward represented by the RRF to be accompanied by reform of the union's political dimensions too.

The new approach to economic intervention promised a positive spillover to political rights. During the years of the financial crisis, EU austerity packages were imposed on member states with little regard for democratic accountability. In the early 2020s, governments and the EU institutions promised a fundamentally different approach. Apparently taking on board the frustrations of the euro-crisis years, governments agreed to the RRF

SNAPSHOT: EUROPE'S NEW POLITICAL ECONOMY   111

quickly and with more flexible procedures. There would be more support for citizens' basic economic and social problems, and this would help underpin support for democracy. Such active help was necessary to recapture some of the trust in democratic institutions that had evaporated in the 2010s.

Crucially, many elements of the emergency framework continued after the worst of the pandemic and were applied in the energy crisis that emerged after Russia's invasion of Ukraine. Many forms of intervention and exception began to look semi-permanent as governments ramped up support to different parts of the economy. Governments effectively ditched the Stability and Growth Pact that had for many years imposed ceilings on deficit spending. The European Commission drew up new fiscal rules that offered more flexibility and country variation related to debt sustainability; these rules would provide European governments with more leeway for reducing debt and gave high debt countries more time to get debt on a downward path. Even the so-called northern frugal states like Germany and the Netherlands accepted this general direction of change, although they quibbled about the details and sought some dilution of the proposals into 2023.

COVID-19 exceptional rules were prolonged and looked set to become quasi permanent in allowing sizeable amounts of national state aid. In 2022, the European Commission signed off 650 billion euros of state aid—even higher than the 384 billion record high during the health emergency in 2020.[1] In 2023 the Commission extended its Temporary Crisis and Transition Framework to allow additional national state aid. A Net Zero Industry Act extended intervention instruments with a sizeable new package of support for renewable energy, and the EU now pushed to relax WTO rules against state subsidies. While EU subsidies rose, the European Commission fashioned a new "economic security strategy" with powers to block imports of goods subsidized by other states and tougher screening measures on inward and outward investment.[2]

The new interventions were aimed at citizens' priorities and helped boost the legitimacy of EU institutions. According to Eurobarometer, in 2023 an overwhelming majority of citizens supported this strong action at both the EU and national government levels, in addition to increased social

---

[1] Figures from Politico Europe, *Brussels Playbook*, January 12, 2023. https://www.politico.eu/new sletter/brussels-playbook/europeans-back-ukraine-hijacking-single-market-arena-quits/.

[2] European Commission and High Representative, *European Economic Security Strategy*, 2023. https://eur-lex.europa.eu/legal-content/EN/TXT/?uri=CELEX%3A52023JC0020.

spending.[3] Moreover, renewed plans for deepening EU reforms ostensibly placed democratic renewal at their heart. The plans raised the possibility of stronger channels of democratic accountability being agreed at the European level. The Conference on the Future of Europe ran over 2021 and 2022 and promised as its centerpiece new forms of citizen engagement on these major EU interventions. The European Commission advanced with new citizen panels on specific pieces of legislation and drew up a Defence of Democracy package in 2023. As more EU funds began to flow, several national governments promised to consult civil society organizations on their RRF programs. A primary component of the plans, democratic engagement for youth also included a special focus on promoting gender equality.

Some writers detected in all this a qualitative shift from the euro crisis to the COVID-19 emergency and beyond. The pandemic pushed the EU another step toward being a "political Europe." This was the first emergency in which crisis management was generated bottom-up, with open debate and public monitoring of governments. The closed, opaque, and top-down style of the eurozone crisis seemed to morph into a more open and engaged decisionmaking style. The very gravity of the pandemic drove more elite direct engagement and communication with the public.[4]

The Specter of Technocratic Statism

Alongside such democratic potential, however, the logic of trustee statism has in many ways emerged reinforced across post-pandemic Europe. Elements of technocratic decision-making intensified as a result of the pandemic emergency. The new recovery funds were decided by governments in marathon summit sessions bereft of citizen involvement. As governments needed to draw up detailed reform plans to receive RRF funds, the process gave the Commission more power over national policies, the ability to insist on more detailed reform milestones and more scope to withhold funds. Member states expressly sought to keep the RRF separate from the EU budget partly to avoid lengthy democratic checks. The fund was embedded

---

[3] European Commission, "Social Europe: Eurobarometer Survey Shows Europeans Support Stronger Social Policies and More Social Spending," February 6, 2023, https://ec.europa.eu/social/main.jsp?catId=89&furtherNews=yes&newsId=10509&langId=en.

[4] L. van Middelaar, *Pandemonium: Saving Europe* (Newcastle upon Tyne: Agenda Publishing, 2021).

SNAPSHOT: EUROPE'S NEW POLITICAL ECONOMY 113

within a more top-down, emergency version of the so-called European Semester—the process by which the EU authorizes national budgets and monitors economic policies—that expressly side-lined social and civic actors and gave the Commission prime influence over recovery plans. All this was adopted under legal procedures that also limited the European Parliament's scrutiny role. The new procedures empowered both technocratic agencies in Brussels and national governments over their parliaments. While member states agreed to consult civil society actors on how funds would be spent, their follow through on this was patchy.[5]

These features were especially present in relation to the climate-change parts of the new EU funding. It was here that the statism of the pandemic fused with the trustee statism of climate action—the latter described in Chapter 3. The EU mandated that 30 percent of RRF funds must be spent on green projects and did this with little citizen input or monitoring.[6] European governments have pushed through hundreds of green projects in express processes that bypass democratic checks. There was little or no prior public debate about the flagship European Green Deal before its very precise climate commitments and financing were agreed within the EU's labyrinthine decision-making processes. The parallel "Fit for 55" package of policies progressed without strong engagement from civic actors and without rigorous assessments of the Green Deal's social impact.

In 2022, governments resisted pressure from the European Parliament to give more information on RRF allocations and also to link the EU's new 72-billion-euro fund for energy poverty to democracy-related criteria. Indeed, as the energy crisis deepened, Germany and France began pushing for further fast-track rules for state aid that expressly bypassed normal democratic processes, and the European Commission proposed simplified executive procedures that directly aim to weaken democratic checks and accountability input into the release of such funding.[7] The EU used the Russian invasion of Ukraine as reason to prolong simplified executive procedures and post-COVID crisis-style policymaking. Perhaps the most striking feature of the new proposed rules on debt is that the Commission would have hugely increased powers to the detriment of national accountability mechanisms.

---

[5] V. Kreilinger, "Next Generation EU and National Parliaments: Taxation without Sufficient Representation?" in *Making EU Representative Democracy Fit for the Future*, ed. G. von Sydow and V. Kreilinger (Stockholm: Swedish Institute for European Policy Studies, 2022), 45–60.

[6] *Konzept #19: What We Must Do to Rebuild* (Frankfurt: Deutsche Bank Research, 2022).

[7] G. Leali, "France and Germany Push for Fast-Track Subsidies After US Row," *Politico*, December 19, 2022.

114 DEMOCRATIC CROSSROADS

Although it brought the prospect of common, EU-level taxes into sight, the RRF funding package did not include any EU-level coordinated plan fully to reinstate the democratic rights that governments had abridged in order to fight the virus. There was no EU democratic upgrade as part of this package, despite the huge financial commitments, the union's new ability to raise debt on capital markets and plans for new EU-level carbon and digital taxes to cover part of the spending. In practice, the EU then struggled to move forward with agreements on common taxes to cover the RRF precisely because it lacked a common base for democratic legitimacy. If one key essence of democracy lies in popular accountability over taxation, the lack of progress on this element of policy was striking. Even as the RRF funds were rolled out, there was a conspicuous lack of detailed democratic debate or engagement over the thorny question of how the 750 billion euros would be repaid. Far from the new economic intervention serving as a platform for deeper and more effective representation over common EU-level taxation, this question constantly slipped from the policy agenda.

The dearth of transparency was reflected in political frustration within member states. Italy ended up with a coalition government formed in large measure to help manage the RRF funds, again usurping domestic democratic competition. The opaque nature of EU decisions was one among many reasons behind the far-right Brothers of Italy's victory in 2022 elections; yet incoming prime minister Giorgia Meloni then centralized powers over RRF funds in her office and undercut authorities' independent monitoring powers over these funds. Sensitivities around decisions over EU funds brought down the Portuguese government in 2021 and were a running source of tension between government and opposition parties in Spain. In Poland, the opposition and civil society groups pushed the government to open a series of consultations on the RRF as the government sought to keep tight control over the funds. France's Green party signed a deal with far-left France Insoumise that involved adopting a more anti-EU position and began to speak out about how EU rules were hollowing out local input into tackling climate change.

In an example of civic micropolitics, a new generation of informal civil society movements emerged across Europe to try to recapture local-level input into EU crisis responses, reflecting the feeling that these were not opening major decisions to citizen voices.[8] The innovative Make.org grew as an open platform fostering citizen engagement around key EU issues, linked to local

---

[8] N. Milanese, K. Nicolaidis, and R. Youngs, "Informal Civil Society: A Booster for European Democracy?," *Carnegie Europe*, March 23, 2022.

funding schemes and cooperation with CSOs too; it focused on the energy crisis and citizen input into the RRF precisely because of a fear that these were tipping the scales more toward top-down, closed-door decision-making. By 2022, social and civic actors had pushed hard and reclaimed some of their influence over the RRF process, as they pressed the Commission and member states to relax their top-down crisis procedures and adopt a slightly more inclusive decision-making mode.[9]

A new EU Social Climate Fund introduced in 2023 promised citizen engagement, but civil society increasingly criticized its top-down processes. As part of unlocking this fund to mitigate energy and transport poverty, governments were obliged to draw up "Social Climate Plans." These plans needed to include a summary of "stakeholder consultation processes" and explain how citizen input had been incorporated. Although civil society deemed this a positive democratic step, governments then expressly weakened provisions for meaningful participation in negotiations. The fund moved toward a familiar EU format of selective consultation with a certain number of insider civil society organizations rather than a vibrant and open kind of citizen engagement—weakening a possible connection between the new interventionism and democratic accountability.

Assessment: Unresolved Trade-offs

The COVID-19 emergency was of such magnitude that it effectively forced the EU and European governments to reassess their economic models. The pandemic and then the economic shockwaves that continued in its aftermath fashioned a new European political economy: new layers and scales of economic intervention from both EU institutions and member-state governments began to alter the relationship between public authority and citizens. As the pandemic receded, some of the momentum behind this change also subsided, but it has not disappeared entirely. The cost-of-living crisis that hit European societies hard in 2022 helped retain traction behind the new political economy, with both post-pandemic and ecological transition challenges pushing policies in the same direction. Many celebrated

---

[9] B. Vanhercke and A. Verdun, "The European Semester as Goldilocks: Macroeconomic Policy Coordination and the Recovery and Resilience Facility," *Journal of Common Market Studies* (2021), https://doi.org/10.1111/jcms.13267.

116   DEMOCRATIC CROSSROADS

these changes as positive and long overdue. Their impact specifically on democracy was certainly of highly positive potential as the changes seemed to address the very factors that had depleted the quality of European democracy during the 2010s.

And yet the raft of new interventions intensified an ethos of trustee statism that also has problematic implications for democracy. Elements of liberal statism in the emerging political economy have coexisted with a strong dose of trustee statism—although as the EU is not a unitary state, the term trustee neo-interventionism might be more strictly apt in this case. Ironically, while the EU's elitist functional technocracy for years acted in the nefarious service of neoliberalism, it has arguably come to be used now to advance a neo-interventionist agenda. Democracy has always had to tread a path between technocratic and popular excesses: managing the EU's current crises has tilted many new measures toward the former.[10]

The EU and its member-state governments certainly crafted new intervention policies with a view to allaying citizens' democratic disaffection, yet in terms of how these were decided and implemented the dynamics of "crisis Europe" have at least partially offset those of "democratic Europe." The protective "economic security" now seen as vital to shore up democracy within Europe risks clashing with EU commitments to balanced and liberal forms of multilateralism. While the crisis-management imperative was understandable, the sizable resource transfers agreed in the wake of the pandemic have surely increased the need for a more effective democratic oversight that European governments have so far not been willing to countenance. Each successive EU crisis has left in its wake a starker mismatch between deeper economic cooperation and more limited democratic processes. EU emergency politics in the last several years have awoken citizen mobilization and a more politicized European project, but they have also supercharged unaccountable top-down decision-making.[11]

[10] H. Thompson, *Disorder: Hard Times in the 21st Century* (New York: Oxford University Press, 2022).
[11] S. Auer, *European Disunion: Democracy, Sovereignty and the Politics of Emergency* (Oxford University Press, 2022).

7
The New Geopolitics and War on Ukraine

Russia's invasion of Ukraine represented a shocking and violent rupture to global politics. The invasion came on top of several years during which geopolitical tensions had already been sharpening. The rules and institutions of the liberal world order have frayed progressively since the early 2010s. Russia's war on Ukraine has added a whole new level of conflict about geopolitical reordering. The unblunting of geopolitics has in many ways put democracy on the defensive. If for many years the international arena seemed to blow favorable winds into democracy's sails, it has gradually become a source of biting headwinds. For some time, authoritarian powers have been gaining influence and apparently reshaping international politics to their advantage. As it further propels this trend, Russia's invasion of Ukraine is a manifestly transformative moment for the democratic dimensions of the liberal order.

The double movement is that as the threats to democracy have become so increasingly evident and pronounced, they have spurred Western democratic powers and civil society into more concerted action. In the year before Russia's war on Ukraine, some Western states had begun to step up their commitments and coordination to defend democratic norms. The Russian invasion and ongoing fighting in Ukraine have fueled further moves in this pro-democracy direction. The process has been led by a clutch of Western democratic governments and given further impetus by more engaged civic politics too. In terms of the book's analytical categories, this represents a partial revival of liberal statism, in parallel with civic micropolitics.

While war and geopolitical conflict have pushed the defense of democracy to the top of Western foreign policy agendas, however, they have not spurred many non-Western democracies to adopt clear commitments to advance open politics. At the global level, the dynamics of realpolitik are powerful and offset those of a more democratic geopolitics. The new geopolitics—hastened by, but not limited to Russia's invasion of Ukraine—are of far-reaching relevance to global democracy and varied in their impact. The post-invasion geopolitical context has triggered a stronger focus on upholding democratic

Democratic Crossroads. Richard Youngs, Oxford University Press. © Oxford University Press 2024.
DOI: 10.1093/oso/9780197762417.003.0007

118 DEMOCRATIC CROSSROADS

norms from some governments and societies, but also complex divisions among both democratic and authoritarian states.

Democratic Lethargy

In the 2010s, it became increasingly clear that an era of visceral geopolitics was taking shape and began to work ever more palpably to democracy's disadvantage. The international politics of the period became dominated by an increasingly bitter rivalry between the democratic West and authoritarian regimes. Russian and Chinese assertiveness came to act as a disruptive spoiler to those actors desiring more democratic forms of governance. The uncertain future of democracy seemed increasingly inseparable from the parlous fate of the West itself, as domestic and global trends reinforced each other.[1] A "multi-order" world has emerged, in which western "liberal modernity is only a limited part of what is on offer."[2] The decline of Western power and the decline of democracy have seemed like overlapping trends, ever more tightly entwined with each other.

As the 2010s unfolded, many autocracies became adept at taking advantage of the international system. The international liberal order seemed for a long time to go inexorably hand in hand with national-level liberalism; now it became clear that some aspects of liberal order were working better for authoritarian regimes than democracies. While autocracies defended themselves from global liberal influences through blocking tactics and repression, democracies increasingly struggled to defend themselves from global illiberal-authoritarian influences.[3] There was also a link here to the debates over economic models outlined in Chapter 5: competition between economic models and the global-level crisis of neoliberal economics compounded the political travails of Western-democratic models in the international system.[4] Democracy was in essence increasingly caught up negatively in global geopolitical and geo-economic rivalry.

---

[1] E. Luce, *The Retreat of Western Liberalism* (New York: Grove Atlantic, 2017); B. Emmott, *The Fate of the West* (New York: Profile Books, 2017); Y. Mounk and R. Foa, "The End of the Democratic Century," *Foreign Affairs*, March/April, 2018

[2] A. Acharya, "After Liberal Hegemony: The Advent of a Multiplex World Order," *Ethics & International Affairs* 31, no. 3 (2017): 271–285.

[3] A. Cooley and D. Nexon, "The Real Crisis of Global Order: Illiberalism on the Rise," *Foreign Affairs*, December 14, 2021.

[4] A. Tooze, *Shutdown: How Covid Shook the World's Economy* (New York: Viking, 2021).

THE NEW GEOPOLITICS AND WAR ON UKRAINE   119

For the first two decades of the twenty-first century, democratic countries seemed to be almost in denial about these geopolitical risks to democracy. International efforts to defend and extend democratic norms waned over the 2010s. While some international cooperation took place in defense of democratic breakthroughs, a more realpolitik tone became more prominent in international relations. The focus of Western foreign policy shifted to pragmatic cooperation with rising powers, regardless of their political regime.[5] Western cooperation with nondemocracies deepened and the share of development aid going to autocracies increased.[6] The democracy promotion field lost momentum from its high point of the late 1990s. Especially in the US a logic of "restraint" gained currency—on the left as atonement for the failures of interventions in Iraq, Afghanistan and elsewhere, on the right as a tighter focus on immediate national interests—and this cut across any privileged focus on American democratic agency internationally.[7]

President Obama's foreign policy foregrounded pragmatism and realism, even as it was ideologically shaped by liberalism.[8] While the first Obama administration did engage in select democracy issues around the world, it also prioritized security and economic interests over these. This was the case in the Persian Gulf, as well as relationships with autocrats in Central Asia and Africa. In the face of ever more clearly encroaching multipolarity, the Obama administration "moved away from any single, overarching foreign policy narrative rooted in the idea of remaking the world in its own image."[9] The US response to the Arab Spring was mixed, with modest support for democracy where political change at least temporarily occurred—in Tunisia, Egypt, Libya, Yemen—but continued cooperation with resilient autocratic allies such as Bahrain, Saudi Arabia, Jordan, and Morocco.[10] The US tilted toward short-term security and away from nurturing lasting political change

[5] R. Haass and C. Kupchan, "The New Concert of Powers," *Foreign Affairs*, March 23, 2021.

[6] M. de Tollenaere, "Development Assistance in Different Political Regime Contexts," Carnegie *Europe*, January 24, 2023.

[7] RevDem, "Realist Thought Between Empire-Building and Restraint: Matthew Specter on Why a Flawed Tradition Endures," May 7, 2022, https://revdem.ceu.edu/2022/05/07/realist-thought-between-empire-building-and-restraint-matthew-specter-on-why-a-flawed-tradition-endures/.

[8] B. O'Connor and D. Cooper, "Ideology and the Foreign Policy and Barack Obama: A Liberal-Realist Approach to International Affairs," *Presidential Studies Quarterly* 51, no. 3 (2021): 635–666.

[9] T. Carothers, "Democracy Policy Under Obama: Revitalization or Retreat?," *Carnegie Endowment for International Peace*, January 11, 2012, https://carnegieendowment.org/2012/01/11/democracy-policy-under-obama-revitalization-or-retreat-pub-46443.

[10] Carothers, "Democracy Policy Under Obama: Revitalization or Retreat?"

120 DEMOCRATIC CROSSROADS

in the name of long-term security. In this period, multipolarity increasingly militated against US democracy support.[11]

President Trump's foreign policy focused primarily on confrontation with China, especially in trade policy. The Trump administration aimed to reduce foreign aid and tie it more directly to other countries' support for American policies. Compared to his predecessors, Trump showed more willingness to meet with autocrats and frequently praised and professed affinity with authoritarian leaders around the globe. Where his administration pressed regimes hard it was because of their hostility to the US not their authoritarianism: Trump strongly supported Egypt, Israel, and Saudi Arabia, while confronting Iran. In Latin America his administration levied more sanctions against the Venezuelan regime and actively supported opposition leaders there.[12]

European democracy support also plateaued in this period. While the EU continued to produce democracy strategies, its core foreign policy document of the decade, a Global Strategy released in 2016, was far more realpolitik in tone than previous such templates. While the EU offered support to the Arab spring revolts, it then adopted a hands-off approach as Middle Eastern and North African governments pushed back against democracy. Some of the biggest increases in European aid went to authoritarian regimes, especially under a new trust fund structure set up to quell the surge in migrant flows in 2016. The democracy elements of EU peacebuilding and stabilization missions dwindled. European positions toward China softened during the decade. The EU did not once invoke the democracy clause it insisted on in all its external agreements outside of sub-Saharan Africa. It declined to remove trade preferences from countries like Pakistan and the Philippines where human rights worsened.[13]

One more positive democratic hope of the 2010s was that non-Western democracies would start playing a more significant role in pushing back against the authoritarian surge. Many rising powers that prospered strongly in the 2010s were democracies, and they showed some increased interest in shoring up democratic values internationally as they become more powerful foreign-policy actors. However, they declined to develop any decisively

---

[11] R. Pee, "Obama Has Put National Security Ahead of Promoting Democracy Abroad," *The Conversation*, August 10, 2016, https://theconversation.com/obama-has-put-national-security-ahead-of-promoting-democracy-abroad-62711.

[12] Council on Foreign Relations, "Candidate Tracker: Donald J. Trump, 2020," https://www.cfr.org/election2020/candidate-tracker/donald-j.-trump(accessed February 19, 2024).

[13] R. Youngs, *The European Union and Global Politics* (New York: Macmillan, 2021), Chapter 9.

THE NEW GEOPOLITICS AND WAR ON UKRAINE 121

strong or systematic commitments to democracy internationally and the prospect of a wider democratic alliance beyond the transatlantic powers receded toward the end of the decade, especially as democracy weakened in key countries like Brazil, India, and Turkey.

There were certainly examples of these rising democracies contributing to global democratic dynamics. Brazil took on a leading role in Haiti's political and economic reconstruction, while pushing for Latin American regional bodies such as Mercosur and the Organization of American States to adopt strong democracy protection clauses. Argentina, Brazil, and Chile reacted strongly to a 2009 military coup in Honduras and responded to a quite different type of coup against Paraguay's sitting president in 2012. At these same states' behest, the Organization of American States introduced an Inter-American Democracy Charter, and most other Latin American regional organizations also introduced democracy clauses aimed at defending incumbent regimes from coup attempts.

Indonesia pushed hard for the Association of Southeast Asian Nations (ASEAN) to launch dialogue forums on democracy support and agree a commitment to defending democratic norms. The country became a leading diplomatic advocate for political reforms in Myanmar and, to some extent, in Cambodia and Vietnam as well. India played a major role in helping the Nepalese government and Maoist insurgents reach a democratic peace deal in 2006 and developed many pro-democracy initiatives and diplomatic efforts in Sri Lanka. Turkey initially positioned itself as perhaps the most engaged external player in the Arab Spring uprisings of 2011 and committed itself to supporting democratic change in the region. South Africa pushed for a democratic resolution to a 2011 electoral crisis in Côte d'Ivoire and sought to build democracy concerns into regional conflict prevention initiatives.

Many of these non-Western democracies invested money in democracy support and established aid programs that included meaningful amounts of financial backing for political reform initiatives. Indonesia began funding so-called South-South cooperation on democratic governance after 2010. The country's Institute for Peace and Democracy ran a wide range of democracy assistance initiatives in Myanmar and other ASEAN countries, gradually moving into more sensitive areas such as security sector reform. Japan rolled out a widening portfolio of aid projects covering election assistance, police reforms and the rule of law—efforts that amounted to several hundred million dollars per year by the late 2000s. Similarly, Turkey's sizable aid

122 DEMOCRATIC CROSSROADS

budget included funding for judicial reforms, civil society, security-sector reforms, and institution building. South Africa funded election observers in many African countries.

Geopolitical factors were often behind these non-Western strategies. In Asia, leading countries like Japan and India saw democracy support as a means of pushing back against China's rise. For large emerging countries like Brazil and Indonesia, advocacy for democratic causes offered a way to rein-force their claims to regional leadership. And for other actors, like Turkey's ruling Justice and Development Party, democracy promotion was a means of backing close ideological affiliates in other countries. However, in general these geopolitical drivers were mixed, and non-Western democracies were reluctant to mount any really committed defense of democratic norms. Their policies remained relatively modest and, in many cases, became less values-based and more realpolitik as the decade unfolded.

In Africa, the African Charter for Democracy, Elections and Governance seemed to run out of steam and did little to counter the continent's author-itarian turn. In Latin American support for democracy got caught up in the region's fraught division between leftist and right-wing governments; left-leaning democratic governments declined to invoke any democratic clauses or instruments against democratic backsliding observed in Venezuela and Nicaragua. Brazil, India, and South Africa held back from supporting de-mocracy more strongly due to their desire to craft an interlocking set of partnerships with Russia and China under the so-called BRICS banner. The more democratic India-Brazil-South Africa (IPSA) Dialogue Forum issued many statements stressing support for democracy and human rights but faded in importance.

Moreover, there was limited coordination among all these democracies. Proposals for a concert or league of democracies were raised and circulated briefly in the mid-2000s. But neither Western nor non-Western governments pursued these ideas with any conviction, and such thinking soon subsided. European governments were unenthusiastic, fearing that such groupings would undermine the United Nations. The Community of Democracies (CoD) was created in 2000, expanded to 106 members and ran many projects and dialogue forums. However, it fell short of initial ambitions and lost mo-mentum. The CoD included many nondemocratic states, complicating its utility as an operational democracy support body and making it more akin to a venue for inclusive dialogue. A lack of civil society inclusion also contributed to its ultimately disappointing outcome. While the CoD ran useful low-level initiatives, it neither gained high-level strategic traction nor much practical operational democracy support on the ground.

Partial Birth of Democratic Geopolitics

Against this troubling backdrop, as the new decade of the 2020s began democratic states slowly and partially began to respond to the geopolitical threats to liberal values. While Russia's invasion of Ukraine in February 2022 was the crucial strategic turning point, the tide began very gently to turn in the period immediately prior to this. In 2020 and 2021, deepening geopolitical tension in at least some measure became a spur to stronger Western commitments to defend democratic values and the faint stirrings of a more liberal statism. Into the early 2020s, prominent experts were pointing to a more "epochal confrontation" between power and legitimacy—a struggle that began to move from the realms of soft power to harder confrontation.[14]

The COVID-19 pandemic served as a wakeup call. It sharpened the democracy-autocracy cleavage, and turbo-charged the push for Western liberal democracies to work together in recognition that safeguarding international collective action was necessary to uphold their own democratic values.[15] China came out of the pandemic empowered through its tightened links with developing states a result of extensive vaccine diplomacy. As outlined in Chapter 5, China's provision of vaccines around the world and its assertive COVID-19–related diplomacy added a further dimension to sharpened geopolitical rivalries across the world. The geopolitical divide between governance systems permeated the politics of COVID-19 and was in turn deepened by the pandemic.

This sharpened a more general sense of rivalry between the democratic West and China. Many democracies now began to see China as a systemic and belligerent enough threat to band together more conspicuously to defend the liberal order and democracy. China was becoming the replacement of the Soviet threat that glued the West together during the Cold War, with the difference that democracy was now the key dividing line, not capitalism. This was no longer the old democracy promotion agenda—a

[14] L. Diamond, "Democracy's Arc: From Resurgent to Imperiled," *Journal of Democracy* 33, no.1 (2022): 163–179.

[15] J. Ikenberry, "The Next Liberal Order," *Foreign Affairs*, June 9, 2020, https://www.foreignaffairs.com/articles/united-states/2020-06-09/next-liberal-order.

second-order belief that it would on balance be a good thing to have other powers move in a democratic direction. Rather, it seemed to reflect an existential view that defending democracy was a more first-order security imperative. Increasingly, democratic nations began to worry that China was a proximate threat to democracy everywhere, including in their own countries.[16]

As the decade turned and especially after the pandemic, Western democracies introduced trade strategies to wean themselves off a dependency on Chinese exports. They introduced barriers to outside interference in democratic processes, as a response to both Chinese and Russia tactics of incursion: in 2020 and 2012, Western and some non-Western budgets for cyber-security ballooned, as did funding for measures to rebuff outside malign influence over democratic elections. The democratic nations began to explore hard security coordination too, reflecting a concern with defending democracy in the most immediate way. In Asia, the Quad—the four democratic nations of Australia, India, Japan, and the US—awoke from its strategic slumber and promised to become more active, framing its renewed mission more expressly in terms of democracy needing to counter authoritarianism.

When the Biden administration took power, it showed a stronger commitment to democracy than US governments had for many years. President Biden spoke in clear terms about a global contest between democracy and autocracy and the need for democracies to stand up for democracy. As discussed in more detail below, his administration organized a Summit for Democracy at the end of its first year, convening (virtually) more than 100 democracies. The administration moved to impose a higher number of democracy related sanctions. Its new Strategy to Prevent Conflict and Promote Stability defined democracy as a priority.[17] Under active leadership by Samantha Power, the US Agency for International Development designed several new democracy-related aid initiatives and created a dedicated democracy bureau for the first time in USAID's history.

Similar changes were forthcoming in European democracy support. The EU strengthened its commitments under a new Democracy and Human

[16] M. Beckley, "Enemies of My Enemy," *Foreign Affairs*, February 14, 2022.

[17] Office of the Spokesperson, "The U.S. Strategy to Prevent Conflict and Promote Stability: Priority Countries and Region," *media note, US Department of State*, April 1, 2022, https://www.state.gov/the-u-s-strategy-to-prevent-conflict-and-promote-stability-priority-countries-and-region/.

Rights Action Plan for 2020–2024. The union launched a new Global Human Rights Sanctions Regime and increased other sanctions to a record level. The EU increased democracy funding under its 2020–2027 budget and made its funding rules more agile and flexible. In 2021 a new Team Europe Democracy initiative got member states contributing to joint democracy programs and efforts around the world. A so-called Global Gateway initiative promised mixed public-private funds that would be an alternative to China's Belt and Road Initiative and a way of funding infrastructure compatible with democratic values. A handful of European governments introduced their own national democracy strategies separate from EU-level initiatives and increased funding under these. While there were limits to all these policy instruments—democracy aid levels remained relatively modest and there were many authoritarian states where European aid increased—taken together they represented a renewed commitment to democracy support.[18]

Japan also began to strengthen its commitments to defending democratic values, especially through policy initiatives like the Free and Open Indo-Pacific concept, its bilateral security agreements with India and Australia, and multilateral agreements with other democracies such as the Japan-EU Economic Partnership Agreement. Its foreign aid began to focus more on good governance and some rights issues. South Korea moved in a similar direction, increasing its contributions to the UN Democracy Fund and its own bilateral good governance funding in developing countries. South Korea also took an unprecedented step in imposing government sanctions against Myanmar after the military coup in 2021. It also launched democracy projects beyond its immediate region, in places like Bangladesh, Gambia, Kenya and Senegal. Some Latin American democracies finally sought to mobilize regional clauses and policy tools against authoritarianism in Venezuela and Nicaragua as well as right-wing authoritarian populism in El Salvador and elsewhere.

In India, even as Prime Minister Modi's government menaced democratic freedoms domestically, it placed greater stress on India's democracy as the key to its global identity. India increased amounts of political aid through its Development Partnership Administration, and it restarted its funding for the UN Democracy Fund and participation in Community of Democracies ministerial meetings. Through a unit of its electoral commission focused

---

[18] European Democracy Hub, "European Democracy Support Annual Review 2021," *Carnegie Europe*, January 24, 2022.

126   DEMOCRATIC CROSSROADS

specifically on external support, India deployed sizable teams and significant resources to train electoral officials and monitor elections in countries like Libya, Namibia, and South Africa. The Indian government was increasingly keen on using its democracy as a strategic tool and wanted to push back against Chinese authoritarian influence. After border clashes with Chinese forces in 2020, India became tougher in framing the risks of Chinese authoritarianism—even if it tended to see Western democracy support as akin to liberal imperialism and Modi's rather civilizational view of Indian identity in the world often sat uneasily with his democracy and rights narrative.

A significant development in these incipient democratic geopolitics came when the Biden administration held a Summit for Democracy in December 2021, with the aim of kickstarting strategic coordination between democratic governments around the world. Over one hundred participating governments made commitments both to improve democracy within their own countries and do more to protect democracy internationally. While the summit was broadly a democratic gathering, political interests and rivalries were not entirely absent from the arrangements. After much debate, the Biden administration invited 110 leaders. While these represented governments that were democratic in some kind or degree, the US excluded some states such as Bolivia, Bosnia, Gambia, Hungary, Lebanon, and Sri Lanka that had higher democracy scores than some of those that were invited.

Democracies around the world participated in the summit, with varying degrees of enthusiasm. South Korea and Japan participated, even though they were concerned about the US using the summit too prominently as an anti-China alliance. The Indian government engaged with the summit process, even though the fact that the summit was being hosted by the United States lessened its enthusiasm. The US and other Western states stated a commitment to be fully open to non-Western powers' concerns and ideas to get them to participate fully in the summit process. The UK had already invited Korea, India, and Australia into the G7 summit in 2021. Still, non-Western democracies complained that the summit was molded around the US's judgments of other states' democratic credentials and its own geostrategic interests. While broadly positive toward international cooperation on democracy, they did not want to be associated with any new democratic interventionism. Some Asian invitees like Malaysia, Mongolia, and Pakistan did not attend, allegedly for fear of stirring Chinese resentment. The summit's mixed reception and results showed that more assertive and coordinated democratic action was beginning to stir but still very tentatively.

Democratic Resolve

This was the haltingly shifting context in the run up to Russia's assault on Ukraine, as some governments began to realize the need to act more concertedly in the face of authoritarian threats. After Russia launched its full-scale invasion of Ukraine, the geopolitical panorama moved into a new era and this faintly incipient trend took more solid form. Russia's invasion was first and foremost a direct attack on Ukraine's sovereignty and territory and a breach of international law. To many, it also represented a more indirect threat to democracy as a system of governance. This was because President Putin's motivations had to do with Ukrainians' efforts to map out their own separate identity, political future, and sense of self-determination. Apart from its country-specific impacts on Ukraine, the conflict has influenced the broader geopolitical balance between authoritarian and democratic dynamics.

Democratic Framing

Support for democracy was not the central element in Western policy responses to the invasion in February 2022, yet in several ways the war provided a fillip to their democratic commitments. In rhetoric reflecting a quality of liberal statism, Western governments framed the outbreak of war as a battle between authoritarianism and democracy as systemic alternatives. The invasion acted as a catalyst for Western democratic nations to move up several gears in their formal commitments to build broader diplomatic alliances in favor of democracy. Many Western leaders and policymakers within and outside Ukraine have conceived the country's fight for survival as a fight for democracy. In Western policy responses, the defense of sovereignty and the defense of democracy have partially fused with each other and with defense of rules-based order too. An increasing number of governments have defined democracy support as a priority within their national security strategies since early 2022.[19] The war has made authoritarianism appear a

[19] Democracy Reporting International, *Democracy as an Aspect of Security Policy: Perspectives from Europe and Beyond* (Berlin: Democracy Reporting International, 2023).

more real and tangible risk and has demonstrated the geopolitical costs of prioritizing accommodation with autocratic regimes. Here, the internal and external strands of empowered liberal statism appear tightly entwined with each other.

President Zelensky has constantly insisted that the war is not simply a war between two states but between two political visions. Casting the war in terms of wider global geopolitics, he argued the overarching strategy must be to ensure "a world equipped to deal with tyrants."[20] At least in their rhetoric, many democratic leaders concurred with the Ukrainian president. President Biden proclaimed: "We are engaged anew in a great battle for freedom. A battle between democracy and autocracy. Between liberty and repression."[21] A new 2022 US National Security Strategy mentioned democracy 99 times and painted the picture of a "contest for the future of our world" between China, Russia, and other autocrats "working overtime to undermine democracy and export a model of governance marked by repression at home and coercion abroad." Its starting assumption was that "democracies and autocracies are engaged in a contest to show which system of governance can best deliver for their people and the world."[22]

President Macron stressed the war's wider political implications too: "Democracy . . . has been called into question right before our eyes. Our freedom and the freedom of our children are no longer a given. Now more than ever, they require courage and the willingness to fight for them." The consequence of the war was that "now Europe must agree to pay the price of peace, freedom and democracy."[23] Chancellor Scholz said the war had made Germany realize "the value of democracy and liberty, and the fact that they are worth defending" and also acknowledged the outcome had a wider global importance to the extent that "the autocrats of the world are watching very closely to see if Putin succeeds."[24] Latvian president, Egils Levits insisted that the war compelled European governments to correct their previous lack

---

[20] Speech delivered to Forum 2000, Prague, September 2022.

[21] President Joe Biden (@POTUS), March 26, 2022, https://twitter.com/POTUS/status/15077821 39315638283.

[22] The White House, *National Security Strategy 2022*, October 2022, https://www.whitehouse. gov/wp-content/uploads/2022/10/Biden-Harris-Administrations-National-Security-Strategy-10.2022.pdf.

[23] Emmanuel Macron, "Address to the Nation," Elysée, March 2, 2022, https://www.elysee.fr/en/ emmanuel-macron/2022/03/02/address-to-the-nation.

[24] O. Moody, "Olaf Scholz: War in Ukraine Has Made Germany Realise Democracy Is Worth Fighting For," *The Times*, July 18, 2022.

THE NEW GEOPOLITICS AND WAR ON UKRAINE   129

of willingness to fight for democracy: "Awareness of these past mistakes in western Europe has grown a very great deal and . . . positions for the defence of democracy are being adopted."[25]

President of the European Commission, Ursula von de Leyen struck a similar tone: "This is about autocracy against democracy . . . This watershed moment in global politics calls for a rethink of our foreign policy agenda. This is the time to invest in the power of democracies. This work begins with the core group of our like-minded partners: our friends in every single democratic nation on this globe." A joint statement by von der Leyen and Canadian premier Justin Trudeau declared that the invasion "underscored the need for democracies to strengthen international cooperation and coordination to stand up against authoritarianism and to develop new approaches to promote and protect democracies around the world."[26] Japan's prime minister Fumio Kishida asserted: "Collaboration among countries sharing universal values becomes ever more vital . . . Ukraine may be East Asia tomorrow."[27] Taiwan's president Tsai Ing-wen spoke about the need for "democracies to come together to stem the tide of authoritarianism" and asserted "we are ready to strengthen our collaboration with like-minded countries to safeguard the liberal democratic world order."[28]

A common refrain from Western democratic leaders has been that the war brings to an end the age of democratic passivity. They have routinely professed more commitment to defend democracy as the war has made it painfully clear that democratic freedoms have to be fought for—and as the war has dragged on, fought for over a sustained period of time. In June 2022, NATO's new Strategic Concept defined "advancing authoritarianism" as the defining threat and promised to increase support to nonmembers to resist autocratic challenges. The concept was not only much tougher on Russia, but for the first time identified China as part of this nondemocratic challenge.

---

[25] O. Moody, "With New Tanks and Jets Ukraine Can Win the War," *The Times*, September 2, 2022.

[26] U. von der Leyen and J. Trudeau, "Joint Statement by President von der Leyen and Prime Minister Trudeau," *European Commission*, March 23, 2022, https://ec.europa.eu/commission/pres scorner/detail/sv/statement_22_1989.

[27] P. Nicholls, "Ukraine Plight Could Be Replicated in East Asia, Japan's Kishida Warns," *Reuters*, May 6, 2022, https://www.reuters.com/world/asia-pacific/peace-stability-taiwan-strait-is-critical-japanese-pm-2022-05-05/.

[28] See Tsai Ing-wen on YouTube, https://www.youtube.com/watch?v=LXjdGhIgyGE&t=492s (accessed February 19, 2024).

130 DEMOCRATIC CROSSROADS

Compared to previous strategic concepts, this new version was more strikingly replete with language on defending democratic values as the driving logic of NATO security policy.[29] The EU's new Strategic Compass similarly noted that security policy must now be framed around a "competition of governance systems."[30] In December 2023, the EU also introduced its own Defence of Democracy package that pinpointed Russian and other threats to liberal politics. Also relevant to democracy-defense, the Japanese government introduced an upgraded version of the Free and Open Indo-Pacific strategy in March 2023.

While mainly about state policies, the democracy framing seemed to resonate at societal level too. Positive views toward Putin and Russia among supporters of European right-wing populist parties declined dramatically.[31] The invasion undercut the flirtation of many Western citizens with Russia-friendly illiberalism. Putin's actions undermined the appeal of his rightist and leftist imitators that had menaced democracy in the West. Ukraine's stirring civic nationalism provided a more positive link between democracy and national identity. Citizens of many countries mobilized in unprecedented fashion to support Ukrainians. Three quarters of Polish citizens participated in humanitarian work related to the Ukraine war. Poles and citizens of other eastern European states self-organized on a huge scale to respond to the refugee influx, with many going to the border to help directly.[32] Suggesting a private-sector element too, the IMF notes that investment flows have become more correlated with political alliances and are "increasingly concentrated among countries that share similar geopolitical views."[33]

[29] NATO 2022 Strategic Concept, June 29, 2022. https://www.nato.int/nato_static_fl2014/assets/pdf/2022/6/pdf/290622-strategic-concept.pdf.

[30] Council of the European Union, *A Strategic Compass for Security and Defence*, 7371/22, March 2022. https://data.consilium.europa.eu/doc/document/ST-7371-2022-INIT/en/pdf.

[31] M. Fagan and L. Clancy, "Among European Right-Wing Populists, Favorable Views of Russia and Putin Are Down Sharply," *Pew Research Center*, September 23, 2022, https://www.pewresearch.org/fact-tank/2022/09/23/among-european-right-wing-populists-favorable-views-of-russia-and-putin-are-down-sharply/.

[32] M. Juczewska, "Guests Not Refugees: Massive Grassroots Humanitarian Action in Poland Supporting the Ukrainian War Refugees," *Institute of World Politics*, March 16, 2022, https://www.iwp.edu/articles/2022/03/16/guests-not-refugees-massive-grassroots-humanitarian-action-in-pol and-supporting-the-ukrainian-war-refugees/.

[33] International Monetary Fund *World Economic Outlook 2023 Navigating Global Divergences*, IMF, 2023.

Combined Security Dynamics

Although much of the rhetorical framing has been strong and unequivocal, Western strategies related to the war have in practice been less clear cut, and this has become more evident the longer the fighting has continued. Perhaps unsurprisingly, they have contained a combination of upgraded backing for democratic norms with more realpolitik concerns made more acute by the war. The US's 2022 security strategy acknowledged that defending democracy was now a higher priority, but as just one element of the country's geostrategy—as in previous security strategies. It committed the US to doing more to support democracy but also to working with authoritarian regimes on "shared challenges." Cooperation with "like-minded" states was not entirely synonymous with an alignment of democracies. US security strategy would build a lattice of many cross-cutting forms of cooperation, some about democracy but many of them not.[34]

Most directly, during the course of 2022 the US sought alliances with many nondemocratic nations against Russia, including in Africa, Asia, and Latin America. The US rebuilt relations with Egypt, restarting arms sales and military aid there, and in late 2023 signed a new strategic partnership with Vietnam, for example. In some countries, limits to democracy support persisted for other strategic reasons. For example, Biden eschewed any criticism of President Obrador and signed new accords on migrant returns with Mexico—here, the US's strategic concerns retained dynamics quite separate from Ukraine related geopolitics.

Similar balances emerged in European policies too. The EU took one of its clearest geopolitical steps when it agreed to make Ukraine a candidate for EU membership. It also offered candidate status to Moldova and more conditionally to Georgia, having rebuffed these three states in their efforts to gain accession for many years. European powers had done so on the grounds that placating Russia was more important than bringing neighboring partners fully into a club ostensibly based on democratic values. While Baltic and eastern European member states had long pushed for the EU to open its doors to Georgia, Moldova, and Ukraine, other states were not keen as they gave higher priority to managing relations with Russia than to pushing EU enlargement as a tool for defending democratic norms. The Russian invasion

---

[34] The White House, "National Security Strategy," October 2022, https://www.whitehouse.gov/wp-content/uploads/2022/10/Biden-Harris-Administrations-National-Security-Strategy-10.2022.pdf.

132   DEMOCRATIC CROSSROADS

was of such consequence that almost immediately these skeptical states reversed their position and came to support the EU's expansion into the former Soviet, eastern region. Leaders also launched a separate, continent-wide European Political Community in October 2022 and billed this as a potential alliance to defend democracy.

Yet diplomats from some European countries—notably, France and Germany—were also hesitant about the democracy-versus-autocracy prism as this would cut across other strategic aims and partnerships. EU High Representative Josep Borrell suggested that the EU did not seek to confront a bloc of nondemocratic countries as the core logic of global order. Indeed, Borrell said "We are too much Kantian, not enough Hobbesian," and talking about the democracy-autocracy divide: "I would not insist on it a lot."[35] The invasion intensified the EU's commitment to being a geopolitical power, and this narrative was more about hard-headed self-interest than about democratic values. The European Political Community included autocratic Azerbaijan, Serbia, Turkey, and several hybrid regimes. While the UK offered strong support to Ukraine, many elements of its democracy support globally weakened over 2022 and 2023; its updated security strategy said explicitly that policy would not be structured around a democracy-versus-autocracy divide and that there would be deeper cooperation with states holding different values.[36]

Most directly as a response to the invasion, Western powers forged new energy partnerships with autocratic regimes as they sought to replace Russian oil and gas supplies—regimes just as or even more repressive than Russia's government. The US adopted a more pragmatic line toward Venezuela for oil supplies. European states and the US signed many new energy deals with Gulf suppliers. European states signed well over 50 new energy accords in 2022 and 2023, most of these with nondemocratic countries. France and Greece welcomed Saudi leaders on renewed official visits, while Italy signed new deals with Algeria and Libya. The EU signed an accord with Azerbaijan to double gas supplies as well as green hydrogen, and a new aid package too. EU governments framed a raft of new climate-change partnerships as part of the strategic effort to wean Europe off Russian oil and gas, as the geopolitical

[35] J. Borrell, "EU Ambassadors Annual Conference 2022: Opening Speech by High Representative Josep Borrell," *European Union External Action*, October 10, 2022, https://www.eeas.europa.eu/eeas/eu-ambassadors-annual-conference-2022-opening-speech-high-representative-josep-borrell_en.
[36] Government of the United Kingdom, "Integrated Review Refresh 2023: Responding to a More Contested and Volatile World" (London: His Majesty's Government, March 2023), 9.

THE NEW GEOPOLITICS AND WAR ON UKRAINE   133

and climate crises intertwined with each other. Diplomats acknowledged that the EU agreed to increase climate funding to developing countries—many with authoritarian governments—partly because it sought allies in support of Ukraine.

If initially many Western governments talked of confronting a tightened Russia-China axis, as the war continued, they increasingly fashioned a differentiated strategy between the two powers. They sought ways to drive a wedge between Russia and China and to work with the latter on select challenges. Most democratic nations were not willing to put their commercial relations with China at risk. UK prime minister Rishi Sunak defined a strategy of "robust pragmatism" on China that sounded to many like a softened line. On China, the West's policy was still commercial engagement mixed with geopolitical containment, with few meaningful democracy components in China itself. A raft of European leaders' visits to China in 2023 clearly demonstrated this trend; French and Chinese diplomats even worked together on a possible peace plan for Ukraine.

More positively in terms of pro-democratic security dynamics, there was spillover from the Ukraine invasion to Western concerns with Taiwan's democracy. President Zelensky called on the international community to support Taiwan's democracy before Beijing attacked and not to repeat the mistakes Europe made with Ukraine in waiting to help until after invasion. Multiple Asian leaders commented that the Ukraine invasion served as the region's wake-up call with regards a potential Chinese attack on Taiwan.[37] When US speaker Nancy Pelosi visited in 2022 and this led to China imposing a four-day blockade of the seas around Taiwan, she framed her aim expressly in terms of defending democratic values. Several European nations also adopted this democracy-defense narrative and began to rethink their Asia-Pacific strategies in this direction. Several EU states and the UK criticized China's belligerent tone toward Taiwan after Pelosi's visit and moved to arrange their own visits—although other member states, like France, remained more equivocal.

---

[37] J. Rogin, "Zelensky Calls for International Support for Taiwan Before China attacks," *Washington Post*, June 11, 2022, https://www.washingtonpost.com/opinions/2022/06/11/zelensky-calls-for-support-taiwan-before-china-attacks-ukraine-russia/.

Democracy Aims within Ukraine

Of most direct relevance, many new pro-democracy programs gained scale and traction in Ukraine itself. Aid flowed to Ukraine in an unprecedent effort to shore up a democratic nation. In the first year of the war, the country received $158 billion (143 billion euros) of aid, half of this from the United States. The US added to its humanitarian aid a sizeable injection of democracy and human rights assistance in 2023. The European Commission set up a Ukraine Reconstruction Platform and offered another 18 billion euros of funding for 2023. Among the aims of this support were countering disinformation, responding to energy sector cyber-attacks and documenting human rights violations.[38]

Western powers and Ukrainian politicians framed the defense of sovereignty and the defense of democracy as synonymous with each other, although in practice there were some tensions between these two aims. Some saw a disjuncture between the democracy narrative and much diplomacy which in practice aimed more at shoring up the principle of sovereignty.[39] Clearly, the vast majority of international funding went to help Ukraine fight the war and also to help Ukrainian citizens displaced by the conflict. The priority focus was on military aid to help fight the war, especially as Ukrainian forces seemed to lose some momentum in late 2023 and early 2024, and funds were also required for covering core budgetary expenses and humanitarian relief. Unsurprisingly, perhaps, in the midst of war, democracy support was a secondary concern. Normal politics was suspended in Ukraine; as invariably is the case in war, the government took on emergency measures that gave it more absolute power.

If this was necessary for fighting the war, the democracy component of external support has also gained traction. Most international funding and support flowed to the government, and many equated defending democracy with supporting Zelensky, given the president's universally admired heroic stoicism during the war. Yet external powers also began to press for

[38] Kiel Institute for the World Economy, "Ukraine Support Tracker," last updated February 24, 2023, https://www.ifw-kiel.de/topics/war-against-ukraine/ukraine-support-tracker/.
[39] S. Wertheim, "The One Key Word Biden Needs to Invoke on Ukraine," *The Atlantic*, June 11, 2022.

THE NEW GEOPOLITICS AND WAR ON UKRAINE   135

Table 7.1 Aid to Ukraine

Country (or EU)	Total Bilateral Aid Commitments in EUR Billion	Total Bilateral Aid Commitments as % of GDP
EU	84.99	0.54
United States	67.71	0.32
Germany	22.06	0.57
United Kingdom	15.66	0.55
Denmark	8.76	2.41
Norway	7.57	1.72
Japan	7.53	0.17
Netherlands	6.21	0.67
Canada	5.78	0.32
Poland	4.30	0.69
Sweden	2.97	0.51
Switzerland	2.38	0.33
Belgium	2.22	0.41
Finland	1.92	0.71
France	1.80	0.07
Czech Republic	1.33	0.52
Italy	1.30	0.07
Estonia	1.21	3.55
Lithuania	0.93	1.54
Spain	0.93	0.07
South Korea	0.88	0.05
Austria	0.80	0.18
Slovakia	0.69	0.65
Australia	0.57	0.04
Latvia	0.42	1.15
Croatia	0.28	0.44
Bulgaria	0.25	0.32
Greece	0.19	0.09
Luxembourg	0.13	0.17
Romania	0.13	0.05
Ireland	0.12	0.03
Slovenia	0.08	0.14
Portugal	0.08	0.03
Turkey	0.07	0.01
Taiwan	0.06	0.01
Hungary	0.05	0.03
New Zealand	0.04	0.02

This table includes countries' aid commitments to Ukraine from January 24, 2022 to January 15, 2024, based on data from the Kiel Institute for the World Economy's Ukraine Support Tracker, https://www.ifw-kiel.de/topics/war-against-ukraine/ukraine-support-tracker/.

136   DEMOCRATIC CROSSROADS

more structural governance reforms. They exerted pressure over corruption concerns, even related to officials who had acted bravely in the war. They spoke out in concern that the Ukrainian government was using wartime powers to restrict civil society and media critics.

This focus on governance reform was seen especially in the EU setting a wide range of demanding democracy conditions that Ukraine had to meet to move forward with its accession negotiations. The EU set and monitored highly detailed pre-conditions on the selection of constitutional court judges, anti-corruption measures, money laundering, de-oligarchization, media pluralism, and a minorities law. These helped leverage more reform commitments from a Ukrainian government keen not to give European member states any excuse to delay EU membership talks. As it fought the war, in 2022 and 2023 the government moved forward with judicial reforms and a major clampdown on corruption. It agreed to strengthen democratic accountability in the security and law enforcement sector, to follow European standards in its media and minorities laws, and to sign key international laws on money laundering and counterterrorism, all in response to EU pressure. A large-scale EU-supported project began in 2023 to strengthen Ukrainian civil society for "participatory reconstruction and post-war recovery."

Democracy concerns also became more notable in Western positions on how the conflict might end. For at least some Western powers, in the initial phases of the war the priority was clearly to contain the conflict rather than to engage unequivocally in favor of democracy scoring a decisive victory over autocracy. France and Germany in particular, as well as the EU and some other European governments, were drawn to a negotiated solution built around compromises on both sides. As Russian violence hardened, their positions moved to highlight Ukrainian democratic self-determination. They placed greater stress on insisting that any such deal must be Ukraine's choice. Some European governments have still clung to a degree of pragmatic quest for conflict containment and debate deepened from late 2023 over whether the best way to defend democracy would be to encourage Ukraine to sue for peace or to weaken Russia as much as possible on the battlefield. Yet the driving sentiment of Ukrainian civic resistance—detailed in the following chapter—has gradually pushed Western powers toward a stronger focus on democratic self-determination as a core to their conflict strategy.

International Democracy Support

The war has also catalyzed some Western democracy commitments more globally. Prodded by the invasion, the US began a range of new democracy funding initiatives beyond Ukraine. The US committed $1.1 billion to a Presidential Initiative for Democratic Renewal, with a wider promise of $9.5 billion total democracy support for three years.[40] The Biden administration requested $3.15 billion for democracy aid in 2024, double the amount allocated in the last year of the Trump administration. It supported new satellite technology to defend democracy activists, created a new post for democratic renewal abroad, and launched a European Democratic Resilience Initiative with $320 million in funding. The USAID agency committed to increase its financial support for "democratic bright spots," including through new Partnerships for Democratic Development to strengthen ties with reformist governments.[41] The US also promised more democracy support in conflict states under its new Strategy to Prevent Conflict and Promote Stability.[42]

Western governments either accelerated or beefed-up many initiatives that had been introduced before the war started. Building on pre-war commitments, funding increased significantly for democracy foundations like the US National Endowment for Democracy, the Taiwan Foundation for Democracy, and the Netherlands Multiparty for Democracy. A large number of international initiatives on democracy were created in 2021 and 2022 and strengthened after the war started, including an International Fund for Public Interest Media, a Global Media Defense Fund, a Tech for Democracy Initiative led by Denmark, a Freedom Online Coalition, a Digital Public Goods Alliance, and others. The G7 announced a Partnership for Global Infrastructure and Investment to wean developing states off China's Belt and Road Initiative, with an aim to mobilize $600 billion, the US committing $200 billion of this.

---

[40] The White House, "Remarks by President Biden at the Summit for Democracy Virtual Plenary on Democracy Delivering on Global Challenges," March 29, 2023, https://www.whitehouse.gov/briefing-room/speeches-remarks/2023/03/29/remarks-by-president-biden-at-the-summit-for-democracy-virtual-plenary-on-democracy-delivering-on-global-challenges/.

[41] S. Power, "How Democracy Can Win," *Foreign Affairs*, February 16, 2023.

[42] United States Strategy to Prevent Conflict and Promote Stability, 2020, https://www.state.gov/wp-content/uploads/2021/01/2020-US-Strategy-to-Prevent-Conflict-and-Promote-Stabilit-508c-508.pdf.

138   DEMOCRATIC CROSSROADS

The war generated more formal commitments behind such initiatives and made democracy support organizations more willing to take risks in their work. The invasion galvanized some civil society dimensions of international democracy support. Examples of new civic initiatives included a Democratic Coalition for Ukraine and a Prague Manifesto for Free Ukraine. The American Coalition for Ukraine formed in the wake of the invasion and hosted several high-profile meetings. Societal donations from around the world have been forthcoming to aid Ukraine's war effort. Scores of tech initiatives have formed with individual experts based in many different countries pushing back against Russian disinformation and monitoring Russian attacks and plans. Citizen donations from around the world raised several hundred million dollars for President Zelensky's "United 24" initiative to defend, sustain and rebuild Ukraine. Civil society also pressured social media platforms and some big tech companies tried to reposition themselves as supporters of Ukrainian democracy.

Still, Western states' financial commitments to democracy support continue to be relatively modest and a small fraction of military spending. The new geopolitical determination behind democracy has not been strong enough to reverse the problems facing democracy support on the ground as regime restrictions and attacks on civil society have become more draconian in most states.[43] The war triggered only modest increases in European democracy funds; most EU donors still did not specify or allocate exact amounts of funding for democracy, even as they insisted this was their priority aim associated with the war.[44] The UK created an Integrated Security Fund to boost security support globally, yet its democracy support flatlined after the war started.[45] Even after its post-2022 increases, the US budget for democracy was still small compared to other parts of the aid budget, and moreover it funded many initiatives about generic rights-based themes without any strategies for dealing with democratic regression in individual countries.[46] Western democracy policies have moved up a gear due to the

[43] N. Cheeseman and M. Desrosiers, "Learning to Do No Harm to Democracy in Engagement with Authoritarian States," *Carnegie Europe*, March 15, 2023, https://carnegieeurope.eu/2023/03/15/learning-to-do-no-harm-to-democracy-in-engagement-with-authoritarian-states-pub-89255.

[44] European Democracy Hub, *European Democracy Support Annual Review 2022*, January 30, 2023.

[45] Independent Commission for Aid Impact, "The UK's Approach to Democracy and Human Rights," January 2023, https://icai.independent.gov.uk/wp-content/uploads/The-UKs-approach-to-democracy-and-human-rights_ICAI-review.pdf.

[46] J. Temin, "The US Doesn't Need Another Democracy Summit," *Foreign Affairs*, March 27, 2023.

Mixed Global Dynamics

war, but they remain relatively low key and secondary compared to other elements of global geopolitical relations and rivalries.

Mixed Global Dynamics

While Western democratic governments have framed the postwar geopolitical context as one pitting democracy against autocracy, this position has not resonated so clearly in other parts of the world. Even if some modest global democratic coordination moved forward in 2022 and 2023, most non-Western democracies were not strongly committed to this, and they have not fully embraced the argument that the Ukraine conflict and its wider ramifications are primarily about a battle for democratic values. Nor has there been uniformity among authoritarian regimes, and this has also diluted the clarity of any democracy-autocracy binary divide as an organizing logic of international politics.

Global dynamics in the invasion's aftermath were varied and far from straightforward. Most democratic states outside the West were critical of Russia and stressed the need to defend democracy. Over 140 states voted against Russia in the first UN vote on the invasion, again in an October 2022 vote in relation to annexation of eastern Ukrainian territories, and in another February 2023 motion calling on Russia to withdraw its troops. Polling suggested that pro-Russian sentiment evaporated in 2022 not just within the West but also in middle-income democracies like Argentina, Chile, and African states, as well as Asian democracies like Korea and Japan.[47] Yet the abstainers in UN votes on the conflict included large democracies like India, Indonesia, Mongolia, and South Africa. Outside the West, only Japan, South Korea, and Taiwan adopted sanctions against Russia. Democracies outside Europe and North America generally condemned the invasion but did not support punitive approaches toward Russia, as shown in Table 7.2.

Non-Western democracies' line was nuanced: they often insisted they were supportive of democratic norms internationally, but that support for democracy was not synonymous with sanctions on Russia. They have pursued hedging strategies that have not entailed support for Russia, but a reticence to get involved in the conflict or actively help Western democracies

---

[47] R. Foa et al., *The Global Satisfaction with Democracy Report 2020* (Cambridge: Centre for the Future of Democracy, 2020), https://www.cam.ac.uk/system/files/report2020_003.pdf.

140 DEMOCRATIC CROSSROADS

Table 7.2 Democracies not applying sanctions

Democracies Not Sanctioning Russia
Argentina
Botswana
Brazil
Cabo Verde
Chile
Colombia
Costa Rica
Dominican Republic
Ghana
Guyana
India
Indonesia
Israel
Jamaica
Lesotho
Malaysia
Mauritius
Moldova
Mongolia
Namibia
Panama
Philippines
Serbia
South Africa
Sri Lanka
Suriname
Thailand
Timor-Leste
Trinidad and Tobago
Uruguay

This table shows partial or full democracies that have not sanctioned Russia since its invasion of Ukraine, as of mid-March 2023.

in their support of Ukraine.[48] These democracies' core argument is that they must safeguard economic interests, even if Russia's invasion raises worrying dangers for the future. In one illustrative case, Mongolian leaders insisted that, sandwiched between two authoritarian giants, they had good reasons to support the global defense of democracy, but could not jeopardize economic ties with China or Russia.[49] Since the war started, China has gained support for its new Global Security Initiative from a wide range of states, including democracies like Mongolia and Uruguay, and more than 70 countries have signed up to its Global Development Initiative.[50]

Indian responses to the war contained some of this nuance. Russia's postwar deepened links with China and indeed Pakistan rung alarm bells for India and sharpened its interest in democratic nations coordinating more effectively. India increased funding for external democracy support initiatives in 2022 and 2023, and prime minister Modi became more outspoken against Russian actions and violence in Ukraine. Yet his government recoiled from Western narratives of democracy support. Indian purchases of Russian energy and weapons increased, and one early 2023 poll suggested over half the Indian population saw Russia as an ally.[51] In July 2023, India hosted a summit of the Shanghai Cooperation Organization. It argued that the democracy agenda must first entail a democratization of global governance and not be reduced to Western nations pressing other powers to be tough on Russia; while the West prevaricated on this wider democratization of international affairs, India's line on war-related geopolitics would not align with Western concerns.[52] In turn, Western powers have made more effort to court India, in part on the grounds of it being a democracy, but also as a counterweight to China and Russia—regardless of its current democratic regression.[53]

Latin American democracies criticized the invasion and rejected Russia as an observer in the Organization of American States but sought to keep some distance from US efforts to bring democracies together. When the

---

[48] M. Spektor, "In Defence of the Fence-Sitters," *Foreign Affairs*, May/June 2023.

[49] R. Lloyd Parry, "Cold War Fears of Mongolia, Caught Between Two Big Brothers," *The Times*, March 14, 2023.

[50] J. Kynge, "China Hit By Surge in Belt and Road Bad Loans," *Financial Times*, April 16, 2023.

[51] T. Ash, I. Krastev, and M. Leonard, "United West, Divided from the Rest: Global Public Opinion One Year into Russia's War on Ukraine," *European Council on Foreign Relations*, February 22, 2023, https://ecfr.eu/publication/united-west-divided-from-the-rest-global-public-opinion-one-year-into-russias-war-on-ukraine/.

[52] S. Jagtiani and S. Wellek, "In the Shadow of Ukraine: India's Choices and Challenges," *Survival* 64, no. 3 (2022): 29–48.

[53] M. Molander, "European Leaders Should Raise Human Rights Concerns: Modi," *Human Rights Watch*, May 3, 2022.

142 DEMOCRATIC CROSSROADS

White House excluded the leaders of Cuba, Nicaragua, and Venezuela from the Summit of the Americas in 2022 and sought to focus this forum on democracy support, the presidents of El Salvador, Guatemala, Honduras, and Mexico boycotted the event.[54] Chile was the only country from the region that clearly condemned the invasion and did not say that blame was shared between Russia and the West. Some Latin American democracies went beyond simply refusing to impose sanctions on Russia: Argentina's president was in Moscow the day before the invasion, promising to be "Russia's gateway to Latin America."

From early 2023, newly elected President Lula tried to position Brazil as an impartial peace mediator, pushing Western states to cease aiding Ukraine. Latin American states welcomed Venezuela back into their leaders' summits and President Lula was especially keen on restoring engagement with President Maduro, suggesting he had been unfairly defined as authoritarian. Leaders from the region prevented an Ibero-American summit in March 2023 from even mentioning the invasion of Ukraine.[55] Despite the invasion, Argentina and Mexico pushed to join the BRICS format alongside Russia and China.[56] Some civil society pressure has emerged in Latin America against governments' ambivalence in defending Ukrainian citizens' democratic freedom.[57]

In Africa, positions have not divided neatly along a democracy-autocracy axis. The continent's most influential democracy, South Africa, declined to participate in the Summit for Democracy process and President Cyril Ramaphosa squarely blamed NATO for the war.[58] While the South African government insisted it was neutral in the conflict, the US saw it as helping Russia and potentially even breaking sanctions to do so. South Africa sent its defense minister to Russia for cooperative talks on security and even participated in naval exercises with the Russian fleet in late 2022.[59] South

---

[54] C. Osborn, "A Disjointed Western Hemisphere Gathers," *Foreign Policy*, June 10, 2022, https://foreignpolicy.com/2022/06/10/summit-americas-biden-los-angeles-boycotts-health-migration/.

[55] M. Gonzalez and F. Manetto, "La comunidad iberoamericana se consolida pese a sus divisiones y debilidades," *El Pais*, March 25, 2023.

[56] "China and Russia's Growing BRICS Bloc Speeds Decline of US Influence," *Newsweek*, June 1, 2023.

[57] J. Gabriel Vasquez, "Mas alla de las ideologías: como hablar de Ucrania en America Latina," *El Pais*, February 2, 2023.

[58] T. Cocks, "South Africa's Ramaphosa Blames NATO for Russia's War in Ukraine," *Reuters*, March 18, 2022, https://www.reuters.com/world/africa/safricas-ramaphosa-blames-nato-russias-war-ukraine-2022-03-17/.

[59] J. Eligon, "South Africa and Russia Are Old Friends—A War Isn't Going to Change That," *New York Times*, February 17, 2023.

Africa—and also democratic Indonesia—forwarded "peace plans" that offered Russia formalized control over eastern Ukraine. Still, while African democracies refused to impose sanctions, they also cooled in their relations toward Russia. In UN votes on the war, African autocracies abstained or voted with Russia, while democracies—Botswana, Cabo Verde, Ghana, Malawi, Mauritius, Nigeria, Kenya, Seychelles, Sierra Leone, Zambia—voted most frequently against Russia. Most African democracies did not attend a Russia-Africa summit in July 2023. Showing the range of views emerging, South Africa's opposition alliance was strongly against the government's co-operation with Russia.

Russia's trade, investment and aid presence has dwindled in Africa as a whole; its main influence comes from military co-operation and arms sales and these are skewed toward autocratic regimes like Algeria, Egypt, and Uganda, while the Wagner Group has deployed to assist nondemocratic regimes retain power. The actions of these Russian mercenaries have made some democratic states, like Zambia, keener to join democratic coordination efforts. While some African democracies have continued to buy weapons from Russia, in general they have become more hesitant to build relations through this security template. While the reticence of African democracies fully to side with Western democracies was a salutary counter to the global democracy narrative, the democracy-autocracy dynamic has not been entirely absent from the continent.[60]

The mixed global dynamics were on display at a second Summit for Democracy that took place in March 2023. For some Western and Asian democracies, the war gave this summit process sharper purpose. The Korean, Dutch, Costa Rican, and Zambian governments stepped forward to share hosting duties with the US and make the initiative more genuinely global. In the period between the first and second summits, the process gathered some momentum. Even as differences emerged over Russia's war in Ukraine, many democracies proposed new avenues of cooperation, including Indonesia, Mexico, Chile, Taiwan, Japan, and South Korea.[61] The US invited 112 leaders to the second summit; 90 turned up. The second summit involved a large number of events and dialogues and the participation of hundreds of political and civic actors.

[60] R. Gopaldas, *Will the Invasion of Ukraine Change Russia-Africa Relations?* (Washington, DC: Carnegie Endowment for International Peace, 2023).
[61] For these details, see International IDEA's Summit for Democracy Commitment Dashboard at https://summitfordemocracyresources.eu/commitment-dashboard/ (accessed February 19, 2024).

144 DEMOCRATIC CROSSROADS

In a summit declaration, leaders agreed to work toward "stronger domestic, regional, and global partnerships that are more assertive in countering authoritarianism" and to cooperate on a range of other issues like climate change and development.[62] Governments agreed to so-called platforms for cooperation on certain issues, to which some countries contributed new funds; they drew up new cooperative principles on surveillance technology, youth democracy, women's empowerment, corruption, and many other issues. Leaders made national statements, generally insisting that they had fulfilled their commitments from the first summit; 30 states announced new, more ambitious reform commitments. Several civil society coalitions played a prominent role and the civic strand has become a more central pillar of the summit process. Building on the second summit, in March 2024 South Korea hosted a third meeting of the process (co-chaired together with the Danish and Kenya governments) and this further deepened coordination on a similar range of issues.

For all the activity and commitments, however, these second and third summits were relatively low key. Of the 90 states at the second summit, only 74 signed the declaration, and 13 of these formally disassociated themselves from parts of the text. There was no process to evaluate how far governments had in fact met their reform commitments. The summits hardly appeared in the international media. The summit process did not gain its own resources or institutional structure. The summits have resembled closed conferences, valuable and interesting but not platforms for political coordination on actual democracy-support policy.[63] The process seems to have eschewed overarching, geopolitical questions and has focused on dialogues about generic themes like corruption. The summit process gave birth to a lot of processes and initiatives and events, but with little sign of its leading to common strategies toward, say, China, Russia, or autocratization in specific countries. The process has steered clear of directly addressing the strategic fallout from Russia's invasion of Ukraine; the 2024 summit produced only a chair's summary that made no mention of the ongoing war or geopolitical conflicts.[64]

[62] Declaration of the Summit for Democracy, March 29, 2023, https://www.state.gov/declaration-of-the-summit-for-democracy-2023/#:~:text=We%2C%20the%20leaders%20of%20the,%2C%20sustainable%20development%2C%20and%20security.

[63] International IDEA, "Democratic Engagement after Two Summits for Democracy" (Stockholm, 2023).

[64] https://s4dkorea.kr/.

US officials have openly lowered their ambition, saying that their aim was not to organize any proto alliance of democracies but more modestly to share work on protecting democracy at home.[65]

Separate from the Summit for Democracy process, new cooperation between Western and non-Western democracies developed in 2022 and 2023 on security issues. Governments framed this security cooperation as being about defending democracies from autocratic threats—even if they did not match it with a similar level of support for democratic norms internationally. Since the war started, the main policy upgrade has been in security ties between Western and Asian democracies in the Indo-Pacific; these are about defending democracy in the sense of dissuading Chinese expansionism, rather than about standard democracy support programs. The UK and Japan signed what they baptized their Hiroshima security accord, while the UK and France joined together in 2023 for a permanent maritime presence in the Indo-Pacific.

In general, multiple hesitancies and caveats have diluted the drive behind international democracy initiatives as the war has continued. Non-Western democracies complained not so much about democracy-support aims in principle, but about having to sign up to a Western geostrategic agenda. Their gripe was that the West expected help now on Ukraine when over many years it had ignored threats to democracy in other regions—and indeed was often the source of those problems. They recoiled from the Western line that democracy's fate now hinged on events in Ukraine; in most places of the world, democracy was still conditioned by very local, internal political factors quite separate from the invasion and new geopolitical context. In late 2023, differences over the renewed violence between Israel and Palestinians reinforced these divergent perspectives between democracies over broader geopolitical issues; non-Western democracies seemed rather firmer in their support for Palestinian than Ukrainian self-determination, in contrast to Western positions. To the extent that they offered some backing to Ukraine, democratic governments outside the West were more comfortable with framing this as a necessary defense of sovereignty rather than democracy. For their part, as the war continued, the US and European powers gradually stepped back from criticizing other powers for not being sufficiently tough on Russia.

---

[65] International IDEA, "Democratic Engagement after Two Summits for Democracy."

146   DEMOCRATIC CROSSROADS

If there were strategic differences among democracies, there was also notable variation between authoritarian regimes—this further muddying the divide between different types of political regime. Certainly, some authoritarian states seemed to share the prognosis of a sharper democracy-autocracy binary. They doubled down on cooperation in a way that reinforced a growing divide with democratic nations, and to a degree pushed the latter to give further emphasis to the defense of democracy. The deepening of China-Russia cooperation was a turning point in their joint actions against democratic self-determination. China lifted its veto against Iran being admitted into the Shanghai Cooperation Organization and this body took on more purpose in countering international democracy support. In the authoritarian Middle Eastern region, regimes fanned the flames of an anti-Westernism that boosted their own hold on power. And some saw war-related sanctions dividing the global economy, meaning a division of globalization into blocs led respectively by Western democracies and a Chinese-Russian authoritarian alliance.

Yet trends did not point unequivocally toward a fully united authoritarian bloc, uniformly committed to undermining global democracy. While there were many meetings between nondemocratic states, they did not generate the kind of concrete policy initiatives that democratic countries advanced. The putative authoritarian grouping did not coordinate any kind of operational autocracy-promotion equivalent to the Summit for Democracy process. China did not expressly set itself to lead a battle for autocracy, even if many of its international actions gave support to authoritarian regimes. While the Ukraine invasion seemed to push it toward a more overt strategy of contention with the democratic world, it did not move to run an open autocracy promotion policy as such.

During a meeting with Biden, President Xi insisted that China did not see "democracy versus authoritarianism" as "the trend of the times."[66] For all the geopolitical tension, war, and talk of decoupling, China's trade with the West is still over 20 times greater than its trade with Russia. A few days before the 2023 US-led Summit for Democracy, China organized its International Forum on Democracy that also attracted over a hundred states, including some democracies. Moreover, some autocratic regimes felt increasingly uneasy with their ties to Russia. This was evident in Central Asia, for instance,

---

[66] "Xi to Biden: Knock Off the Democracy vs. Autocracy Talk," *Reuters*, November 14, 2022, https://www.reuters.com/world/asia-pacific/xi-biden-knock-off-democracy-vs-autocracy-talk-2022-11-14/.

where Kazakhstan in particular sought counterbalancing partnerships with democratic states and questioned the Russian-led Collective Security Treaty Organization. In Central Asia, younger people now talked of the need for "decolonialization" from Russia as a framing to press governments for reforms and more effort to excise Russian influences.

Assessment: A Democratic War, for Some

Geopolitical dynamics have shifted dramatically over the last decade. They have changed in many ways and for many reasons. One prominent dimension is the evolving relationship between the changing patterns of international politics, on the one hand, and the global state of democracy, on the other hand. As geopolitical tensions have sharpened so they have come to have a stronger shaping impact on democratic politics. After years in which these geopolitical changes were gathering force, Russia's invasion of Ukraine added a dramatic turning point to this fraught and uncertain international environment, a third crisis of far-reaching importance alongside the climate crisis and the COVID-19 emergency.

The actions of authoritarian regimes outside their own borders represent a heightened challenge for supporters of democratic reform and the international system no longer provides favorable following winds for democratization. This was evident as the decade of the 2020s got underway. The era seemed to be one of authoritarian gains stealing a march over increasingly defensive and uncertain democratic states. The shifting patterns of global power seemed to be working clearly to democracy's disadvantage. China's influence was rapidly expanding, Russia increasingly assertive and other nondemocratic states more self-confident in sustaining their autocracy. If international-system change had any causal impact on domestic politics, it appeared to be as a strong contribution to the autocratization that defined the 2010s.

The tragedy that began in February 2022 has added more variation to this panorama. Western democracies were not pre-emptively seeking a democracy-versus-autocracy contest but felt pushed into this as Russia crossed so many redlines of rule-breaking international action. Prominent analysts detect a reinvigorated commitment to defending liberal order and democratic norms since the war began.[67] They have argued that the battle for

---

[67] L. Way, "The Rebirth of the Liberal World Order," *Journal of Democracy* (March 2022), https://www.journalofdemocracy.org/the-rebirth-of-the-liberal-world-order/.

148 DEMOCRATIC CROSSROADS

Ukraine should be interpreted as a broader battle for democracy and against autocratic and illiberal values. In the uncertain early months of 2022, a commonly made observation was that the war unleashed far stronger determination to defend the liberal order.[68] With the war continuing at the time of writing, a common line is that democracy's global future will hinge on how events unfold in Ukraine. Some eminent writers see this as a turning point after the years of Western democracies "conceding the tradition of democracy."[69] A "democratic realism" suggests that the tensions underlying the war are about different political-regime preferences more than purely immediate interests or security calculations.[70]

This chapter has detailed the concrete policy developments that have given some substance to these outlooks. The war has spurred a new determination on the part of Western democratic countries and a raft of new policies aimed at shoring up democracy across the world and pushing back against authoritarian actions. A Summit for Democracy process began and gained some traction, albeit as a low-level forum for thematic coordination rather than a high-level geopolitical initiative. Many Western governments have framed the Ukraine war in these global systemic terms much more than they did with previous conflicts in Iraq, Afghanistan, or Libya. Even if much of the promise of a new democratic dawn has been exaggerated hyperbole, there has been some real substance behind these commitments too.

Many Western leaders, journalists and analysts have expressed a clear conviction that the war has generated a dynamic of democratic redemption. The unity between Western democratic nations has been stronger than most expected. Moves to resist and isolate Russia have broadened into a tougher attitude from many democratic nations toward authoritarian assertiveness in general. Western leaders have repeatedly proclaimed that the community of democratic nations no longer stands passively indulgent of autocracy.

Western democratic governments have adopted more of a securitized identity in this environment of heightened geopolitical risk. To recall the book's analytical categories, these reflect the dynamics of empowered

---

[68] K. Schake, "Putin Accidentally Revitalized the West's Liberal Order," *The Atlantic*, February 28, 2022, https://www.theatlantic.com/international/archive/2022/02/vladimir-putin-ukraine-invasion-liberal-order/622950/.

[69] T. Snyder, "Ukraine Holds the Future," *Foreign Affairs*, September/October 2022; L. Diamond, "All Democracy Is Global," *Foreign Affairs*, September/October 2022.

[70] E. Jones, "War in Ukraine: Democratic Realism," *Encompass*, August 2022, https://encompass-europe.com/comment/the-war-in-ukraine-democratic-realism.

THE NEW GEOPOLITICS AND WAR ON UKRAINE   149

states seeking to protect democratic norms—the liberal statism laid out in Chapter 2. This empowered state agency has been evident both within and between states, tying together domestic politics and liberal multilateralism. It has gone beyond the traditional democracy promotion agenda of funding a few civic or opposition leaders toward a far wider notion of the concept: much of it is about shoring up Western democracies themselves, giving them the means of more effective self-defense and also for wider sets of alliances and more economic autonomy to cut debilitating dependencies on autocracies. Western democracy support has begun to mold itself to a more overtly political agenda—not just helping reformers overcome their local undemocratic elites but pushing back a more systemic anti-democratic tide of geopolitical risk even in democracy's supposed heartlands.

The longstanding realist call for the West to acknowledge Russian interests in eastern Europe has become harder to sustain in the face of Putin's egregious breach of so many basic international rules and this perspective lost weight in Western policy after February 2022. The conflict has been about the very Ukrainian agency that realists have subordinated to supposedly prudent calculations of interest between great powers. The implication for this book's subject matter is that the conflict casts doubt on the realist separation of interstate relations from domestic politics: Ukraine's domestic politics have become a core matter of international geopolitics.

The geopolitics of this conflict over democracy have been not only about state power but also about societal reactions and actions. Support within Ukraine and for Ukraine from outside has involved a strong civil society dimension. Both in the role played by nonstate actors in Ukraine and in the influence of such actors in organizing international support, a new focus of civic geopolitics has taken shape. Referring back to the analytical framework, the concepts of empowered liberal statism and civic micropolitics have to some degree worked together in shaping the upgraded defense of democracy. The war has intensified the democracy-related influences that transit back and forth between local politics and the overarching structural dynamics of global order.

A more skeptical line is that the democracy components of the conflict are relatively insubstantial. Critics insist that the framing of the war as a democracy-reaffirming battle against autocracy has been exposed as an "unwarranted exuberance."[71] They doubt that the war has much international

[71] G. Packer, "A New Theory of American Power," *The Atlantic*, November 21, 2022.

150 DEMOCRATIC CROSSROADS

relevance for democracy: democratic governments outside the West have not taken up the framing that the Ukraine war is about a global battle for democratic values and they still do not fully see democracy support as being part of geostrategic reasoning.[72] These governments do not see themselves as siding with Russia, but do not want to bear costs for a war they see as being mainly about European order and not global democracy—the latter depending on other factors more strongly.

Non-Western democracies have spoken out against Russian actions, and some have stepped up their support for democratic coordination and initiatives, but they have not committed strongly to this agenda in a way that fully multilateralizes or de-Westernizes democracy support. Their complex policy mix is perhaps more akin to what might be termed pluri-alignment than the nonalignment of previous periods. Moreover, Western governments themselves have adopted much security-oriented pragmatism as well, in an ad hoc mix of toughened realism and democracy support. Western powers have sought alliances with nondemocracies in the name of buttressing the place of democratic regimes in the international order.[73] Ukrainians have inspired the democratic world and yet this inspiration has—notwithstanding all the stirring speeches—not translated into really ambitious or far-reaching upgrades to pro-democracy policies. The fact that the US and some of its democratic allies have become more assertive in their rhetorical defense of democracy does not in itself constitute a more effective attack on the underlying drivers of democratic regression.

While the skeptics are right to highlight all this, they risk being overly dismissive of the conflict's democratic resonance.[74] It is easy and obvious to point out that the responses have not divided neatly into a democracy-autocracy binary and that many non-Western democracies have been soft toward Russia. However, many err in holding that this means there has been no democracy component at all to the conflict and its aftermath. The fact that no single neat divide has emerged between democracies and autocracies has become something of a strawman, as this does not preclude more meaningful and dynamic democratic international action.

---

[72] S. Menon, "The Fantasy of the Free World," *Foreign Affairs*, April 4, 2022, https://www.foreign affairs.com/articles/united-states/2022-04-04/fantasy-free-world.

[73] H. Brands, "The Age of Amorality," *Foreign Affairs*, March/April 2024.

[74] M. Leonard, "Xi Jinping's Idea of World Order," *European Council on Foreign Relations*, April 5, 2023, https://ecfr.eu/article/xi-jinpings-idea-of-world-order/.

It would be remiss to ignore the mobilizing power that democratic identity has had within Ukraine and how this has come to pervade many European and North American responses. In contrast to a point routinely made by democracy skeptics, while Western support has mainly been aimed at protecting Ukraine's sovereignty, this has gone hand in hand with more focus on improving its democracy too. More overlap is evident now between the aims of maintaining order and protecting democracy, even if these do not fuse entirely in a single policy. The Russian attack has certainly alerted democratic governments everywhere to the need to make their own open political systems more robust and effective.

It is perhaps hardly surprising that Western foreign policies since the invasion have not been purely concerned with democracy or that democratic governments outside the West have different strategic perspectives. Yet the strategic rivalry between democracy and autocracy has become more significant even if not the dominant organizing principle of international politics. A defining feature of geopolitics after the war is the deepening of multiple differentiated patterns of cooperation, engagement, and rivalry; if most of these cut across political regime types, democracy dynamics do define one set of these new global-order patterns. Geopolitics has certainly become more multidirectional, as the war has hastened a messy order with elements of democratic coordination and zero-sum rivalry coexisting.[75]

In sum, it is analytically significant that the war has become a major factor in reshaping the international politics of democracy and democratization. There is a line of connection, even if feint, between specific postwar democracy-defense policies, on the one hand, and the political dynamics that condition the structure of global order, on the other hand. The tragedy in Ukraine has unlocked stronger democratic commitment even if this has not yet found strong enough practical expression in international policies to constitute a fully transformative change. The invasion has moved the needle on democratic geopolitics, and liberal-statist and civic-led influences have both played their role in this adjustment.

---

[75] R. Higgott and S. Reich, "The Age of Fuzzy Bifurcation: Lessons from the Pandemic and the Ukraine War," *Global Policy* 13, no. 5 (2022): 627–639.

8

Snapshot: Ukraine's Democratic Resilience

The previous chapter detailed the international dimensions of the Russian invasion of Ukraine and assessed how far this has galvanized wider global support for democratic norms. Yet the invasion has also had implications for debates and political actions related to democracy at the local level within Ukraine itself. Indeed, it is within Ukraine that perhaps the strongest defense of democratic values has taken shape. Intense citizen engagement in the pursuit of better democracy extended across Ukraine in the invasion's shadow. This is tightly connected to the categories of the book's analytical framework, as this is an especially critical and compelling case of an intensified civic micropolitics mobilizing in favor of democratic values and self-survival. Ukraine's domestic resilience shows how the concept of civic micropolitics helps capture one important response to the geopolitics of conflict. This is a highly significant case of a crisis in geopolitics driving a tightened focus on democracy.

Accountability in War

Before the invasion, Ukraine's democracy was not in especially good shape. After taking power in 2019, President Zelensky's government centralized security powers, filled key positions with supporters and charged previous president Petro Poroshenko with treason in a clearly political move that cast doubts on judicial independence. Some observers doubted how far the Russian invasion turned this situation around. It was understandable that the government introduced martial law that curtailed civil liberties and centralized executive control over many decisions, as is normal in war time. However, critics felt that the government also went too far in using the emergency rules to silence criticism and constrict civil society and the press.[1]

---

[1] T. Colton, "Ukraine and Russia: War and Political Regimes," *Journal of Democracy* 33, no. 4 (2022): 20–36.

Democratic Crossroads. Richard Youngs, Oxford University Press. © Oxford University Press 2024.
DOI: 10.1093/oso/9780197762417.003.0008

SNAPSHOT: UKRAINE'S DEMOCRATIC RESILIENCE 153

Rather than passively accepting these restrictions, Ukrainian civil society and other actors kept up their critical scrutiny of the government. Ukrainian citizens did not merely rally around the government and show support for the war effort, but also exhibited a more critical insistence on well-functioning democratic values. Far from accepting that these values might be set aside in the name of warfighting, they stressed a firmer conviction in the importance of democratic reform. In the invasion, citizens were able to see "democracy in action" and came to accord it more significance for dealing with the country's multiple challenges. Levels of support for democracy and the centrality of democracy to Ukraine's identity rose from 2020 and continued to solidify during the war: polls showed that many citizens previously ambivalent about democracy became more fully convinced of its importance. They "rallied around democracy" more than rallying around one leader or set of government actions.[2]

In an influential template—the so-called Lugano declaration—civil society organizations presented their own agenda to set the parameters for postwar reconstruction. Central to this was the insistence that democratic quality must not be sacrificed on the altar of physical reconstruction or uncritical backing of governmental powers. The civil society declaration stated: "The burden of war and the associated suffering should not motivate political elites and some members of society to support authoritarian systems of governance and seek populist solutions . . . the strategy of reconstruction and modernization, and specific plans and projects at all levels should not take place in a narrow circle and under the pressure of current circumstances, but in an open, transparent, inclusive way."[3]

Many examples of this heightened democratic activism could be cited. Anti-corruption campaigns gathered more momentum as the costs of corruption became increasingly evident to the war effort. A new layer of activists emerged to fight corruption, deploying a very direct security narrative that anyone accepting bribes was now in effect helping Russia, as these actions sapped the vitality of Ukrainian resources and resistance. A coalition of civil society organizations mobilized against the government's weak anti-corruption strategy. CSOs began expressing concerns about some government officials already setting themselves up to pocket reconstruction funds

---

[2] O. Onuch, "Why Ukrainians are Rallying Around Democracy," *Journal of Democracy* 33, no. 4 (2022): 37–46.

[3] Civil Society Manifesto 2022 (Lugano Declaration), https://manifesto.org.ua/eng.

154   DEMOCRATIC CROSSROADS

for their own benefit. They played a major role in the disbanding of the Kyiv district administrative court in late 2022, one of the country's most corrupt bodies, and in getting a more committed and less tainted chief public prosecutor appointed. In January 2023 a scandal over corruption in the Ukrainian ministry of defense emerged: Ukrainian civil society revealed this and pushed for action.

Many civil society organizations faced logistical and financial challenges amid the war, often struggling to maintain their activities and make their voices heard, and yet sought to stick to their "old goals" related to human rights and democracy. Civil society played a significant role in pushing for EU candidate status, helping ministries prepare the necessary technical arrangements to win this and pushing to make sure the government committed to reforms to move accession forward. The newly formed International Centre for Ukrainian Victory lobbied intensely and effectively for international support.[4] The Centre for Civic Liberties was awarded the 2022 Nobel prize for peace and kept rights issues firmly on the political agenda.[5] A major focus of critical civil society pressure was the government's tightened control over the security services—with local groups expressing far more concern over this than Western governments did. Civil society also expressed concerns over the government taking emergency control over companies for the war effort. CSOs pressed hard for a stronger registry of oligarchs than that included in a law proposed shortly before the invasion, trying to reduce the influence of both Russian-linked and more national-oriented oligarchs.

Even as established CSOs have grappled with the longstanding need for stronger institutional development of the civic sphere, a new generation of democratic activists has emerged because of the invasion. The civil society organization Horizons of Change embarked on new work to foster local democratic participation. It channeled a growing desire among citizens to engineer open political decision-making. The organization insisted people were alert to the danger of the government usurping more powers and the need to make sure that ministers did not "get too comfortable" with martial law. Ukrainian activists' use of ironic political humor against the political elite has been striking during the war. They have pressed for more decentralization, reflecting a widespread conviction that

---

[4] International Center for Ukrainian Victory website, https://ukrainianvictory.org (accessed April 28, 2023).
[5] Centre for Civic Liberties website, ccl.org.ua (accessed April 28, 2023).

SNAPSHOT: UKRAINE'S DEMOCRATIC RESILIENCE 155

the empowering of local government during the 2010s has provided one of the strongest sources of resilience during the invasion—new community groups have been highly attentive to any risk of the central government reappropriating powers.

There has been a dramatic expansion in the number and range of analytical centers to meet demand for assessment of the war. These have kept a sharp eye on civil liberties and trends in democracy, putting pressure on the government and generating knowledge for the international community. Somewhat at odds with the standard wartime picture, the Russian invasion has generated more critical monitoring, more transparency, more coverage of political developments from within the country and from the wider international community. Ukrainian democracy has become a pivotal issue of international concerns and domestic actors have harnessed this to increase the leverage of their own democratic actions and campaigning.

The more than five million Ukrainians forced to leave the country include many citizens active in political and civic organizations. There were efforts to help these Ukrainian refugees continue their democracy work from Poland and other countries. These citizens kept remarkably active in democracy related actions from outside the country in extremely trying circumstances. They sought international funds to do so, and donors responded through new, flexible funding schemes. Some of the most effective pro-democracy pressure and campaigning came from such temporarily displaced civic figures, pressing the government for reforms even amid war-driven national unity. Compared to other conflict contexts, there have been especially notable efforts by this new diaspora to retain links with in-country civic groups.

Civic criticism has pushed the government to implement some governance reforms. Ministers have talked increasingly about postwar rebuilding being used to jump to a postindustrial economic model based on local community green growth. In June 2023, the Ukrainian government launched an online platform giving citizens engagement in relation to reconstruction decisions and contracts—indeed, pushing participation beyond such provisions in other European states. The Ukrainian parliament has remained open and online pluralism has been strong. De facto decentralization has deepened as each province, district and city has taken on new responsibilities related to the invasion. Cooperation has improved between civil society and political parties, even if this link remains a relative weak point in Ukraine compared to other countries. If tensions over language and ethnicity were rising before the war, they have subsided since early 2022: bearing the brunt of Russian

156 DEMOCRATIC CROSSROADS

attacks in the east, ethnic Russians have aligned with a more strongly unified civic democratic patriotism.

Civic Engagement

In addition to the societal focus on democratic reform, a wider and more disparate ethos of civic resilience has also taken shape across Ukraine in response to Russia's invasion. It is this element that provides one of the most distinctive, stirring and perhaps improbable instances of local participative renovation in recent years. As Ukrainian towns and villages were bombarded by Russian forces in early 2022, citizens self-organized and provided a wide range of social, economic, emergency, and political functions. This intense conflict-driven mutualism has strengthened and extended across the country. While such solidarity is often seen in societies under attack, in Ukraine this aspect of the war has been especially striking and significant for the quality of democratic engagement.[6]

Ukrainians have expressed a particularly high level of civic duty: active democratic engagement is now understood as part of core national responsibility.[7] After the invasion, some 80 percent of the population participated in some form of collective civic action.[8] Since the invasion, around 1700 civil society and volunteering organizations have been created in Ukraine to deal with humanitarian aid alone.[9] Most of these are not formalized CSOs but new informal movements. Some of these movements emerged out of the COVID-19 pandemic, repurposing for the conflict. Unprecedented scales of crowdfunding have been directed to emergency supplies and the army. Community groups, social movements, hackers, and business leaders have coordinated in offering services to the population. A Local Democracy Network brought these community groups together to amplify their impact. In the second half of 2023, community forums proliferated across the

---

[6] Drawn from K. Zarembo, "Civic Activism against Geopolitics: the Case of Ukraine," in *Global Civil Society in a Geopolitical Age: How Great Power Competition Is Reshaping Civic Activism*, ed. R. Youngs (Brussels: Carnegie Europe, 2022), 55–60.

[7] Onuch, "Why Ukrainians are Rallying Around Democracy."

[8] "The Eighth National Poll: Ukraine During the War," *Rating Group*, April 8, 2022, https://rati nggroup.ua/en/research/ukraine/vosmoy_obschenacionalnyy_opros_ukraina_v_usloviyah_voyny _6_aprelya_2022.html.

[9] United Kingdom Humanitarian Innovation Hub, "Enabling the Local Response: Emerging Humanitarian Priorities in Ukraine March–May 2022," June 2022, https://www.humanitarianoutco mes.org/sites/default/files/publications/ukraine_review_2022.pdf.

SNAPSHOT: UKRAINE'S DEMOCRATIC RESILIENCE   157

country to monitor the government's use of international reconstruction aid. Ukrainian civic leaders talk of a "citizen-led war."

This civic resilience emerged out of a decade in which new and dynamic forms of citizen engagement proliferated across Ukraine, spreading out into small towns and involving more citizens from local communities. Even as Ukrainian governments stalled on reforms and as membership of formal CSOs plateaued in the late 2010s, an informal and community-rooted civic sphere was thickening in the adversity of Russian threats. These locally rooted hubs, spaces and clubs were key to civic mobilization in the war around an ethos of community responsibility.[10] Monitoring the dramatic expansion of such initiatives after February 2022, one writer suggests that "self-organization is part of the impulse that justifies Ukraine's very existence."[11] Volunteer groups have gained as much trust and support among the population as the president and behind only the army as the most trusted institutions in the country.[12]

These actions were led by civic groups that formed after the 2014 Euromaiden uprising, like the Hospitalliers, Come Back Alive, and Prytula foundations that support fighting forces, alongside many new and small-scale initiatives. The emblematic AutoMaidan movement from the 2014 revolts repurposed to coordinate emergency supplies. Green Odessa and other environmental groups became leaders in delivering emergency relief, providing medical services and organizing logistics for resistance forces. A Civic Readiness project has worked to coordinate citizens' mobilization to back up the armed forces and from this generate new community leadership figures engaged in politics. Another project provided modular housing for those bombed out of their flats and encouraged community organization around such rebuilding. Civic leaders refer to a "new democratic leadership" emerging from these volunteer initiatives and insist that Ukrainian citizens will not tolerate "a return to the old leaders." A new Youth Democratic Movement embodies this shift. These kinds of new movements have worked to find ways to keep the volunteering and united solidarity going in the longer term.

[10] K. Zarembo and E. Martin, "Civil Society and Sense of Community in Ukraine: From Dormancy to Action," *European Societies* (2023), doi: 10.1080/14616696.2023.2185652.
[11] E. Channell-Justice, *Without the State: Self-Organization in Ukraine* (Toronto: University of Toronto Press, 2022).
[12] Kyiv International Institute of Sociology, *Omnibus Opinion Poll*, December 2022. https://euro maidanpress.com/2023/01/13/trust-in-ukraines-president-increased-three-fold-in-2022-army-still-most-trusted-institution-poll/.

158   DEMOCRATIC CROSSROADS

The digital dimensions of this intensified volunteer-mutualism have been especially strong. During the 2010s, Ukraine was an international leader in the development of so-called civic tech and after the invasion this helped spur a major leap forward in digital activism. Digital activists helped to keep the state functioning in the early days and weeks of the war when Ukrainian forces were clearly on the backfoot. Digital platforms then helped ensure that basic services were delivered even to the millions of people displaced from their homes. Civil society organizations ran digital tools that kept people connected and helped to keep some elements of normal economic and social activity running even as citizens hunkered down in basements and bomb shelters.

Digital tools were crucial in crowdfunding resources for military equipment like satellites and medical equipment. Displaced people had all their citizenship documents made available on their phones through a game-changing app originally developed for anti-corruption goals. Ukrainian CSOs have also been especially effective in countering Russian disinformation and have been successful in this by building inclusive civic networks working on this issue across different parts of society.[13] In 2023 civic-tech activists helped extend an emblematic online platform, Prozorra, that increased transparency in public procurement contracts, to ensure against officials syphoning off slices of the international aid that was now pouring into the country.

Notably, civic engagement included functions related directly to the war and protecting Ukraine from Russian attacks. Ukrainian society became a de facto defense actor, through an expansion of the self-defense units set up during the Euromaidan demonstrations and volunteer battalions following the beginning of hostilities in the east. Partisan movements spread in the most forcefully occupied territories, sometimes shading into local guerrilla movements.[14] Many of the democracy and human rights focused organizations that had grown through the 2010s took on new purposes related to the war, using their structures to assist society in very direct ways. These bodies helped to procure military equipment for Ukrainian troops and provide logistical services like medical or clerical work, even at the frontlines. They were involved in the monitoring and oversight of defense-related issues and

---

[13] A. Fivenson, G. Petrenko, V. Vichova, and A. Polescuk, *Shielding Democracy: Civil Society Adaptations to Kremlin Disinformation about Ukraine* (Washington, DC: National Endowment for Democracy, 2023).

[14] V. Vdovychenko, "Shaping Up Social Resistance: Zelenskyy's Approach to Rearranging Ukraine," in *Volodymyr Zelenskyy's Presidency and the Impact of the Russia-Ukraine War*, ed. A. Reichardt and T. Stepniewski (Lublin: Institute of Central Europe, 2022), 61.

military operations in the Donbas region. That is, civil society performed the function of a security provider, helping to compensate for stretched state institutions and resources.

The new layer of informal civic organization even extended to Ukraine's occupied territories, where civil society defense functions merged with civic protest and resistance. Most formal CSOs from the occupied parts of Donbas had already been forced to leave. After February 2022, informal civil society mobilization sought to counter the effects of Russian forces assuming control. The grassroots New Druzhkivka movement organized volunteers in Donbas against occupation. Independent media outlets have reported stories of the war under occupation, examples including Mist Kherson and Gwara Media in Kharkiv. Public protests in Kherson, Kakhovka, Melitopol, and other cities lasted several weeks, and as these lacked any centralized organizational structure, Russian forces struggled to extinguish them. Even after Russian forces opened fire on protests, spontaneous actions continued. People would walk individually and apparently without motive in a park and then suddenly fuse together in a march under "Kherson is Ukraine" banners taking a photo of themselves and then quickly disbanding.

As conditions worsened under Russian occupation, more and more people formed under-the-radar organizational clusters geared toward procuring food and medicine for those in need. Volunteers also offered psychological help and information on survival tactics. Citizens coordinated with Radio Liberty to get out messages about Russian forces' whereabouts. The so-called Yellow Ribbon or Yellow Stripe movement gained high profile as its members began tying ribbons with the yellow of the Ukrainian flag in public places. Often, actions were carried out by sole individuals in a way that made Russian control more difficult. These kinds of efforts were aimed especially at countering Russian narratives and disinformation. One notable focus was to stress the significance of the EU's decision to make Ukraine a candidate state, as civic activism used this to inspire firmer resistance against the Russian occupation. These may have been very small-scale actions, but they helped stiffen resolve and pushed the central government to redouble efforts to regain captured cities. They acted as an antidote to the notion that Donbas was happy to be annexed into Russia.[15]

---

[15] For more detail on these examples, see K. Zarembo, "Civic Activism against Geopolitics: The Case of Ukraine," in *Global Civil Society in a Geopolitical Age*, ed. R. Youngs (Brussels: Carnegie Europe, 2022).

Assessment: War Citizenry

In the period prior to the Russian invasion, Ukrainian democracy appeared caught in a common post-transition trap. The stirring Euromaidan revolt of 2014 ushered in a formally democratic government and many areas of political reform progressed during the 2010s. Yet the country's putative transition appeared stalled on many fronts and many democratic reformers increasingly expressed frustration at the lack of deep, structural political change. As international indices downgraded Ukraine's democratic status in the early 2020s, the country was widely quoted in writings and debates on global democracy as an increasingly typical example of promising democratic transitions unwinding. Ukraine seemed symptomatic of the broader international democratic malaise that so dominated attention in the 2010s.

The invasion generated a different set of political dynamics. Many of these put democracy under more severe strain. The invasion threatened the very existence of an independent Ukrainian democratic system, while wartime emergency powers placed understandable limitations on political rights and freedoms. Yet in a striking instance of double movement, it also prompted an intense ethos of democratic protection and regeneration. Ukrainian civil society fought against Russian occupation to preserve its sovereignty and territorial integrity, while democratic identity also became a mobilizing catalyst for its self-defense. Defending sovereignty was framed and conceived as defending a distinctive belief in political freedom that distinguished Ukraine from its would-be occupier and gave a rallying core to its resistance. This has fashioned one of the most stirring and consequential cases of civic micropolitics of recent years, a showcase for one of the key categories defined within the book's analytical framework.

As the previous chapter charted the democracy-defense elements of international policies related to the invasion, so the violent lurch into a new geopolitical context has reshaped Ukrainian internal politics too. More active commitments to democratic norms are understood to be part of the country's democratic advantage and part of its core plea for international support. While the war is about hard, military defense, it also has an important civic element. This should not be overly idealized—Ukrainian civil society suffers from the same limitations as elsewhere—but it is an element that has been especially strong in Ukraine relative to other conflict scenarios in recent years. Ukraine's military resistance would not have been possible without the multiple forms of democratic engagement outlined above. These actions have kept issues of democracy on the agenda and have catalyzed new political reform energy. Ukrainian civil society has moved into co-creating democratic reforms together with state authorities, beyond its standard advocacy role.

The invasion may have provided the shock that will ensure there is no return to the status quo ante in Ukraine, as Russia's war of aggression has raised the level of national consciousness and amplified expectations of change: historically, wars have been among the biggest drivers of political and social change and this may also be the case for Ukraine, provided that it wins.[16] There is certainly less tolerance amongst Ukrainian citizens of democratic shortcomings since the invasion and the government has been pushed to respond with reform commitments. A tightened interaction has developed between the new spirt of civic micropolitics, on the one hand, and a state empowered by the invasion, on the other hand. The war's still uncertain outcome means these democratic trends could be quashed; for now, they stand as an inspiring exemplar of active and engaged citizenship.

---

[16] Economist Intelligence Unit, *Democracy Index 2022*, 20.

9

Conclusion

Every era's challenges can seem especially daunting, complex, and defining from up close, in their moments of maximum intensity. The current age is not unique in facing unsettling turbulence and structural transformation. Yet there is widespread agreement that its turmoil presents multiple tests that are especially far-reaching and systemic. The view is repeated often today that major history-shaping forces have returned to the forefront of global politics. If political history is never entirely stilled, in the last several years its driving features have been strikingly unfixed and powerful in their impulse to reordering. This volatile mutability has reopened debates about many generation-prevailing precepts and patterns of institutional order. Established trends and assumptions have been shaken hard by dramatic crises that are either new or of a fast-deepening magnitude.

The effects of climate change and other aspects of ecological crisis have become increasingly tangible and severe. Many countries around the world have in the last few years suffered record-breaking heatwaves, droughts, storms, hurricanes, floods, and wildfires, and these extreme events have begun to drive political change. The COVID-19 pandemic brought much of the world to a virtual standstill for nearly two years in a way previously unseen, and this experience has left behind strains and adjustments of long-term significance. And, on top of these already extreme calamities, came the murderous cataclysm of Russia's invasion of Ukraine. Crucially, the three very different crunch points can all be similarly conceived as world-historic transformative crises that propel and mold political change.

These powerful driving forces have opened a new phase of debate about global democracy. For well over a decade, a standard and fairly uniform narrative of democratic decline has rooted itself firmly at the heart of political and analytical debates. The storyline of this period has been one of chastening clarity: after years of apparently breezy assumptions that

Democratic Crossroads. Richard Youngs, Oxford University Press. © Oxford University Press 2024.
DOI: 10.1093/oso/9780197762417.003.0009

CONCLUSION   163

democracy was on an inexorably upward trajectory, a multitude of troubles has reigned back the aspirational horizons of political liberalism and fueled the sinister creep of authoritarian illiberalism. But in the current era of overlapping climate, pandemic, and geopolitical crises, is this still the sole political script that should command analytical attention? The crises are certainly profound enough to invite searching questions in this regard. Are these three crises reinforcing authoritarian dynamics and tipping the scales even further against democratic potential? Or are they awakening a more varied set of developments that offer the prospect of stronger democratic resilience and political renewal?

If these macro-challenges have entailed great political drama at the policy level, they equally invite more analytical reconsiderations about the international politics of democracy. They present different kinds of causal drivers, both in favor of democracy and against it. They suggest a need to reassess what kinds of factors are set most powerfully to drive political trends—the vital question of what causes global politics to move in either democratic or authoritarian directions. The era raises important questions of a highly conceptual nature. Do the three crises spotlighted in this book indicate that democracy's fate is now driven more decisively by enveloping, global changes? Or are local forces, varying across states and communities, more consequential in explaining how these overarching shifts play themselves out politically?

This concluding chapter draws out similarities and differences across the three areas of crisis. It also reflects on the relationships between them, aiming to paint a more comprehensive picture of the new era that is marked heavily by these very different kinds of challenge. The conclusions are preliminary more than definitive, as the political ramifications of climate, post-pandemic, and geopolitical crises will take time to run their course; these closing reflections are offered as a guide to the kinds of questions and issues likely to be of consequence in conditioning future democratic trends and against which still-evolving political adjustments can be measured. The assessment here turns first to the role of these three crises as drivers of political change. A second focus is on unpacking the twin concepts of empowered states and micropolitics that have run as a thread through the book. And a third reflection considers where these current trends leave the prospects for positive democratic transformation flowing from the climate change, pandemic, and geopolitical crises.

Crises as Political Driver

The book shows how major, exogenous crises and shocks have begun to drive political change. As reiterated through the book, this does not mean that other drivers have lost their powerful influence: the identity, economic, leadership and other factors that have attracted analytical attention over the last decade and more remain pertinent, as do additional sources of overarching structural change, like the role of technological developments. However, the chapters bring to the fore a new conjuncture of factors reshaping democracy's fate and trajectory across the world. The three crises are not equal in either the magnitude of their impact or the form of that impact. They are at different stages in their political impact too. Still, generalizing their combined effect it can be concluded that they alter the dynamics of democratization and autocratization across the world, even though they do not yet add up to a decisive watershed for global democracy.

The book does not present any kind of conclusive, final statement on or picture of these three drivers of change. It shows that the crises have opened different pathways of possible political transformation without being fully determinant in themselves. The three crises are likely to condition political change in eclectic ways for some time into the future. It will take time to determine their ultimate effects, with a lag time between their opening of political flux and the ultimate result of that change. This is especially the case with regards to the climate crisis and the Russian invasion of Ukraine. It may be possible to reach more of an advanced judgment over the political impact of COVID-19, but even here the shockwaves from the pandemic continue to ripple through political, economic, and social systems.

The book sketches a framework for identifying and measuring reshaped influences over democratization and autocratization as these evolve over the years to come. In this vein, the foregoing chapters point to many general and common trends, but also significant variation in outcomes. Two axes of variation are evident: differences between the three crises as drivers of change; and differences in crisis-related outcomes across countries.

Variation between Crises

The dynamics of the three crises as drivers of political change differ in important ways. The first challenge of climate and ecological crisis has been

CONCLUSION 165

brewing for many years and has in the last several years assumed towering proportions as the era's defining test. As climate and ecological considerations have come to dominate so many policy spheres—redirecting economic, technology, industrial, trade, fiscal, and many other strategies—so they have come to influence the organization of different political orders. The increasingly catastrophic effects of environmental collapse have moved the issue from an over-the-horizon concern to a more immediate crisis-tinged driver of political change. If erstwhile frameworks for explaining both democratization and autocratization have tended to include climate change as a secondary factor, if at all, the events of the last several years show that it must now be incorporated and conceived as a variable of first-order importance for the fate of different kinds of regime type.

The COVID-19 pandemic, the book's second crisis, appeared more suddenly as a driver of political change. In the midst of COVID-19 a common refrain was that nothing in politics would ever be the same again. The empty streets and lives placed on hold created such a shock around the world that few doubted such dramatic sentiment. As most countries have moved into a post-pandemic period of recuperation from the crisis, so it has become clearer that the effects have not been quite as seismic as seemed inevitable between 2020 and 2022. Some historians draw parallels in recalling that there were limits to the transformative effects of previous global catastrophes.[1] Yet, of longer-term significance, the pandemic has set in course processes of social and economic adjustment that are driving political change—again, either replenishing democracy or ossifying autocracy.

With regards the third crisis of geopolitical turmoil, Russia's war in Ukraine represents the most intrinsically political of the three crises covered in the book and its eruption as a driver of democracy-related debates is unequivocal. The conflict came atop an already-accumulating set of geopolitical tensions and has intensified these to fever pitch. Not all these tensions are about a democracy-autocracy divide, and the war itself is rooted in many other considerations beyond this issue; yet the invasion clearly sets in train a dramatic cascade of effects for systems of political governance. While historically involvement in war has tended to have a negative impact on levels of democracy, for direct belligerents and in neighboring countries to conflicts,

---

[1] N. Ferguson, *Doom: The Politics of Catastrophe* (New York: Penguin, 2021).

166   DEMOCRATIC CROSSROADS

Russia's war in Ukraine seems to have unleashed at least some more potent democratic dynamics.[2]

Any attempt to apportion exact degrees of weight or causality to each crisis would be difficult and present an arbitrary exactness. Yet the preceding chapters do bring to the fore some clear contrasts. Of the three, the geopolitical crisis triggered by Russia's invasion of Ukraine has had the strongest and most direct effect on upgrading formal state commitments to protect and advance democratic norms. The greater alignment of Western and some Asian democracies reflects how far the invasion has given a fillip to international coordination around democracy support; even though the post-invasion world order is messy, these efforts to protect democracy have certainly moved up a gear within this general systemic imprecision. Climate change and ecological crisis are more of a background swirl, set to reinvigorate democratic engagement and contestation to the most all-pervasive extent in the longer-term. The COVID-19 pandemic was the most dramatic, world-stopping event that appeared politically all-determining for an intense two years before subsiding and acting as an indirect driver of social and economic adjustments that in turn have political implications.

If the pandemic appeared to be the most favorable of the three crises to authoritarian dynamics, it has over time come to leave a more diverse legacy. Climate change has had the most mixed outcome in terms of putting both democratic and nondemocratic systems of governance under strain, but it is also the crisis that has engendered the most widespread wave of new civic, democratic engagement. The Ukraine conflict has generated strong Western democratic narratives, and yet this particular conflict is relatively unique in the way it fuses the defense of sovereignty and democracy; the same clarity of commitment is not seen in Western democracy support elsewhere.

One useful guide might be to distinguish between the three crises' immediate and long-term effects. Some analysts see a sharper distinction opening between long embedded or distal features, intermediate drivers of long-term democratic development, and proximate causes of more dramatic political changes.[3] To some extent this template of causal levels is helpful

---

[2] M. Coppedge, B. Denison, P. Friesen, L. Tiscornia, and Y. Xu, "Chapter IV: International Influence: The Hidden Dimension," in *Why Democracies Develop and Decline*, ed. M. Coppedge, A. Edgell, C. Knutsen, and S. Lindberg (Cambridge: Cambridge University Press, 2022), 80–118.

[3] M. Coppedge, A. Edgell, C. Knutsen, and S. Lindberg, "Chapter VIII: Causal Sequences in Long-Term Democratic Development and Decline," in *Why Democracies Develop and Decline*, ed. M. Coppedge, A. Edgell, C. Knutsen, and S. Lindberg (Cambridge: Cambridge University Press, 2022), 215–261.

CONCLUSION   167

to understanding the evolving impacts of the three crises examined in this book: the very dramatic immediacy of the war on Ukraine contrasts with the incremental structuration of the climate crisis. Yet the three challenges also cut across these temporal distinctions: all of them work to remold underlying political and social structures, and all of them have entailed a degree of immediate crisis.

Variation Across Countries

Alongside the differences between the three crises, they share one point in common: none has been so strong that is has emasculated other, more locally rooted factors. As the foregoing chapters make clear across all three crises, there has been significant variation in outcome across countries and this reflects the influence of these local drivers. Apart from the fact that the respective crises have simply had more severe or immediate effects on some countries than on others, variation results from many local political factors and these caution against overly bold claims about all-prevailing zeitgeists. The power of the three crises relative to local factors varies across different national contexts. A key finding is that the relationship between external and internal change is far from constant across the contrasting regions of the world. The three crises create a set of powerful overarching dynamics at the level of structural environmental, socioeconomic, and geopolitical change; their ultimate outcomes are mediated through local national and subnational conditions.

The COVID-19 pandemic has left a legacy deeply troubling for open politics in some countries and has in some places provided a cloak for harsher authoritarian surveillance and control. In other countries it left democratic freedoms intact, while having its most notable impact in thickening the civic sphere and opening the way to more inclusive economic policymaking and rights-protecting state action. Likewise, Russia's war in Ukraine has put some authoritarian systems on the defensive, left others largely untouched, and empowered still others. It has ignited noble democratic conviction in Ukraine, its region, and some Western states, while having little resonance to democratic claims in other parts of the world. Many trends in global politics continue, separate from the Russian invasion. Most states in the world still work to position themselves between China and the US as the means of protecting their interests in an international system dominated by rivalry

168 DEMOCRATIC CROSSROADS

between these two powers, and interstate geo-economics weighs heavily relative to democracy-related dynamics.

The book also sheds light on the democracy-related *interactions* between the three crises and how these differ across contrasting political contexts. Although a standard line is that the crises reinforce each other's negative effects, the foregoing chapters suggest a more varied picture. Spillover effects between different strands of the poly-crisis can be detrimental but also beneficial to global democracy. The war and the pandemic have together revealed certain structural dysfunctions of authoritarianism and have jointly given a fillip to democratic dynamics.[4] Equally, the narratives of democratic pushback against Russia and the urgency of green transition have fused together and reinforced each other. The post-pandemic reassessment of economic models and the dynamics of geopolitical crisis also influence each other: relative levels of economic success and social stability between regime-types have come to form part of the arsenal of democracy-autocracy rivalries. In myriad ways, the coincidence of the three crises compounds the overall magnitude of political change underway in many places around the world.

Statism and Localism

These overlapping shifts are not only driving changes in the overall balance between democracy and autocracy, but also exert a more qualitative impact on political forms. The book shows that the location of power and sites of political activity are moving upward and downward at the same time. While there may be many reasons for this beyond the issues highlighted in this book, the three crises of climate change, COVID-19 and geopolitical turbulence are certainly an important part of the explanation for this dual up-down movement. Each of the proceeding chapters reveals the increasing prominence of the two trends and how in each policy area they are most often unfolding in parallel with each other. This demonstrates the centrality of what the book's analytical framework has termed the empowered state and micropolitics: there is much evidence to suggest that these twin dynamics are coming to define the current era.

---

[4] Z. Beauchamp, "A Bad Year for the Bad Guys," *Vox*, December 19, 2022, https://www.vox.com/policy-and-politics/2022/12/19/23453073/2022-year-democracy-russia-ukraine-china-iran-america-brazil.

CONCLUSION 169

Neo-Statism

Climate change, post-pandemic socioeconomic challenges and geopolitical conflict are all driving a reassessment of the state and its role in attenuating crisis and existential threats. Separately and combined, these crises have shone a sharper spotlight on the need for an empowered state. Each of the three crises has caused policymakers and analysts to call for ambitious levels of support and financing through state and international bodies. Each has buttressed calls for unprecedented levels of financing and state power. Governments around the world have begun to empower states as an integral part of embryonic moves toward ecological society, post-pandemic rebuilding, and securitized geopolitics.

This change is significant but still partial. States do not yet possess the powers or resources to deal fully or effectively with ecological collapse, to resolve economic turmoil or to offer effective protection against geopolitical risks. The erstwhile case for the minimalist state may have collapsed, but the era of empowered states is not yet fully unfurled—at least in most countries. Still, the basic case for an empowered state has become ever more compelling in the context of these epoch-defining challenges. Deeper change may be needed, but the terms of debate about public authority have undeniably evolved in the last several years and the three crises are a powerful driver of this incipient shift. What remains harder to determine is the political impact of this shift, that is this book's central concern: namely, the impact of the new statism on political systems and governance models around the world.

A pressing question is whether the increasingly empowered Leviathan is a democratically empowering or disempowering Leviathan. The trends in relation to climate crisis, post-pandemic restructuring, and geopolitical conflict are not conclusive in this regard and point in different political directions. In some ways new state powers offer a clearly positive potential for democratic renewal. State-led climate action is vital to saving democracy in a very direct, physical sense, as well as to dealing with the social impacts of energy transition that otherwise could fuel anti-democratic frustration. States empowered in the COVID-19 pandemic acted to preserve the kind of social fabric upon which democracy depends, while also acknowledging the need to redress the socioeconomic marginalization that undermines a de facto equality of democratic rights. And strong state action has self-evidently sought to preserve core principles of democratic order in and after the Ukraine war. Some aspects of empowered state agency have helped mold

170 DEMOCRATIC CROSSROADS

stronger linkages between local-level democratic renewal and interstate liberal multilateralism.

Yet other parts of the new statism appear more problematic for democratic renewal and the prospects of democratization around the world. Several types or levels of concern emerge from the book's analysis. One is that highly authoritarian state machinery is emerging empowered from the era of crisis and change. Another relates to the weak accountability over empowered states that marks the large number of hybrid regimes that combine elements of autocracy with weak democracy. And another concern is the trend toward technocratic statism in democratic states that is not overtly anti-democratic but curtails the breadth and vibrancy of citizens' influence. In many cases empowered state agency has been deployed for relatively inward-looking agendas and to the detriment of deeper rules-based multilateralism. Variants of trustee statism counterbalance more liberal forms of statism, and they caution against categoric generalizations about the empowered state's impact on democracy and democratization.

Micropolitics

The trend of micropolitics is equally as significant, a double movement in parallel with and offsetting the new statism. The development of more localized forms of citizen organization and engagement has been apparent and gathering pace in many countries around the world for quite some number of years. Yet it is clear from the foregoing chapters that this emergent trend has been given a decisive prompt forward by the more recent issues associated with climate crisis, health emergencies and the need for societal resilience against geopolitical threats. These micropolitics have a distinguishing feature that sets them apart from formally organized civil society, as forms of community participation are gaining ground that are led by those most directly impacted by political decisions. Their ethos is of a participative enrichment to and remolding of mainstream liberal-democratic templates.

With both the pandemic and environmental crisis, as well in the ethos of Ukrainian civic resilience, what is often called a democracy of the commons has gained ground, based around a mutualization and shared management of local economies. This involves citizens not just pushing for formal political change but taking more active control at community level.[5] One prominent

---

[5] E. Jourdain, *Esprit—La Démocratie des Communs* (Revue Esprit, 2022): 31–34.

CONCLUSION 171

figure defines this trend as "the localization of resistance" across the areas of health, climate action and conflict.[6] This makes both a direct contribution to democracy as it adds a layer of activism aimed at democratic renewal and an indirect one as it more generally thickens a social fabric and strengthens community resilience against repressive intrusion. The emerging micropolitics does not replace other levels of civic engagement but adds a more strongly rooted foundation to democratic renewal—and it is striking how the three very different crises addressed in this book have had at least some similar localist effects in this sense.

This micropolitics carries with it interesting implications. It is curiously a form of democratic renewal supported and now encouraged by both rightist and leftist forces on the political spectrum. Many on the right see it as heralding a welcome return to traditional community. For the left it symbolizes a potentially more radical and empowered form of mobilization against the inequities of the status quo. It is also significant that this kind of micropolitics stands as an understated corrective to higher-level, macro democratic trends. It is still generally not well captured in big-picture analyses of the state of democracy. And it is not fully picked up and reflected in the democracy indices that command so much attention and that each year for the last decade have reported ever-spiraling democratic regression. Moreover, the civic micropolitics detailed through this book are increasingly evident across all types of political regime, from consolidated democracies to hybrid regimes and fully authoritarian states.

As with the rise of the empowered state, this micropolitics has not been axiomatically or uniformly beneficial for democracy or democratization. Some localized mobilization is tipping into an often-violent questioning of state authority as this fails to deal with climate crisis, COVID-19 or geopolitical conflict—a questioning pursued in ways not conducive to positive political liberalization. Some of it has mobilized around agendas and values that are illiberal or even anti-democratic or simply in denial of climate, health, economic, and geopolitical challenges. Some of it is also anti-internationalist and has acted as one factor holding governments back from more fully effective multilateral coordination on the three crises: although much civic mobilization has partially pushed state authorities into more

---

[6] D. Miliband, "The Global Battle Against Impunity," The Rachman Review podcast, *Financial Times*, January 19, 2023. https://shows.acast.com/therachmanreview/episodes/the-global-battle-against-impunity.

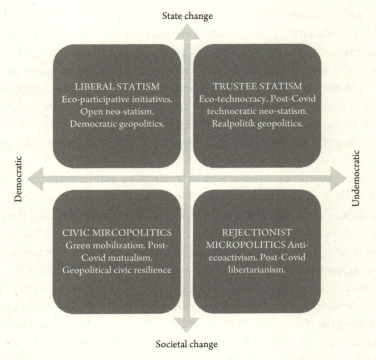

Figure 9.1 Analytical categories, results

international cooperation, some it pulls in the opposite direction. A rejectionist micropolitics unfolds alongside a civic micropolitics, another facet of the double movement that now colors and stretches global trends in democracy. Figure 9.1 shows the variation of trends across the analytical categories introduced in Chapter 2.

Statism-Micropolitics Balances

While the general trends in neo-statism and micropolitics apply in each of the three areas of transformation examined in the book, the balance between these two dynamics differs across the three crises and across different countries. Civic micropolitics has gathered its most notable presence in relation to climate change and ecological crisis. State agency has become stronger in this area of policy, but the relative weighting toward local-level mobilization and organization is in overall terms greater than in relation to the other two crises. Responses to the Russian invasion of Ukraine are mainly about more securitized national-state agency, and this is the area where the democracy agenda has become most tightly associated with efforts at inter-state democratic coordination. Civic micropolitics have become a defining feature of political resistance within Ukraine itself, although even here the war has perforce triggered a concentration of state power. In relation to COVID-19, civic micropolitics were generally strongest where governments' health emergency measures were most conspicuously lacking, while in the post-pandemic phase the balance has generally shifted from the civic sphere toward empowered neo-statism. Local mobilization has arisen most extensively in states that already exhibit a degree of political space, although new informal micropolitics have also become a way for populations to seek influence in more closed regimes too.

All this invites recognition of the locally specific factors that determine the balance between levels of agency and whether empowered states and micropolitics have pro- or anti-democratic effects. It has become increasingly important to chart the precise combination of and interaction between the new statism and localist civic politics. To the extent that good quality democracy and indeed democratizing reform away from autocracy require both strong state capacities and strong societies, the twin rise of these two trends would seem to augur well for democratic potential. Yet as the book has shown, the tensions between them are notable too: the new statism often risks suffocating democratic localism, while conversely hyperlocalist challenges can undercut public authority within the wider political system.

One much cited analysis from the end of the 2010s lamented that trends at both state and society level were heading in democracy-weakening rather than democracy-strengthening directions and that the combination of the two was especially problematic: in some countries stronger state powers have not been matched by societal control, while in others the state has effectively become too weak to underpin open politics.[7] The evidence presented in this book offers a more varied and balanced picture in this regard. Such negative trends persist but more democratic state-and-society combinations are also gaining momentum. In this sense, as climate, pandemic and geopolitical factors have exerted their influence into the 2020s, they are beginning to alter the overarching dynamics of global democratization and autocratization.

---

[7] D. Acemoglu and J. Robinson, *The Narrow Corridor: How Nations Struggle for Liberty* (New York: Penguin, 2020), 474, 483.

174 DEMOCRATIC CROSSROADS

The fact that negative perspectives on democracy have been so dominant in the last decade makes the more positive dynamics of renewal especially interesting from an analytical point of view, even if their reach is subject to clear limitations.

Democratic Transformations?

The book's attempt to explain emerging political trends may help more normative reflections about the future of global democracy. At the policy level, for a decade or more those concerned with preserving and fostering liberal political values have grappled with the challenge of how to push back against the much-commented authoritarian surge. To this end, the book's analysis offers a number of possible pointers toward the future. Several implications emerge from its explanatory framework in terms of both the promising avenues for democratic renewal and, more negatively, the additional problems emerging that could compound the dynamics of global authoritarianism and de-democratization.

The overall assessment suggests a degree of balance. Democracies have shown tenacity in the buffeting of the three crises of climate emergency, the pandemic and geopolitical conflict, yet there is clearly a need for deeper reform and rethinking of democracy. The different crises show there is rising demand for democratic renewal and a need for reforms to ensure that democracy can better deal with systemic shocks. So far, across these different crises, Western democracies have seemed unable to move into a different gear in their responses or shift out of the comfort zone of "normal times" politics in a way that preserves liberalism's wider appeal.[8]

While the impacts and policy responses have been mixed and there is much still to nourish democratic pessimism, the three crises have tentatively opened the door of democratic transformation. This is perhaps not a conclusion of absolute clarity—the simultaneous deepening of double-movement dynamics both favorable and unfavorable to deeper democratization is a theme that runs through the book. Yet it is hopefully one that points toward a more balanced framework for analyzing democratic trends. This book has paid particular attention to the emerging dynamics of and opportunities

---

[8] B. Macaes, *Geopolitics for the End Times: From the Pandemic to the Climate Crisis* (London: Hurst, 2021).

CONCLUSION 175

for positive democratic renewal. It does so not to idealize this momentum or downplay the factors working against democracy, but to highlight that a fully rounded picture requires more focus on the incipient possibilities of democratic renewal driven by the three major challenges—in addition to the heavier and better-established focus on democratic regression.

While stressing the openings toward democratic transformation, the foregoing chapters show just as clearly that democratic change has not been far reaching enough. If the three shifts are to leave a more unequivocally positive mark on global democracy, deeper democratic renewal will be needed. Societies need to be able to better withstand the immediate effects of crises. Civic micropolitics still needs to be embedded into mainstream politics. The best of participation and technocracy would need to combine in a fusion of micropolitics and empowered states in the service of better democracy—a more organically rooted democracy, buttressed by an empowering Leviathan. A mutually enhancing fusion of democratic mobilization and state-empowerment is needed, in the sense of citizens actively engaging with and through their states to deliver better public goods related to climate change, health and other imperatives. Renewal must still probe the right combination of active popular engagement with restraints both on power and also on the illiberal risks of popular will.[9]

New and deeper forms of global cooperation on democracy will also be vital, as these have yet to appear in full enough form as a response to authoritarian geopolitics. If global strategic rivalry is not to militate more decisively against open politics, liberal statism will need to drive a more democratic form of geopolitics, while civic micropolitics must also still do more to focus on this issue. Efforts to uphold democracy internationally will need to mold themselves around very different kinds of diplomatic format and find a more balanced coverage of Western and non-Western states' varied concerns. Through stronger coordination, democracies will need a weight in numbers that allows them to support democracy less equivocally while also defending necessary areas of engagement with autocracies. Longstanding patterns of democracy support will need to give way to wider networks of many actors defending the security and prosperity of democracies and closing vulnerabilities to autocratic influence. More inclusive democratic networks will need to link these international elements of democracy to the

---

[9] J. Keane, *The Shortest History of Democracy* (Melbourne: Schwartz Books, 2022), 61–65.

176 DEMOCRATIC CROSSROADS

core national and subnational challenges related to climate change and economic problems much more effectively than in the past.

More broadly, government and civic reformers will need to show greater willingness to look outside standard templates of democracy. A common refrain of the last several years is the need for a new social contract: but it is not clear still what this entails and what it implies for democracy. Some thinkers argue that such a menu of democratic renewal is currently held back by failure to imagine a different democracy.[10] While this book has not offered a conceptual exploration of different models of democracy, it has provided a rich array of empirical examples of novel democratic practices that could embellish standard liberal democracy and push it in more participative directions.

All of this comes with a caveat that the trends examined in the book are still unfolding in a highly changeable fashion. In some ways, narratives around democracy's advantages have regained ground as a result of international events—the Russian war on Ukraine and also citizens' desire to have a say in managing ecological emergencies and the fall-out from the COVID-19 pandemic. However, the three crises' evolution is fluid and could either provide a fillip to authoritarian powers or to the cause of democracy. Each has much distance still to run and their combined fall-out will shape global politics for years to come. Each critical juncture will cut deeper and in more changeable ways before their eventual effects show themselves with any definitive clarity. Much more analytical work will be needed to unpack their impact as they unfold. The balance between the different factors examined in the preceding chapters will undoubtedly change over time—the balances between democratic and anti-democratic dynamics, and those between upward and downward dynamics in political agency.

This book should be seen as a modestly preliminary map of conceptual pointers to guide the future analysis of these fluctuations. The unspent dynamics of change reinforce the notion and significance of democracy standing at crucial crossroads. Crises often cut with a double-edged bite. They generate an instinct for political control and for securitized management of risk.

---

[10] G. Mulgan, *Another World Is Possible: How to Reignite Social and Political Imagination* (London: Hurst, 2022).

CONCLUSION 177

They also shake existing systems, social contracts, assumptions and models and open windows of transformative opportunity. This uneasy combination will mark political trends for many years. In an era of sharpened political agency and action, propelled by dramatic shifts and crises, democracy's fate is more openly up for grabs than it has been for many years.

Bibliography

Abadi, C. "What If Democracy and Climate Mitigation Are Incompatible?" *Foreign Policy*, January 7, 2022. https://foreignpolicy.com/2022/01/07/climate-change-democracy/.

Accetti, C. *What Is Christian Democracy? Politics, Religion and Ideology*. New York: Cambridge University Press, 2019.

Acemoglu, D., and J. Robinson. *The Narrow Corridor: How Nations Struggle for Liberty*. New York: Penguin, 2020.

Acharya, A. "After Liberal Hegemony: The Advent of a Multiplex World Order." *Ethics & International Affairs* 31, no. 3 (2017): 271–285.

Acosta, C., and M. Abi-Habib. "Protests Erupt in Cuba Over Government Response to Hurricane Ian." *New York Times*, September 30, 2022. https://www.nytimes.com/2022/09/30/world/americas/cuba-hurricane-ian-protests.html.

Agren, D. "Mexico Protesters Fear US-Owned Brewery Will Drain Their Land Dry." *The Guardian*, February 4, 2018. https://www.theguardian.com/world/2018/feb/04/mexico-water-brewery-mexicali-constellation-brands.

Alexander, J. *Citizens: Why the Key to Fixing Everything Is All of Us*. London: Canbury Press, 2021.

Ali, Z. "The Escazú Agreement: A Landmark Regional Treaty for Environmental Defenders." *Universal Rights Group*, February 10, 2021. https://www.universal-rights.org/contemporary-and-emerging-human-rights-issues/the-escazu-agreement-a-landmark-regional-treaty-for-environmental-defenders/.

American Bar Association. "COVID-19 Related State of Emergency Measures: Impact and Responses." February 8, 2022. https://www.americanbar.org/groups/human_rights/reports/covid-19-related-state-of-emergency-measures-impact-and-response/.

Amnesty International. "China: Unfair Trials of Prominent Activists an Attack of Freedom of Association." June 21, 2022. https://www.amnesty.org/en/latest/news/2022/06/china-unfair-trials-of-prominent-activists-an-attack-of-freedom-of-association/.

Auer, S. *European Disunion: Democracy, Sovereignty and the Politics of Emergency*. New York: Oxford University Press, 2022.

Averchenkova, A., O. Plyska, and J. Wahlgren. *Addressing the Climate and Environmental Crises through Better Governance: The Environmental Democracy Approach in Development Cooperation*. London: Westminster Foundation for Democracy, 2022.

Avramovska, E., J. Lutz, F. Milačić, and M. Svolik. *Identity, Partisanship, Polarization: How Democratically Elected Politicians Get Away with Autocratizing Their Country*. Vienna: Friedrich Ebert Stiftung, 2022. https://library.fes.de/pdf-files/bueros/wien/19536-20220926.pdf.

Azevedo, I., M. R. Davidson, J. D. Jenkins, V. J. Karplus, and D. G. Victor. "The Paths to Net Zero." *Foreign Affairs* 99, no. 3 (2020): 18–27.

Babelon, I., N. Nickel, and P. Pierri. "A Novel Approach to Local Climate Action in France." *Carnegie Europe*, April 22, 2021. https://carnegieeurope.eu/2021/04/22/novel-approach-to-local-climate-action-in-france-pub-84363.

Bartels, L. *Democracy Erodes from the Top*. Princeton, NJ: Princeton University Press, 2023.

Beauchamp, Z. "A Bad Year for the Bad Guys." *Vox*, December 19, 2022. https://www.vox.com/policy-and-politics/2022/12/19/23453073/2022-year-democracy-russia-ukraine-china-iran-america-brazil.

180 BIBLIOGRAPHY

Beckley, M. "Enemies of My Enemy." *Foreign Affairs*, February 14, 2022.

Benoit, C., and C. Hay. "The Antinomies of Sovereigntism, Statism and Liberalism in European Democratic Responses to the COVID-19 Crisis: A Comparison of Britain and France." *Comparative European Politics* 20 (2022): 390–410.

Bernhard, M. "Chronic Instability and the Limits of Path Dependence." *Perspectives on Politics* 13, no. 4 (December 2015): 976–991.

Biden, J. (@ POTUS). "We are engaged anew in a great battle for freedom." *Twitter*, March 26, 2022. https://twitter.com/POTUS/status/1507782139315638283.

Boese, V., S. Lindberg, and A. Lührmann. "Waves of Autocratization and Democratization: A Rejoinder." *Democratization* 28, no. 6 (2021): 1202–1210.

Boix, C. "Development and Democratization." *Institut Barcelona d'Estudis Internacionals (IBEI)* (2009). https://www.jstor.org/stable/resrep14156.

Bordoff, J., and M. O'Sullivan. "Green Upheaval: The New Geopolitics of Energy." *Foreign Affairs*, November 30, 2021. https://www.foreignaffairs.com/articles/world/2021-11-30/geopolitics-energy-green-upheaval.

Borner, S. "Is the Coronavirus Going to Reshape the European Welfare State?" *Social Europe*, November 3, 2020. https://socialeurope.eu/is-the-coronavirus-going-to-reshape-the-europ ean-welfare-state.

Borrell, J. "EU Ambassadors Annual Conference 2022: Opening Speech by High Representative Josep Borrell." *European Union External Action*, October 10, 2022. https://www.eeas.eur opa.eu/eeas/eu-ambassadors-annual-conference-2022-opening-speech-high-representat ive-josep-borrell_en.

Brancati, D. *Democracy Protests: Origins, Features, and Significance*. Cambridge: Cambridge University Press, 2016.

Brands, H. *The Age of Amorality, Foreign Affairs*, March/April 2024.

Bremer, I. *The Power of Crisis: How Three Threats—and Our Response—will Change the World*. New York: Simon & Schuster, 2022.

Brownlee, J., and K. Miao. "Debate: Why Democracies Survive." *Journal of Democracy* 33, no. 4 (October 2022): 133–149.

Bua, A., and S. Bussu. "Reclaiming Participatory Governance: Social Movements and the Reinvention of Democratic Innovations." *Participatory and Deliberative Democracy*, May 3, 2022. https://deliberativehub.wordpress.com/2022/05/03/reclaiming-participatory-gov ernance-social-movements-and-the-reinvention-of-democratic-innovations/.

Burck, J., T. Uhlich, C. Bals, N. Höhne, L. Nascimento, M. Tavares, and E. Strietzel. "Climate Change Performance Index 2023." *CCPI* (2022). https://ccpi.org/download/climate-cha nge-performance-index-2023/.

C19 People's Coalition. Accessed April 28, 2023. https://c19peoplescoalition.org.za/.

Capoccia, G., and R. Kelemen. "The Study of Critical Junctures: Theory, Narrative, and Counterfactuals in Historical Institutionalism." *World Politics* 59, no. 3 (April 2007): 341–369.

Carayannis, E., D. Campbell, and E. Grigoroudis. "Democracy and the Environment: How Political Freedom is Linked with Environmental Sustainability." *Sustainability* 13, no. 10 (2021): 5522. https://doi.org/10.3390/su13105522.

Carothers, T. "Democracy Policy Under Obama: Revitalization or Retreat?" *Carnegie Endowment for International Peace*, January 11, 2012. https://carnegieendowment.org/2012/01/11/democracy-policy-under-obama-revitalization-or-retreat-pub-46443.

Carothers, T. "Is the Global Tide Turning in Favor of Democracy?" Washington, DC: Carnegie Endowment for International Peace, 2023.

Carothers, T., and B. Press. "Understanding and Responding to Global Democratic Backsliding." *Carnegie Endowment for International Peace*, October 20, 2022. https://carnegieendowment.org/2022/10/20/understanding-and-responding-to-global-democra tic-backsliding-pub-88173.

BIBLIOGRAPHY 181

Carroll, W. "Fossil Capitalism, Climate Capitalism, Energy Democracy: The Struggles for Hegemony in an Era of Climate Crisis." *Socialist Studies* 14, no. 1 (2020): 1–26.

Centre for Civic Liberties. Accessed April 28, 2023. ccl.org.ua.

Centre for Democracy Innovation. Accessed February 20, 2024. https://www.nationalciviclea gue.org/center-for-democracy-innovation/.

Channell-Justice, E. *Without the State: Self-Organization in Ukraine.* Toronto: University of Toronto Press, 2022.

Cheeseman N., and M. Desrosiers. "Learning to Do No Harm to Democracy in Engagement with Authoritarian States." *Carnegie Europe*, March 15, 2023. https://carnegieeurope.eu/ 2023/03/15/learning-to-do-no-harm-to-democracy-in-engagement-with-authoritarian-states-pub-89255.

CIVICUS. *2021 State of Civil Society Report.* https://civicus.org/state-of-civil-society-report-2021/.

Club of Madrid. *Democracy & Emergencies: Lessons from the Covid-19 Pandemic for Democratic Resilience,* 2021. https://clubmadrid.org/global-commission-on-democracy-and-emergencies/.

Cocks, T. "South Africa's Ramaphosa Blames NATO for Russia's War in Ukraine." *Reuters,* March 18, 2022. https://www.reuters.com/world/africa/safricas-ramaphosa-blames-nato-russias-war-ukraine-2022-03-17/.

Coldwell, W., and K. Chaddah. "Beyond Extinction Rebellion: The Protest Groups Fighting on the Climate Frontline." *The Guardian*, October 30, 2021. https://www.theguardian.com/ environment/2021/oct/30/beyond-extinction-rebellion-the-protest-groups-fighting-on-the-climate-frontline.

Colton, T. "Ukraine and Russia: War and Political Regimes." *Journal of Democracy* 33, no. 4 (2022): 20–36.

Conway-Lamb, W., N. Curato, K. de Pryck, S. Elstub, A. Morán, M. Ross, E. Sanchez, N. Sari, S. Tiliteke, L. Veloso, and H. Werner. *Global Assembly on the Climate and Ecological Crisis: Evaluation Report,* June 2023. chrome-extension://efaidnbmnnnibpcajpcglclefind mkaj/https://researchprofiles.canberra.edu.au/files/82182314/Global_Assembly_Evalua tion_Report.pdf.

Cooley, A., and D. Nexon. "The Real Crisis of Global Order: Illiberalism on the Rise." *Foreign Affairs*, December 14, 2021.

Coppedge, M., A. Edgell, C. Knutsen, and S. Lindberg. "Chapter I: V-Dem Reconsiders Democratization." In *Why Democracies Develop and Decline*, ed. M. Coppedge, A. Edgell, C. Knutsen, and S. Lindberg, 1–28. Cambridge: Cambridge University Press, 2022.

Coppedge, M., A. Edgell, C. Knutsen, and S. Lindberg. "Chapter VIII: Causal Sequences in Long-Term Democratic Development and Decline." in *Why Democracies Develop and Decline*, ed. M. Coppedge, A. Edgell, C. Knutsen, & S. Lindberg, 215–261. Cambridge: Cambridge University Press, 2022.

Coppedge, M., B. Denison, P. Friesen, L. Tiscornia, and Y. Xu. "Chapter IV: International Influence: The Hidden Dimension" in *Why Democracies Develop and Decline*, ed. M. Coppedge, A. Edgell, C. Knutsen, & S. Lindberg, 80–118. Cambridge: Cambridge University Press, 2022.

Corrales, J. "Democratic Backsliding through Electoral Irregularities: The Case of Venezuela." *European Review of Latin American and Caribbean Studies*, no. 109 (2020): 41–65.

Council of the European Union. *A Strategic Compass for Security and Defence*, 7371/22, March 2022. https://data.consilium.europa.eu/doc/document/ST-7371-2022-INIT/en/pdf.

Council on Foreign Relations. "Candidate Tracker: Donald J. Trump, 2020." https://www.cfr. org/election2020/candidate-tracker/donald-j.-trump.

Counterpoint and OSEPI. *Green Wedge? Mapping Dissent Against Climate Policy in Europe.* Counterpoint, 2021. https://counterpoint.uk.com/projects/climate-policy-in-a-post-covid-19-europe/.

182 BIBLIOGRAPHY

Curato, N., J. Vrydagh, and A. Bächtiger. (2020) "Democracy without Shortcuts: Introduction to the Special Issue." *Journal of Deliberative Democracy* 16, no. 2 (2020): 1–9.

De Tollenaere, M. "Development Assistance in Different Political Regime Contexts." *Carnegie Europe*, January 24, 2023.

De Wilde, P. "The Quality of Representative Claims: Uncovering a Weakness in the Defence of the Liberal World Order." *Political Studies* 68, no. 2 (2019): 271–292.

Delina, L. "Climate Mobilizations and Democracy: The Promise of Scaling Community Energy Transitions in a Deliberative System." *Journal of Environmental Policy and Planning* 22, no. 1 (2020): 30–42.

Delina, L. *Emancipatory Climate Actions: Strategies from Histories.* New York: Palgrave Pivot, 2019.

Della Porta, D. *Mobilizing for Democracy: Comparing 1989 and 2011.* Oxford: Oxford University Press, 2014.

Democracy Reporting International. *Democracy as an Aspect of Security Policy: Perspectives from Europe and Beyond.* Berlin: Democracy Reporting International, 2023.

di Cesare, D. *The Time of Revolt.* Cambridge: Polity, 2022.

Diamond, L. "All Democracy Is Global." *Foreign Affairs*, September/October 2022.

Diamond, L. "Democracy's Arc: From Resurgent to Imperiled." *Journal of Democracy* 33, no. 1 (January 2022): 163–179.

Diamond, L. "Democratic Regression in Comparative Perspective: Scope, Methods, and Causes." *Democratization* 28, no. 1 (2020): 22–42.

Drezner, D. "Turns Out Covid-19 Didn't Reshape Global Politics." *Foreign Policy*, September 29, 2022.

Dudley, H., A. Jordan, and I. Lorenzoni. "Independent Expert Advisory Bodies Facilitate Ambitious Climate Policy Responses." *ScienceBrief Review*, March 2021.

Dunt, I. *How to Be a Liberal: The Story of Freedom and the Fight for its Survival.* Kingston upon Thames: Canbury Press, 2022.

Eckersley, R. "Ecological Democracy and the Rise and Decline of Liberal Democracy: Looking Back, Looking Forward." *Environmental Politics* 29, no. 2 (2020): 214–234.

Economist Intelligence Unit. *Democracy Index 2021: the China Challenge*, 2022. https://www.eiu.com/n/campaigns/democracy-index-2021/.

Economist Intelligence Unit. *Democracy Index 2022: Frontline Democracy and the Battle for Ukraine*, 2023. https://www.eiu.com/n/campaigns/democracy-index-2022/.

Edelman Trust Barometer. Accessed February 20, 2024. https://www.edelman.com/trust/2021-trust-barometer.

Eligon, J. "South Africa and Russia Are Old Friends—A War Isn't Going to Change That." *New York Times*, February 17, 2023.

Emmott, B. *The Fate of the West.* New York: Profile Books, 2017.

Encarnación, O. "Latin America's Abortion Rights Breakthrough." *Journal of Democracy* 33, no. 4 (2022): 89–103.

Energy Democracy Alliance. www.energy-democracy.net.

ESO, *Future Energy Scenarios 2022.* https://www.nationalgrideso.com/future-energy/future-energy-scenarios.

European Commission. "Social Europe: Eurobarometer Survey Shows Europeans Support Stronger Social Policies and More Social Spending." February 6, 2023. https://ec.europa.eu/social/main.jsp?catId=89&furtherNews=yes&newsId=10509&langId=en.

European Commission and High Representative. European Economic Security Strategy, 2023. https://eur-lex.europa.eu/legal-content/EN/TXT/?uri=CELEX%3A52023JC0020.

European Democracy Hub. "European Democracy Support Annual Review 2021." *Carnegie Europe*, January 24, 2022.

European Democracy Hub. "European Democracy Support Annual Review 2022." *Carnegie Europe*, January 30, 2023.

Extinction Rebellion. Accessed April 27, 2023. https://rebellion.global/.

BIBLIOGRAPHY 183

Extinction Rebellion (UK). Accessed April 27, 2023. https://www.xrdemocracy.uk/.

Fagan, M., and L. Clancy. "Among European Right-Wing Populists, Favorable Views of Russia and Putin Are Down Sharply." *Pew Research Center*, September23, 2022. https://www.pewresearch.org/fact-tank/2022/09/23/among-european-right-wing-populists-favorable-views-of-russia-and-putin-are-down-sharply/.

Falanga, R. *Citizen Participation during the Covid-19 Pandemic*. Bonn: Friedrich Ebert Stiftung, 2020. https://repositorio.ul.pt/bitstream/10451/45726/1/ICS_RFalanga_Citzen.pdf.

Feldstein, S. *The Rise of Digital Repression: How Technology is Reshaping Power, Politics, and Resistance*. Oxford: Oxford University Press, 2021.

Feldstein, S., E. Ferreyra, D. Krivokapić, and B. Kerley. "The Global Struggle over AI Surveillance." *National Endowment for Democracy*, 2022. https://www.ned.org/wp-content/uploads/2022/06/Global-Struggle-Over-AI-Surveillance-Emerging-Trends-Democratic-Responses.pdf.

Ferguson, N. *Doom: The Politics of Catastrophe*. New York: Penguin, 2021.

Fivenson, A., G. Petrenko, V. Vichova, and A. Polescuk. *Shielding Democracy: Civil Society Adaptations to Kremlin Disinformation about Ukraine*. Washington, DC: National Endowment for Democracy, 2023.

Flores, A., J. C. Cole, S. Dickert, K. Eom, G. M. Jiga-Boy, T. Kogut, R. Loria, M. Mayorga, E. J. Pedersen, B. Pereira, E. Rubaltelli, D. K. Sherman, P. Slovic, D. Västfjäll, and L. Van Boven. "Politicians Polarize and Experts Depolarize Public Support for COVID-19 Management Policies Across Countries." *PNAS* (2022). https://www.pnas.org/doi/10.1073/pnas.2117543119.

Foa, R. S., A. Klassen, M. Slade, A. Rand, and R. Collins. *The Global Satisfaction with Democracy Report 2020*. Cambridge: Centre for the Future of Democracy, 2020. https://www.cam.ac.uk/system/files/report2020_003.pdf.

Foroohar, R.. "After Neoliberalism: All Economics Is Local." *Foreign Affairs*, October 28, 2022. https://www.foreignaffairs.com/united-states/after-neoliberalism-all-economics-is-local-rana-foroohar.

Forum 2000, Prague, September 2022.

Freedom House. *Freedom in the World 2024 The Mounting Damage of Flawed Elections and Armed Conflict*, 2024. https://freedomhouse.org/report/freedom-world/2022/global-expansion-authoritarian-rule.

Fridays for Future. Accessed April 27, 2023. https://fridaysforfuture.org/.

Frontline. *Annual Report 2021*. https://www.frontlineplc.cy/annual-report-2021/.

Fukuyama, F. *The Origins of Political Order: From Prehuman Times to the French Revolution*. New York: Farrar, Straus and Giroux, 2011.

Fukuyama, F. "The Pandemic and Political Order: It Takes a State." *Foreign Affairs* 99, no. 4 (July/August 2020): 26–30.

Gabor, D. "The European Green Deal Will Bypass the Poor and Go Straight to the Rich." *The Guardian*, February 19, 2020.

Gabriel Vasquez, J. "Mas alla de las ideologías: como hablar de Ucrania en America Latina." *El Pais*, February 2, 2023.

Garton Ash, T., I. Krastev, and M. Leonard. "United West, Divided from the Rest: Global Public Opinion One Year into Russia's War on Ukraine." *European Council on Foreign Relations*, February 22, 2023. https://ecfr.eu/publication/united-west-divided-from-the-rest-global-public-opinion-one-year-into-russias-war-on-ukraine/.

Gerbaudo, P. *The Great Recoil: Politics after Populism and Pandemic*. London: Verso, 2021.

Gerbaudo, P. "A Post-Neoliberal Paradigm Is Emerging: Conversation with Felicia Wong." *Agenda Publica*, November 4, 2022. https://agendapublica.elpais.com/noticia/18303/post-neoliberal-paradigm-is-emerging-conversation-with-felicia-wong.

Gerschewski, J. "II. Autocratization and Democratic Backsliding: Taking Stock of a Recent Debate." In *Democracy Promotion in Times of Uncertainty: Trends and Challenges*, 5–9. Frankfurt: Peace Research Institute Frankfurt, 2018), 6.

184 BIBLIOGRAPHY

Gerschewski, J. "Erosion or Decay? Conceptualizing Causes and Mechanisms of Democratic Regression." *Democratization* 28, no. 1 (2021): 43–62.

Global Assembly. "Community Assembly Toolkit." Accessed February 20, 2024. https://globala ssembly.org/resources/brand-imagery/GA_DIY-Toolkit_v5.1.pdf.

Global Assembly. "People's Declaration for the Sustainable Future of Planet Earth." Last updated December 18, 2021. https://globalassembly.org/declaration.

Global Assembly. *Report of the 2021 Global Assembly on the Climate and Ecological Crisis: Giving Everyone a Seat at the Global Governance Table*, 2022. https://globalassembly. org/resources/downloads/GlobalAssembly2021-FullReport.pdf.

GlobalFocus. *Democratic Resilience Index*. Bucharest: GlobalFocus Center, 2021. https://www. global-focus.eu/wp-content/uploads/2021/09/Democratic-Resilience-Index.pdf.

Global Witness. "Last Line of Defence." *Global Witness*, September 13, 2021. https://www. globalwitness.org/en/campaigns/environmental-activists/last-line-defence/.

Gonzalez, M., and F. Manetto. "La comunidad iberoamericana se consolida pese a sus divisiones y debilidades." *El Pais*, March 25, 2023.

Gopaldas, R. *Will the Invasion of Ukraine Change Russia-Africa Relations?* Washington, DC: Carnegie Endowment for International Peace, 2023.

Government of the United Kingdom. "Integrated Review Refresh 2023: Responding to a More Contested and Volatile World." London: His Majesty's Government, March 2023.

Graham, M., and M. Svolik. "Democracy in America? Partisanship, Polarization, and the Robustness of Support for Democracy in the United States." *American Political Science Review* 114, no. 2 (May 2020): 392–409.

Granados, O. "Las minas españolas resucitan." *El Pais*, August 21, 2021. https://elpais.com/ economia/2021-08-22/las-minas-espanolas-resucitan.html.

Gray, J. *The New Leviathians: Thoughts after Liberalism*. London: Penguin, 2023.

Gueorguiev, D. *Retrofitting Leninism: Participation Without Democracy in China*. Oxford: Oxford University Press, 2021.

Guriev, S., and D. Treisman. *Spin Dictators: The Changing Face of Tyranny in the 21st Century*. Princeton, NJ: Princeton University Press, 2022.

Haass, R., and C. Kupchan. "The New Concert of Powers." *Foreign Affairs*, March 23, 2021.

Hall, D., S. Kaye, and C. Morgan. "How the Pandemic Has Accelerated the Shift Towards Participatory Public Authorities." In *Democracy in a Pandemic: Participation in Response to Crisis*, ed. T. Hughes and G. Smith, 145. London: University of Westminster Press, 2021.

Hall, P., and C. Taylor. "Political Science and the Three New Institutionalisms." *Political Studies* 44, no 4 (1996): 936–957.

Hamid, S. *The Problem of Democracy*. Oxford: Oxford University Press, 2022.

Henley, J. "Energy Citizenship: Europe's Communities Forging a Low-Carbon Future." *The Guardian*, September 3, 2022. https://www.theguardian.com/environment/2022/sep/03/ energy-citizenship-europes-communities-forging-a-low-carbon-future.

Hicken, A., S. Baltz, and F. Vasselai. "Chapter VI: Political Institutions and Democracy." In *Why Democracies Develop and Decline*, ed. M. Coppedge, A. Edgell, C. Knutsen, and S. Lindberg, 161–184. Cambridge: Cambridge University Press, 2020.

Hickman, L. "James Lovelock: Humans Are too Stupid to Prevent Climate Change." *The Guardian*, March 29, 2010.

Hicks, J. *Donor Support for "Informal Social Movements."* K4D Helpdesk Report 1140, *Institute of Development Studies* (2022). doi: 10.19088/K4D.2022.085.

Higgott, R., and S. Reich. "The Age of Fuzzy Bifurcation: Lessons from the Pandemic and the Ukraine War." *Global Policy* 13, no. 5 (2022): 627–639.

Hollingsworth, J., and J. Kwon. "South Korea Sees the Largest Turnout in Almost 30 Years in Election Held During Coronavirus Outbreak." *CNN*, April 16, 2020. https://www.cnn.com/ 2020/04/15/asia/south-korea-election-intl-hnk/index.html.

Huang, K., and M. Han. "Did China's Street Protests End Harsh COVID Policies?" *Council on Foreign Relations*, December 14, 2022. https://www.cfr.org/blog/did-chinas-street-prote sts-end-harsh-covid-policies.

BIBLIOGRAPHY   185

Huber, M. *Climate Change as Class War: Building Socialism on a Warming Planet*. London: Verso, 2022.

Ikenberry, J. "The Next Liberal Order." *Foreign Affairs*, June 9, 2020. https://www.foreignaffairs.com/articles/united-states/2020-06-09/next-liberal-order.

International Monetary Fund *World Economic Outlook 2023 Navigating Global Divergences*, IMF, 2023.

Independent Commission for Aid Impact. "The UK's Approach to Democracy and Human Rights." January 2023. https://icai.independent.gov.uk/wp-content/uploads/The-UKs-approach-to-democracy-and-human-rights_ICAI-review.pdf.

Ing-wen, T. "President Delivers Video Address at Copenhagen Democracy Summit." *YouTube*, June 10, 2022. https://www.youtube.com/watch?v=LXjdGhIgyGE&t=492s.

International Center for Ukrainian Victory. Accessed April 28, 2023. https://ukrainianvictory.org/?fbclid=IwAR3l2Cjgxvd7cZXTaV5bxjQhshxiPMSLseaG0k7kdchXeiOB7RZri8q3vG4.

International IDEA. "Democratic Engagement after Two Summits for Democracy." Stockholm: International IDEA, 2023.

International IDEA. *The Global State of Democracy Indices*. Accessed April 28, 2023. https://www.idea.int/gsod-indices/covid19globalmonitor.

International IDEA. *Summit for Democracy Commitment Dashboard*. Accessed February 20, 2014. https://summitfordemocracyresources.eu/commitment-dashboard/.

International IDEA. "Taking Stock of Global Democratic Trends Before and During the Covid-19 Pandemic." December 9, 2020. https://www.idea.int/publications/catalogue/global-democratic-trends-before-and-during-covid19.

IPCC. Sixth Assessment Report. Geneva: Intergovernmental Panel on Climate Change, 2022.

Jack, V. "Ukraine War Heats up Energy Poverty Debate." *Politico*, May 17, 2022.

Jagtiani, S., and S. Wellek. "In the Shadow of Ukraine: India's Choices and Challenges." *Survival* 64, no. 3 (2022): 29–48.

Jensen, L. "Avoiding 'Too Little Too Late' on International Debt Relief." *United Nations Development Programme*, October 11, 2022. https://www.undp.org/publications/dfs-avoiding-too-little-too-late-international-debt-relief.

Jones, E. "From the End of History to the Retreat of Liberalism." *Survival* 59, no. 6 (2017): 165–174.

Jones, E. "War in Ukraine: Democratic Realism." *Encompass*, August 2022. https://encompass-europe.com/comment/the-war-in-ukraine-democratic-realism.

Jourdain, E. *Esprit—La Démocratie des Communs*. *Revue Esprit* 6 (2022): 31–34. https://www.cairn.info/revue-esprit-2022-6-page-31.htm.

Juczewska, M. "Guests Not Refugees: Massive Grassroots Humanitarian Action in Poland Supporting the Ukrainian War Refugees." *Institute of World Politics*, March 16, 2022. https://www.iwp.edu/articles/2022/03/16/guests-not-refugees-massive-grassroots-humanitarian-action-in-poland-supporting-the-ukrainian-war-refugees/.

Keane, J. *The Shortest History of Democracy*. Melbourne: Schwartz Books, 2022.

Kempf, J. "Has democracy regressed back to 1986?" *Democracy Paradox*, March 16, 2023.

Kiel Institute for the World Economy. "Ukraine Support Tracker." Last updated February 24, 2023. https://www.ifw-kiel.de/topics/war-against-ukraine/ukraine-support-tracker/.

Kleinfeld, R. "Five Strategies to Support US Democracy." Washington, DC: Carnegie Endowment for International Peace, 2022.

Knutsen, C., and S. Skaaning. "Chapter II: The Ups and Downs of Democracy, 1789–2018." In *Why Democracies Develop and Decline*, edited by M. Coppedge, A. Edgell, C. Knutsen, and S. Lindberg, 29–54. Cambridge: Cambridge University Press, 2022.

Konzept #19: What We Must Do to Rebuild. Frankfurt: Deutsche Bank Research, 2022.

Kreilinger, V. "Next Generation EU and National Parliaments: Taxation without Sufficient Representation?" In *Making EU Representative Democracy Fit for the Future*, ed. G. von Sydow and V. Kreilinger, 45–60. Stockholm: Swedish Institute for European Policy Studies, 2022.

186 BIBLIOGRAPHY

Kulin, J., I. Sevä, and R. Dunlap. "Nationalist Ideology, Right-Wing Populism, and Public Views about Climate Change in Europe." *Environmental Politics* 30, no. 7 (2021): 1111–1134.

Kutlay, M., and Z. Onis. "Liberal Democracy on the Edge? Anxieties in a Shifting Global (Dis) order, *Alternatives: Global, Local, Political* 48, no. 1 (2022). https://doi.org/10.1177/030437 54221096511.

Kyiv International Institute of Sociology. *Omnibus Opinion Poll,* December 2022. https://euro maidanpress.com/2023/01/13/trust-in-ukraines-president-increased-three-fold-in-2022-army-still-most-trusted-institution-poll/.

Kynge, J. "China Hit By Surge in Belt and Road Bad Loans." *Financial Times,* April 16, 2023.

Lakhani, N. "A Just Transition Depends on Energy Systems That Work for Everyone." *The Guardian,* November 13, 2022. https://www.theguardian.com/environment/2022/nov/12/cop27-dash-for-gas-africa-energy-colonialism.

Lamour, C., and P. Carls. "When COVID-19 Circulates in Right-Wing Populist Discourse: The Contribution of a Global Crisis to European Meta-Populism at the Cross-Border Regional Scale." *Journal of Contemporary European Studies* (2022). https://www.tandfonline.com/doi/full/10.1080/14782804.2022.2051001.

Langer, G. "Pandemic Surge Damages Trump, Boosting Biden's White House Bid: POLL." *ABC News,* July 19, 2020. https://abcnews.go.com/Politics/pandemic-surge-damages-trump-boosting-bidens-white-house/story?id=71779431.

Latour, B. *After Lockdown: A Metamorphosis.* Cambridge: Polity, 2021.

Lawlor, M. *Final Warning: Death Threats and Killings of Human Rights Defenders: Report of the Special Rapporteur on the Situation of Human Rights Defenders.* Geneva: United Nations, 2021.

Leali, G. "France and Germany Push for Fast-Track Subsidies After US Row." *Politico,* December 19, 2022.

Lech, M. "Mutual Aid and Self-Organisation: What We Can Learn from the Rise of DIY Responses to the Pandemic." In *Democracy in a Pandemic: Participation in Response to Crisis,* ed. T. Hughes and G. Smith, 124–132. London: University of Westminster Press, 2021, 124–132.

Lee, T. "The Rise of Technocracy and the COVID-19 Pandemic in Taiwan: Courts, Human Rights, and the Protection of Vulnerable Populations." *German Law Journal* 22, no. 6 (September 2021): 1115–1132.

Lent, J. "Coronavirus Spells the End of the Neoliberal Era. What's Next?" *Open Democracy,* April 12, 2020. https://www.opendemocracy.net/en/transformation/coronavirus-spells-the-end-of-the-neoliberal-era-whats-next/.

Leonard, M. "Xi Jinping's Idea of World Order." *European Council on Foreign Relations,* April 5, 2023. https://ecfr.eu/article/xi-jinpings-idea-of-world-order/.

LePan, N. "Rare Earth Elements: Where in the World Are They?" *Visual Capitalist,* November 23, 2021. https://www.visualcapitalist.com/rare-earth-elements-where-in-the-world-are-they/.

Li, E. "Eric Li on the Failure of Liberal Democracy and the Rise of China's Way." *The Economist,* December 8, 2021. https://www.economist.com/by-invitation/2021/12/08/eric-li-on-the-failure-of-liberal-democracy-and-the-rise-of-chinas-way.

Li, Y., and J. Shapiro. *China Goes Green: Coercive Environmentalism for a Troubled Planet.* Cambridge: Polity, 2020.

Lieven, A. *Climate Change and the Nation State: The Realist Case.* London: Allen Lane, 2020.

Lindvall, D. *Democracy and the Challenge of Climate Change.* Stockholm: International IDEA, 2021.

Litobarski, J. "What Comes after Neoliberalism? A New Social Contract." *Friends of Europe,* January 25, 2022. https://www.friendsofeurope.org/insights/what-comes-after-neoliberal ism-a-new-social-contract/.

Lloyd Parry, R. "Cold War Fears of Mongolia, Caught between Two Big Brothers." *The Times,* March 14, 2023.

BIBLIOGRAPHY 187

Luce, E. *The Retreat of Western Liberalism*. New York: Grove Atlantic, 2017.

Macaes, B. *Geopolitics for the End Times: From the Pandemic to the Climate Crisis*. London: Hurst, 2021, 54–55.

Macfarlane, L. "Covid Has Forced a Neoliberal Retreat. But State Intervention Isn't Always Progressive." *University College London News*, April 29, 2021. https://www.ucl.ac.uk/news/2021/apr/opinion-covid-has-forced-neoliberal-retreat-state-intervention-isnt-always-progressive.

Machin, A. "Democracy, Disagreement, Disruption: Agonism and the Environmental State." *Environmental Politics* 29, no. 1 (2020): 155–172.

Macron, E. "Address to the Nation." *Elysée*, March 2, 2022. https://www.elysee.fr/en/emmanuel-macron/2022/03/02/address-to-the-nation.

Malloch-Brown, M. "The Return of Conflict, the Retreat of Democracy." Speech at the Royal College of Defence Studies, London, June 26, 2023.

Mann, G., and J. Wainwright. *Climate Leviathan: A Political Theory of Our Planetary Future*. London: Verso, 2018.

Mason, P. "Ukraine: The Politics of Dying." *Medium*, February 25, 2022. https://medium.com/mosquito-ridge/ukraine-the-politics-of-dying-a37f9f1fe6e9.

Mathieson, K. "Climate Activists Have a New Target: Civilians." *Politico*, May 2, 2023.

Mathieu, E., H. Ritchie, L. Rodés-Guirao, C. Appel, D. Gavrilov, C. Giattino, J. Hasell, B. Macdonald, S. Dattani, D. Beltekian, E. Ortiz-Ospina, and M. Roser. "Policy Responses to the Coronavirus Pandemic." *Our World in Data*, accessed February 20, 2024. https://ourworldindata.org/policy-responses-covid.

Mazower, M. "Keeping the World at Bay: Does Globalism Subvert Democracy or Strengthen It?" *Foreign Affairs*, May/June 2023.

Mazzucato, M. *Mission Economy: A Moonshot Guide to Changing Capitalism*. London: Allen Lane, 2021.

McClure, M. "'Here for Each Other': How COVID-19 Has Changed Community Organizing." *The Chicago Maroon*, February 25, 2021. https://chicagomaroon.com/28315/grey-city/covid-19-changed-community-organizing/.

Mellier, C., and R. Wilson. *A Global Citizens' Assembly on the Climate and Ecological Crisis*. Brussels: Carnegie Europe, 2023.

Menon, S. "The Fantasy of the Free World." *Foreign Affairs*, April 4, 2022. https://www.foreignaffairs.com/articles/united-states/2022-04-04/fantasy-free-world.

Merkel, W., and A. Lührmann. "Resilience of Democracies: Responses to Illiberal and Authoritarian Challenges." *Democratization* 28, no. 5 (2021): 869–884.

Meyer, B. "Populist-Led Governments Are More Likely to Be Punished by the Electorate for Rising Covid-19 Deaths." *LSE*, January 28, 2022. https://blogs.lse.ac.uk/europpblog/2022/01/28/populist-led-governments-are-more-likely-to-be-punished-by-the-electorate-for-rising-covid-19-deaths/

Milanese, N., K. Nicolaidis, and R. Youngs. "Informal Civil Society: A Booster for European Democracy?" *Carnegie Europe*, March 23, 2022.

Miliband, D. "The Global Battle Against Impunity." The Rachman Review podcast, *Financial Times*, January 19, 2023. https://shows.acast.com/therachmanreview/episodes/the-global-battle-against-impunity.

Molander, M. "European Leaders Should Raise Human Rights Concerns: Modi." *Human Rights Watch*, May 3, 2022.

Møller J., A. Schmotz, and S. Skaaning. "Economic Crisis and Democratic Breakdown in the Interwar Years: A Reassessment." *Historical Social Research* 40, no. 2 (2015): 301–318.

Moody, O. "Olaf Scholz: War in Ukraine Has Made Germany Realise Democracy Is Worth Fighting For." *The Times*, July 18, 2022.

Moody, O. "With New Tanks and Jets Ukraine Can Win the War." *The Times*, September 2, 2022.

188 BIBLIOGRAPHY

Moore, F., K. Lacasse, K. J. Mach, Y. Ah Shin, L. J. Gross, and B. Beckage. "Determinants of Emissions Pathways in the Coupled Climate-Social System." *Nature* no. 603 (2022): 103–111.

Moore, M. *Democracy Hacked: How Technology is Destabilizing Global Politics.* London: Oneworld Publications, 2018.

Mounk, Y., and R. Foa. "The End of the Democratic Century." *Foreign Affairs*, March/April, 2018.

Mulgan, G. *Another World Is Possible: How to Reignite Social and Political Imagination.* London: Hurst, 2022.

Naatujuna, D. "Bridging the Gap Between Policy and Action." *UNDP Strategic Innovation*, March 10, 2022. https://medium.com/@undp.innovation/bridging-the-gap-between-policy-and-action-84335c48041.

National Conference on Citizenship. *National Conference on Citizenship 2020 Report.* Accessed February 20, 2024. https://ncoc.org/national-conference-on-citizenship-2020-report/.

NATO 2022 Strategic Concept. https://www.nato.int/nato_static_fl2014/assets/pdf/2022/6/pdf/290622-strategic-concept.pdf.

Nicholls, P. "Ukraine Plight Could Be Replicated in East Asia, Japan's Kishida Warns." *Reuters*, May 6, 2022. https://www.reuters.com/world/asia-pacific/peace-stability-taiwan-strait-is-critical-japanese-pm-2022-05-05/.

Nord, M., F. Angiolillo, M. Lundstedt, F. Wiebrecht, and S. Lindberg. *When Autrocatization is Reversed: Episodes of Democratic Turnaround since 1900*, V-Dem working paper. Gothenburg: V-Dem Institute at University of Gothenburg, 2024.

Norris, P., and R. Inglehart. *Cultural Backlash: Trump, Brexit, and Authoritarian Populism.* Cambridge: Cambridge University Press, 2019.

O'Sullivan, M. *The Levelling: What's Next After Globalization.* New York: PublicAffairs, 2019.

O'Connor, B., and D. Cooper. "Ideology and the Foreign Policy and Barack Obama: A Liberal-Realist Approach to International Affairs." *Presidential Studies Quarterly* 51, no. 3 (2021): 635–666.

Office of the Spokesperson. "The U.S. Strategy to Prevent Conflict and Promote Stability: Priority Countries and Region." *Media note, US Department of State*, April 1, 2022. https://www.state.gov/the-u-s-strategy-to-prevent-conflict-and-promote-stability-priority-countries-and-region/.

Onuch, O. "Why Ukrainians are Rallying Around Democracy." *Journal of Democracy* 33, no. 4 (2022): 37–46.

Open Government Partnership. "Collecting Open Government Approaches to COVID-19." Accessed February 20, 2024. https://www.opengovpartnership.org/collecting-open-government-approaches-to-covid-19/.

Ortiz, I., S. Burke, M. Barrada, and H. Cortes. *World Protests: A Study of Key Protest Issues in the 21st Century.* London: Palgrave Macmillan, 2021.

Osborn, C. "A Disjointed Western Hemisphere Gathers." *Foreign Policy*, June 10, 2022. https://foreignpolicy.com/2022/06/10/summit-americas-biden-los-angeles-boycotts-health-migration/.

Osorio, C. "Francia Márquez visita una Buenaventura que espera su nueva oportunidad." *El Pais*, October 22, 2022. https://elpais.com/america-colombia/2022-10-22/francia-marquez-busca-una-segunda-oportunidad-para-buenaventura.html.

Pacheco-Vega, R., and A. Murdie. "When Do Environmental NGOs Work? A Test of the Conditional Effectiveness of Environmental Advocacy." *Environmental Politics* 30, no. 2 (2020): 1–22.

Packer, G. "A New Theory of American Power." *The Atlantic*, November 21, 2022.

Pee, R. "Obama Has Put National Security Ahead of Promoting Democracy Abroad." *The Conversation*, August 10, 2016. https://theconversation.com/obama-has-put-national-security-ahead-of-promoting-democracy-abroad-62711.

People's Plan for Nature. Accessed February 20, 2024. https://peoplesplanfornature.org/sites/default/files/2022-09/People%27s-Plan-for-Nature-Conversation-guide_1.pdf.

BIBLIOGRAPHY 189

Pickering, J., K. Bäckstrand, and D. Schlosberg. "Between Environmental and Ecological Democracy: Theory and Practice at the Democracy-Environment Nexus." *Journal of Environmental Policy & Planning* 22, no. 1 (2020): 1–15.

Pierson, P. *Politics in Time*. Princeton, NJ: Princeton University Press, 2004.

Pildes, R. "The Age of Political Fragmentation." *Journal of Democracy* 32, no. 4 (2021): 146–159.

Pogrebinschi, T. *30 Years of Democratic Innovation in Latin America*. Berlin: WZB Berlin Social Science Center, 2021.

Pogrebinschi, T. *Innovating Democracy? The Means and Ends of Citizen Participation in Latin America*. Cambridge: Cambridge University Press, 2023.

Polanyi, K. *The Great Transformation: The Political and Economic Origins of Our Time*. New York: Farrar & Rinehart, 1944.

Politico Europe. *Brussels Playbook*, January 12, 2023. https://www.politico.eu/newsletter/brussels-playbook/europeans-back-ukraine-hijacking-single-market-arena-quits/.

Posse, L., and E. Chaimite. "Perceptions of Covid-19 in Mozambique and the Influence of 'Intermediaries.'" *Institute of Development Studies*, November 12, 2020.

Povitkina, M. "The Limits of Democracy in Tackling Climate Change." *Environmental Politics* 27, no. 3 (2018): 411–432.

Power, S. "How Democracy Can Win." *Foreign Affairs*, February 16, 2023.

Rahman, M., N. Anbarci, and M. Ulubasoglu. "'Storm Autocracies': Islands as Natural Experiments." *Journal of Development Economics* 159 (November 2022). https://doi.org/10.1016/j.jdeveco.2022.102982.

Rapeli, L., and V. Koskimaa. "Concerned and Willing to Pay? Comparing Policymaker and Citizen Attitudes towards Climate Change." *Environmental Politics* 31, no. 3 (2022): 542–551.

RevDem. "Realist Thought Between Empire-Building and Restraint: Matthew Specter on Why a Flawed Tradition Endures." May 7, 2022. https://revdem.ceu.edu/2022/05/07/realist-thought-between-empire-building-and-restraint-matthew-specter-on-why-a-flawed-tradition-endures/.

Ringe, N., and L. Renno, eds. *Populists and the Pandemic: How Populists Around the World Responded to COVID-19*. London: Routledge, 2022.

Rockström, J., W. Steffen, K. Noone, A. Persson, F. S. Chapin III, E. F. Lambin, T. M. Lenton, M. Scheffer, C. Folke, H. J. Schellnhuber, B. Nykvist, C. A. de Wit, T. Hughes, S. van der Leeuw, H. Rodhe, S. Sörlin, P. K. Snyder, R. Costanza, U. Svedin, M. Falkenmark, L. Karlberg, R. W. Corell, V. J. Fabry, J. Hansen, B. Walker, D. Liverman, K. Richardson, P. Crutzen, and J. A. Foley. "A Safe Operating Space for Humanity." *Nature* 461 (September 2009): 472–475.

Rogin, J. "Zelensky Calls for International Support for Taiwan Before China Attacks." *Washington Post*, June 11, 2022. https://www.washingtonpost.com/opinions/2022/06/11/zelensky-calls-for-support-taiwan-before-china-attacks-ukraine-russia/.

Romero-Vidal, X., R. Foa, A. Klassen, L. S. Fenner, M. Quednau, and J. F. Concha. "The Great Reset: Public Opinion, Populism, and the Pandemic." *Centre for the Future of Democracy* (2022). https://www.bennettinstitute.cam.ac.uk/publications/great-reset.

Ross, M., B. Ogembo, S. Y. Woo, and F. Rey. "Resisting Colonisation, Avoiding Tropicalisation: Deliberative Wave in the Global South." *Deliberative Democracy Digest*, May 3, 2022. https://www.publicdeliberation.net/resisting-colonisation-avoiding-tropicalisation-deliberative-wave-in-the-global-south/.

Russo, L., and M. Bräutigam. *Harmonized Eurobarometer 2004–2021*. GESIS Leibniz Institute for the Social Sciences, 2023.

Saad-Filho, A. "Coronavirus Crisis and the End of Neoliberalism." *Conter*, April 17, 2020. https://www.conter.scot/2020/4/17/coronavirus-crisis-and-the-end-of-neoliberalism/.

Sabeel Rahman, K. "Statecraft and Policy Design in the New Political Economy." *Hewlett Foundation New Common Sense*, May 2023.

BIBLIOGRAPHY

Sandher, J., and H. Kleider. "Coronavirus Has Brought the Welfare State Back, and It Might Be Here to Stay." *The Conversation*, June 24, 2020. https://theconversation.com/coronavirus-has-brought-the-welfare-state-back-and-it-might-be-here-to-stay-138564.

Savage, L. *The Dead Center*. New York: OR Books, 2022.

Schake, K. "Putin Accidentally Revitalized the West's Liberal Order." *The Atlantic*, February 28, 2022. https://www.theatlantic.com/international/archive/2022/02/vladimir-putin-ukra ine-invasion-liberal-order/622950/.

Schmitt, H., and E. Scholz. *The Mannheim Eurobarometer Trend File, 1970–2002*. Europäische Sozialforschung, Mannheim: Mannheimer Zentrum für, 2005.

Shearman, D., and J. Smith. *The Climate Change Challenge and the Failure of Democracy*. Westport, CT: Praeger, 2007.

Siccardi, F. "Will Green Activism Save Turkey's Democracy?" *Carnegie Europe*, June 30, 2022. https://carnegieeurope.eu/2022/06/30/will-green-activism-save-turkey-s-democr acy-pub-87413.

Silander, D. "Building Democracy: National and International Factors." In *Globalization*, ed. G. Y. Wang. London: Intech Open, 2017. doi: 10.5772/intechopen.71984.

SIPRI. "Addressing the Climate Crisis and Protecting the Future of Democracy." *YouTube*, May 23, 2022. https://www.youtube.com/watch?v=UQ1kyo0OxVk.

Smith, G. *Can Democracy Safeguard the Future?* Cambridge: Polity Press, 2021.

Snyder, T. "Ukraine Holds the Future." *Foreign Affairs*, September/October 2022.

Soifer, H. "The Causal Logic of Critical Junctures." *Comparative Political Studies* 45, no. 2 (2012): 1572–1597.

Spektor, M. "In Defence of the Fence-Sitters." *Foreign Affairs*, May/June 2023.

Staggenborg, S. *Grassroots Environmentalism*. Cambridge: Cambridge University Press, 2020.

Stuenkel, O. "How Brazil's Democracy Stepped Back from the Cliff." *The Globe and Mail*, October 31, 2022. https://www.theglobeandmail.com/opinion/article-how-brazils-democr acy-stepped-back-from-the-cliff/.

Susova-Salminen, V., and I. Svihlikova, eds. "The Covid-19 Pandemic: The End of Neoliberal Globalization?" *Transform Europe*, 2020. https://transform-network.net/wp-content/uplo ads/2023/05/ebook_the_covid-19_pandemic_en_version_final.pdf.

Suss, R. "Horizontal Experimentalism: Rethinking Democratic Resistance." *Philosophy and Social Criticism* 48, no. 8 (2021). doi: 10.1177/01914537211033016.

Szulecki, K., and I. Overland. "Energy Democracy as a Process, an Outcome and a Goal: a Conceptual Review." *Energy Research and Social Science* 69 (November 2020). https://doi. org/10.1016/j.erss.2020.101768.

Teddy, G. "Policy and Implementation Gap: A Multi-Country Perspective." *International Journal of Advanced Research* 7 (2019): 678–704.

Temin, J. "The US Doesn't Need Another Democracy Summit." *Foreign Affairs*, March 27, 2023.

The Economist. *The New Interventionism*. Special report, January 15, 2022. https://www. economist.com/special-report/2022-01-15.

The White House. "National Security Strategy." October 2022. https://www.whitehouse.gov/ wp-content/uploads/2022/10/Biden-Harris-Administrations-National-Security-Strategy-10.2022.pdf.

The White House. "Remarks by National Security Advisor Jake Sullivan on Renewing American Economic Leadership at the Brookings Institution." April 27, 2023. https://www. whitehouse.gov/briefing-room/speeches-remarks/2023/04/27/remarks-by-national-secur ity-advisor-jake-sullivan-on-renewing-american-economic-leadership-at-the-brookings-institution/.

The White House. "Remarks by President Biden at the Summit for Democracy Virtual Plenary on Democracy Delivering on Global Challenges." March 29, 2023. https://www.whitehouse. gov/briefing-room/speeches-remarks/2023/03/29/remarks-by-president-biden-at-the-summit-for-democracy-virtual-plenary-on-democracy-delivering-on-global-challenges/.

BIBLIOGRAPHY 191

Ther, P. *How the West Lost the Peace: The Great Transformation since the Cold War.* Cambridge: Polity Press, 2023.

Thompson, H. *Disorder: Hard Times in the 21st Century.* New York: Oxford University Press, 2022.

Tomini, L. "Don't Think of a Wave! A Research Note about the Current Autocratization Debate." *Democratization* 28, no. 6 (2021): 1191–1201.

Tooze, A. "Democracy in the Age of Polycrisis with Adam Tooze." *ECFR podcast*, June 9, 2023. https://ecfr.eu/podcasts/episode/democracy-in-the-age-of-polycrisis-with-adam-tooze/.

Tooze, A. "Has Covid Ended the Neoliberal Era?" *The Guardian*, September 2, 2021. https://www.theguardian.com/news/2021/sep/02/covid-and-the-crisis-of-neoliberalism.

Tooze, A. *Shutdown: How Covid Shook the World's Economy.* New York: Viking, 2021.

Tooze, A. "Welcome to the World of the Polycrisis." *Financial Times*, October 28, 2022. https://www.ft.com/content/498398e7-11b1-494b-9cd3-6d669dc3de33.

Tormey, S. *The End of Representative Politics.* Cambridge: Polity Press, 2015.

Torney, D. "Deliberative Mini-Publics and the European Green Deal in Turbulent Times: The Irish and French Climate Assemblies." *Politics and Governance* 9, no. 3 (2021). https://www.cogitatiopress.com/politicsandgovernance/article/view/4382.

Trubowitz, P., and B. Burgoon. *Geopolitics and Democracy: The Western Liberal Order from Foundation to Fracture.* New York: Oxford University Press, 2023.

Tucker, A. *Democracy Against Liberalism.* Cambridge: Polity Press, 2020.

United Kingdom Humanitarian Innovation Hub. "Enabling the Local Response: Emerging Humanitarian Priorities in Ukraine March-May 2022." June 2022. https://www.humanitarianoutcomes.org/sites/default/files/publications/ukraine_review_2022.pdf.

United Nations Climate Change. "Action for Climate Empowerment." Accessed February 20, 2024. https://unfccc.int/topics/education-youth/the-big-picture/what-is-action-for-climate-empowerment#eq-3.

United States Strategy to Prevent Conflict and Promote Stability. 2020. https://www.state.gov/wp-content/uploads/2021/01/2020-US-Strategy-to-Prevent-Conflict-and-Promote-Stability-508c-508.pdf.

V-Dem Institute. "The Case for Democracy Week: Combating Climate Change." *YouTube*, livestreamed on March 23, 2021. https://www.youtube.com/watch?v=Mcew0ahVO9E.

V-Dem Institute. *Democracy Report 2024, Democracy winning and losing at the ballot.* Gothenburg: V-Dem Institute at the University of Gothenburg, 2024.

V-Dem Institute. Pandemic Backsliding: Democracy During COVID-19 (March 2020 to June 2021). Accessed February 20, 2024. https://www.v-dem.net/pandem.html.

V-Dem Institute. *V-Party Dataset*, 2022. Accessed February 20, 2024. https://www.v-dem.net/data/v-party-dataset/.

Vachudova, M. "Ethnopopulism and Democratic Backsliding in Central Europe." *East European Politics* 36, no. 3 (2020): 318–340.

van Middelaar, L. *Pandemonium: Saving Europe.* Newcastle upon Tyne: Agenda Publishing, 2021.

Vanhercke, B., and A. Verdun. "The European Semester as Goldilocks: Macroeconomic Policy Coordination and the Recovery and Resilience Facility." *Journal of Common Market Studies* (2021). https://doi.org/10.1111/jcms.13267.

Vdovychenko, V. "Shaping Up Social Resistance: Zelenskyy's Approach to Rearranging Ukraine." In *Volodymyr Zelenskyy's Presidency and the Impact of the Russia-Ukraine War*, ed. A. Reichardt and T. Stepniewski, 61. Lublin: Institute of Central Europe, 2022.

Vince, G. *Nomad Century: How to Survive the Climate Upheaval.* London: Penguin, 2022.

von der Leyen, U., and J. Trudeau. "Joint Statement by President von der Leyen and Prime Minister Trudeau." *European Commission*, March 23, 2022. https://ec.europa.eu/commission/presscorner/detail/sv/statement_22_1989.

Way, L. "The Rebirth of the Liberal World Order." *Journal of Democracy* (March 2022). https://www.journalofdemocracy.org/the-rebirth-of-the-liberal-world-order/.

192 BIBLIOGRAPHY

Welzel, C., S. Kruse, and L. Brunkert. "Why the Future Is (Still) Democratic." *Journal of Democracy* 33, no. 1 (2022): 156–162.

Werner Müller, J. *RevDem podcast*, July 2021. https://www.youtube.com/watch?v=EpKy RWMNR60&list=PL_0phSnA7tyRLbTWOCpRA6poMQf4X20xm&index=37.

Wertheim, S. "The One Key Word Biden Needs to Invoke on Ukraine." *The Atlantic*, June 11, 2022.

Wilkinson, M. *Authoritarian Liberalism and the Transformation of Modern Europe.* New York: Oxford University Press, 2021.

Willis, R. *Too Hot to Handle? The Democratic Challenge of Climate Change.* Bristol: Bristol University Press, 2020.

Wolf, M. *The Crisis of Democratic Capitalism.* New York: Penguin, 2023.

Wu, G. "For Xi Jinping, the Economy Is No Longer the Priority." *Journal of Democracy* (2022). https://www.journalofdemocracy.org/for-xi-jinping-the-economy-is-no-longer-the-priority/.

Wunsch, N., and P. Blanchard. "Patterns of Democratic Backsliding in Third-Wave Democracies: a Sequence Analysis Perspective." *Democratization* 30, no. 2 (2023): 278–301.

Youngs, R. *The European Union and Global Politics.* New York: Macmillan, 2021.

Youngs, R., M. von Bülow, C. Buzasu, Y. Cherif, H. Halawa, M. Ho, M. Kademaunga, A. Larok, P. Marczewski, V. MJ, N. Shapovalova, J. Sombatpoosiri, and O. Zihnioglu. *Civil Society and Global Pandemic: Building Back Different.* Washington, DC: Carnegie Endowment for International Peace, 2021, https://carnegieendowment.org/2021/09/30/civil-society-and-global-pandemic-building-back-different-pub-85446.

Zahra, T. *Against the World: Anti-Globalism and Mass Politics between the World Wars.* New York: Norton, 2023.

Zarembo, K. "Civic Activism against Geopolitics: the Case of Ukraine." In *Global Civil Society in a Geopolitical Age: How Great Power Competition Is Reshaping Civic Activism*, ed. R. Youngs, 55–60. Brussels: Carnegie Europe, 2022.

Zarembo, K., and E. Martin. "Civil Society and Sense of Community in Ukraine: From Dormancy to Action." *European Societies* (2023). doi: 10.1080/14616696.2023.2185652.

Zielonka, J. "Has the Coronavirus Brought Back the Nation-State?" *Social Europe*, March 26, 2020. https://socialeurope.eu/has-the-coronavirus-brought-back-the-nation-state.

Zuboff, S. *The Age of Surveillance Capitalism: The Fight for a Human Future at the Frontier of Power.* London: Profile Books, 2019.

Index

For the benefit of digital users, indexed terms that span two pages (e.g., 52–53) may, on occasion, appear on only one of those pages.

1.5 degrees target, 66
350.org, 43

A22 network, 50
African Charter for Democracy, Elections and
    Governance, 122
Antonio Guterres, UN secretary general, 68
Arab spring, 51, 119–20
ASEAN (Association of Southeast Asian
    Nations), 121
austerity, 109–10
authoritarian reflex, 12

Bachelet, Michelle (UN High Commissioner
    for Human Rights), 46
Belt and Road Initiative (China), 124–25
Biden, President, 39, 124, 128
Borrell, Josep, 132
Brazil
    climate protests, 48
    COVID-19, 83
    foreign policy, 121
    polarization, 77
BRICS, 122, 142
Brothers of Italy, 114

C40 Cities Climate Leadership Group, 57
Carnegie Global Protest Tracker, 92
Centre for Civic Liberties (Ukraine), 154
China
    authoritarianism in green clothing, 32–33
    COVID-19 protests, 93–94
    COVID-19 response, 76
    foreign policy, 123–24
    Global Development Initiative, 139–41
    Global Security Initiative, 139–41
    state interventionism, 102
Choked Up, 45
civic micropolitics, 23–24, 27
Civic Readiness (Ukraine), 157
Civicus Sate of Civil Society Report, 78

civil society organizations, 41–46
Climate Action Network, 66–67
Climate Action Tracker, 30
climate assemblies, 55–58
climate capitalism, 44–45
Climate Change Performance Index, 29–30
climate denial, 55
climate emergencies, 39
climate litigation, 38–39
climate protests, 46–55
Climate Reality project, 43
Collective Security Treaty Organization,
    146–47
community mutualism, 86–92
Community of Democracies, 122–23, 125–26
COP (Conference of the Parties), 66
COP26 Scotland, 69, 70–71
COP27 Egypt, 66–67
Coronavirus Government Response Tracker
    (Blavatnik School), 79–80
cost-of-living crisis, 115–16
COVID-19, 74–108
COVID-19 consultations, 83–86
COVID-19 lockdowns, 76–78
COVID-19 protests, 92
critical junctures, 18
critical minerals, 33

deglobalization, 99
deliberation, 67–71
deliberativa, 67
democracy promotion, 118–27, 134–36, 137–39
democratic regression, 10–11
democratic turnarounds, 19–20
depoliticization, 38
disinformation, 78
double movement, 22, 60, 106–7

E3Zero, 45
eco-authoritarianism, 30–31, 42
eco-co-operativism, 41–42

194 INDEX

ecological authoritarianism, 30–31
ecological democracy, 42
ecological mandarins, 37
economic security, 102–3
Economist Intelligence Unit Democracy Index, 75–76
eco-technocracy, 37, 59–60
Emergency Governance Initiative, 86–87
empowered state, 5 , –25
energy communities, 45
Energy Democracy Alliance, 44–45
energy democracy, 41–42
energy transition, 35
Environmental Reporting Collective, 45
Escazu Treaty, 46
EU
    Conference on the Future of Europe, 111–12
    Defence of Democracy Package, 111–12, 129–30
    Democracy and Human Rights Action Plan, 124–25
    emergency powers, 39
    Eurozone financial crisis, 110–11
    European Semester, 112–13
    Fit for 55, 113
    Global Gateway, 124–25
    Global Human Rights Sanction Regime, 124–25
    Global Strategy, 120
    Net Zero Industry Act, 111
    political union, 110
    Social Climate Fund, 115
    Stability and Growth Pact, 111
    Strategic Compass, 129–30
    Team Europe Democracy, 124–25
    Temporary Crisis and Transition Framework, 111
Eurobarometer, 111–12
European Climate Foundation, 56
European Commission, 111–12, 113
European Court of Human Rights, 38–39
European Democratic Resilience Initiative (US), 137
European Green Deal, 113
European hard-right, 82–83
European Parliament, 112–13
European Political Community, 131–32
existential politics, 27–28
expert-guided democracy, 36–37
Extinction Rebellion, 43, 58

Farmer Citizen Movement (Dutch), 53
financial crisis, 96–97
Forum on Democracy (China), 146–47

France Insoumise party, 114
Free and Open Indo-Pacific, 125, 129–30
Freedom House, 11
Fridays for Future, 43, 49
Front Line Defenders, 52

G7 Partnership for Global Infrastructure, 137
Georgia, EU accession, 131–32
Global Assembly on the Climate and Ecological Crisis, 65–73
Global Climate Strike, 49–50
Global Witness, 52
governability, 79
Great Transformation (book), 22
Green Odessa, 157
Green Trustee Democracy, 36–41
greenwashing, 66–67
Greta project, 45–46

Horizons of Change (Ukraine), 154–55

IBSA (India, Brazil, South Africa), 122
illiberal populism, 12–13
India
    climate protests, 48
    COVID-19 response, 81
    foreign policy, 121, 122, 125–26, 141
    mutualism, 87–88
    village parliaments, 57
Indonesia, foreign policy, 121–22
Inflation Reduction Act (US), 97–98
Innovate for Africa, 88
Innovation for Policy Foundation, 67
Integrated Security Fund (UK), 138–39
Inter-American Democracy Charter, 121
International Centre for Ukrainian Victory, 154
International IDEA, 81–82
international liberal order, 118
IPCC, 40–41
Israel-Palestinian conflict, 145
Iswe Foundation, 67

Jake Sullivan speech, 99–100
Japan, foreign policy, 125
Just Stop Oil, 49, 58

Kazakhstan, protests, 53
Kishida, Fumio, 129
Knowledge network on Climate Assemblies (KNOCA), 56

League of Conservation Voters, 45
Les Soulevements de la Terre, 51–52

INDEX 195

Leviathan
  absent, 24–25
  climate, 31–32
  democratic, 169–70
Levits, president, 128–29
liberal statism, 27, 60–61, 99–101, 106–7, 148–49, 168–74
liberation technology, 14
Local Democracy Network (Ukraine), 156–57
Lula, President, 142

Macron, Emmanuel, 110, 128–29
Make.org, 114–15
Mark Malloch Brown, 101
Meloni, Giorgia, 114
micropolitics, 5–6, 25, 41–46, 72–73, 86–92, 106, 160–61, 168–74
Modi, prime minister, 125–26
Moldova, EU accession, 131–32
Mongolia, climate protests, 49–50
  foreign policy, 139–41
MovementHub, 45
multi-order world, 118

National Endowment for Democracy (US), 137
NATO Strategic Concept, 129–30
neo-statism, 96–104
Netherlands Institute for Multiparty Democracy, 137
new interventionism, 97
Next Generation EU, 109–12

Obama, President, 119–20
oil and gas subsidies, 35
Open Government Partnership, 84
Organization of American States, 121, 141–42

Partnerships for Democratic Development (US), 137
Pass the Mic, 45
Pelosi, Nancy, 133
People's Declaration for the Sustainable Future of Planet Earth, 69, 70
Persian Gulf, 33
planetary stewardship, 37
Planet Patrol, 45
Poder Ciudadano, 90
Polanyi, Karl, 22
poly-crisis, 18
Poroshenko, Petro, 152
post-neoliberalism, 96–104
Power, Samantha, 124

Presidential Initiative for Democratic Renewal (US), 137
Putin, President, 130

Ramaphosa, Cyril, 142–43
Reconstruction Platform, 134
Recovery and Resilience Facility (RRF), 109–10, 112–15
rejectionist micropolitics, 27, 52–55, 63
restraint, US concept, 119
Russia-China axis, 133, 146
Russia, Covid Solidarity, 88–89
Russian invasion of Ukraine, 117–18, 127–39

Scholz, Chancellor, 128–29
Shanghai Cooperation Organization, 141, 146
Shining Hope for Communities (South Africa), 88
South Korea, 125
storm autocracy, 32
Strategy to Prevent Conflict and Promote Stability, 137
Summit for Democracy, 124, 126–27, 143–45

Taiwan, Chinese threat, 133
Taiwan Foundation for Democracy, 137
Taiwan, COVID-19 response, 84–85
Thailand, eco-friendly villages, 43–44
Trudeau, Justin, 129
Trump, President, 120
trustee statism, 27, 59–60, 116, 168–74
Tsai Ing-wen, 129
Turkey
  climate protests, 48
  Covid-19 mutualism, 89
  environmental organizations, 43–44
  foreign policy, 121, 122

UK, COVID-19 mutualism, 90
Ukraine
  civil resilience, 152–61
  COVID-19 mutualism, 88
  decentralization, 155–56
  democracy aid, 134–36
  displaced activists, 155
  Donbas, 159
  EU accession, 131–32
  Euromaidan, 157, 160
  Lugano declaration, 153
  Prozorra, 158
  Russian invasion, 127–39
UN, votes on Ukraine, 139, 142–43
UN Action for Climate Empowerment, 45–46

196 INDEX

US Agency for International Development (USAID), 124–25, 137
UN Democracy Fund, 125–26
UNFCCC (United Nations Framework Convention on Climate Change), 66, 68
UN Summit for the Future, 70–71
US National Security Strategy, 128

variation in democratic trends, 19–23
Varieties of Democracy, 10–11, 79–80
Von der Leyen, Ursula, 129

Wagner group, 143
WTO, 111

Xi, President, 146–47

Yellow Ribbon movement (Ukraine), 159
Yellow Stripe movement (Ukraine), 159
Youth Democratic Movement (Ukraine), 157

Zelensky, President, 128, 152